CW01021150

RUSSIA

CASPIAN SEA

OVERLAND JOURNEY
INDIA TO IRELAND

Doğubeyazit

Tabriz

KEY

ALBORZ MOUNTAINS

Tehran   Damavand

IRAN

AFGHANISTAN

Leh

Yazd

Isfahan   Kerman

Pathankot   Manali

Lahore   McLeod Ganj

Bam

Quetta   Amritsar

HIMALAYA

Zahedan

Multan

NEPAL

PAKISTAN

Delhi

INDIA

CLIMBING
RAMABANG

One Irish climber's explorations in the
Himalaya and his overland trip home

CLIMBING
RAMABANG

With Best Regards,
Gerry Galligan
July 2013

VICARIOUS
PUBLISHING

Vicarious Publishing, Dublin, Ireland.

CLIMBING RAMABANG — GERRY GALLIGAN

First published in 2013 by Vicarious Publishing.

VICARIOUS PUBLISHING

Vicarious Publishing, 63 The Windmill, Sir John Rogerson's Quay, Dublin 2, Ireland.

Copyright © Gerry Galligan 2013.

This book is a work of non-fiction based on the life, experiences and recollections of Gerry Galligan.

Photography: Gerry Galligan unless otherwise credited.

ISBN: 978-1-909461-03-1 (Hardback)

ISBN: 978-1-909461-04-8 (Ebook)

Design and production by Rod Harrison — Vertebrate Graphics Ltd. — www.v-graphics.co.uk

Printed and bound in the UK by T.J. International Ltd, Padstow, Cornwall.

Till a voice, as bad as Conscience, rang interminable changes
On one everlasting Whisper day and night repeated — so:
'Something hidden. Go and find it. Go and look behind the Ranges —
Something lost behind the Ranges. Lost and waiting for you. Go!'

THE EXPLORER, RUDYARD KIPLING, 1898

Contents

PART 1

The Spiti Expedition

An Itch and a Plan

I could blame Roger McMorrow. It was his expedition that planted the seed of an idea in my head several years ago. He and his girlfriend Sara Spencer and two of their friends, all climbers, went to Garhwal in the Indian Himalaya in 2002 with the aim of making the first ascent of an unclimbed six-thousand metre peak. They succeeded and their mountain became known as Draíocht Paravat — Magic Mountain. To make the first ascent of a Himalayan mountain was a dream they had harboured for years. When I saw their photographs of vast glacial valleys and magnificent white summits, that same dream rubbed off on me. What a great thing it must be to venture to places in the world where no one has been. To be first to set foot on high untouched ground; to have the privilege of exploring unknown valleys and experience views not seen. To pioneer. What Roger and Sara did was special and I could think of nothing more alluring. So I swore to myself I would attempt something similar, somewhere in the Himalaya.

Adventure has never been far from my mind. I was born lucky, into a good home, the only son and the youngest in a family of six. My father was an engineer. He was a remarkable man, practical, fair-minded and devoted to his family. He was also mentally and physically strong, and had an interest in travel and adventure. As a young man after the Second World War he served with the British Royal Marines. Engineering as a career interested him. But the RM wouldn't make a provision for this so, dissatisfied, he left the military and joined the Electricity Supply Board at home. A successful career followed where he worked in various power stations around Ireland. Consequently, as a family we moved every few years: to places like Donegal, Offaly, Kerry and eventually settling in Wicklow. When he could, my father took up foreign assignments; serving on power projects in Bahrain in the 1970s and Bhutan in the '80s. I remember postcards of camels and Bedouins in the desert and Buddhist monasteries hanging precariously to cliff faces. And I remember the descriptions and stories he told us: of wealthy Sheiks and opulent life-styles; of Sharia law and grisly scenes of public justice; of cold, desolate Christmas days spent in the Himalaya on meagre rations — butter tea, hard-boiled eggs and Mars bars. I have no doubt that were it not for the demands of a growing family and his sense of commitment to us, he would have pursued an even more adventurous career.

I can say my father's curiosity and adventurous inclination rubbed off on me. I had a happy childhood, mixing easily with others my own age, playing football and soldiers in the streets and fields. My earliest memory as an infant in the late '60s, is of being rowed out to Gola Island, Donegal in a currach on a bright summer's day. I can still see it; the lapping of the waves on the black hull, the oarsman's blue woollen jumper, his white knuckles and black sideburns, and the family singing Báidín Fheilimí. Years later I would be drawn back to Gola as a rock climber. This time with a different family of friends, and all of us excited by the sea cliffs of that magical place.

As a child my first experiences of mountains came from my father's personal accounts of being snow bound on Turlough Hill in the Wicklow Mountains for days, and of drifts so high a man could step over telegraph poles as if they were fence posts. Many Sundays outside the winter months were spent visiting my aunt's cottage in the remote Corriebracks. I loved it there, rambling in the bogs and marshes, looking out for deer, stoat and other fauna. I savoured the fresh air and quietness, the smells of the earth and the different colours and moods. Often the evenings brought out midges which forced us indoors. The cottage had no electricity. As the evenings grew dark we would make tea on a gas stove and crowd around the fire listing to crackling John McCormack records on a vintage gramophone. Late into the night we would pile into the Volkswagen estate and head back over the Wicklow Gap home. I would lie in the back looking up at the stars, thinking about the events of the day and wishing for the journey never to end.

Primary schooling was enjoyable enough — a good mixture of lessons and sports. Secondary school, less so. I had academic ability, but little interest in testing myself or achieving much. At fifteen I couldn't take schoolwork seriously. My parents grew concerned as exam results deteriorated. A change was needed. At sixteen I left day school and went to boarding school at Castleknock. The cultural difference between the two was staggering. The former made up of working and middle class boys like myself, the latter a club of privileged rich boys, many of them spoiled, with heads full of ego and ambition. The move didn't change me. I remained an academic under-achiever. Moreover I felt I didn't belong. These rich kids weren't my kind of people. I considered myself left wing, and I still do, but here I was in a minority, outnumbered by precocious young capitalists. The school was all right. It had a swimming pool, sports pitches and a snooker room, while the food, though questionable in quality, was plentiful. However boarding school felt more like an internment camp than a place of learning. Freedom was curtailed and the daily routine was driven by bells. A walk to the village shop was forbidden and a half-day out to see family required a parental letter and the permission of the President. The confined living conditions didn't help either. There was a lack of personal space. As a result, it was difficult for anyone to relax. As an institution, it was easy for me to reject it. During class-time I often found myself staring out the window, dreaming of liberation and adventures to far-flung places, reading books about adventure and escape. I counted the days left. I am of the view now as I was then, that boarding schools are archaic unnatural environments for any child or teenager to be placed in, away from society, family and friends. They should all be done away with. Time passed, I scraped some qualifications and left the place, thankfully with most of my sanity.

At eighteen I had no career ambition and little appetite for further education. All I wanted to do was be a loafer, wandering around seeing the world. Not that I could have remained at home. Ireland in the 1980s was a bleak place for many young people. A time of economic stagnation, with no jobs, no money circulating and few prospects of a decent future. Going away was the best option. But some skills were needed before leaving. After some parental pressure I did a two-year engineering course at a technical college, following somewhat in my father's footsteps. Then a six-month welding course. After that I went to Australia and spent two and a half years in Sydney, working a variety of jobs: as an estimator, a design-draughtsman, a welder and a sheetmetal worker. Holidays were spent hitch-hiking around the country, up and down the east coast and across to the west. I met all kinds of characters, at work and on the road, and had great craic.

With a visa long expired, I returned home for a few weeks. Then I went to London and got a job on the railways, fixing trains on the overground Brighton to Bedford line. More enjoyment was had here, fraternising with railway headbangers. A rail trip around Europe followed this, roughing it from Paris to Athens. Then I went to America and travelled coast to coast on Greyhounds. Finally in San Francisco I tried to settle down. I came up with a five-year plan. The aim was to work hard and save enough money to return home and set up a business. No particular business, just something that would allow me to be my own boss. But like a lot of great plans, it came to nought.

It was 1990, the first Gulf war was raging and the American economy nose-dived. Jobs were hard to come by. I moved from one low-paying job to another: security guard, crab seller, postal worker, to finally a dishwasher in a flophouse. Dispirited, after eighteen months I gave up and went home.

Life wasn't easy at home. There was still a recession and I spent many months on the dole. Changes were afoot. I had lost my desire to wander. What's more, my rough life-style had caught up with me. A new focus and direction was needed. I gave up booze and soft drugs.

The early 1990s saw a burgeoning computer industry. IT became one of the few areas that seemed to offer quality jobs and opportunities. I did a nine-month computer course and learned all about coding and networking. This led to a one-year contract with a bank as a systems administrator. Since then I have remained in the IT industry, working at various jobs in different companies around Dublin and have developed a reasonably successful career. Outside work, I took up running and circuit training for fitness. This led to an interest in adventure sport. I dabbled in sailing for a while, crewing for work mates in Dublin Bay races and dinghy sailing in Dun Laoghaire and off the west coast. Then one summer morning in 2000, while on a sailing week in Mayo, the weather was particularly calm. Not wishing to waste the day, a group of us decided to walk up the hill of Croagh Patrick. We were rewarded with a marvelous view from the summit looking out over Clew Bay and this inspired me to do more. Returning to Dublin I joined Glenans Hillwalking Club. Before I knew it, I was exploring the hills around Ireland, Scotland and Wales. From then on my interest in the mountains developed. I progressed to scrambling and then rock, ice and alpine climbing. Sailing fell by the wayside. The mountains won me over.

I had been hankering for a big adventure for years. The ones I had in my twenties were borne partly out of curiosity for seeing different places and peoples and experiencing new things. That was the 1980s, I had nothing to loose and everything to learn. But my world had changed since then and I had a good career. I was in my thirties, single, solvent, however the flame of adventure still burned. Mountaineering now offered the means. Also, it is fair to say that being in the hills took over a good chunk of my time, energy and interest. All holidays were spent climbing: in the summer doing routes in the Alps, in winter mixed climbing in Scotland and ice-climbing in Norway and France. Weekends saw me marching across the hills of my native Wicklow and climbing its crags, as well as tackling rock and mountain routes in other parts of the country. I loved being in the hills, and continue to. The freedom they offer, their space, beauty and colours, and the atmospheres they create draw me to them again and again. I wouldn't say mountaineering had become an obsession with me, but I find it more rewarding than chasing other dreams; like making money, amassing possessions and striving for recognition and social success. That said, the mountains have come at a cost to me. Over the years personal relationships have suffered, girlfriends haven't lasted and career progression stalled. But I can't complain. I've led a good life since I stopped wandering as a young fella. But I know that voice of youth in my head is never far away. And sometimes it cries out, urging me on another adventure. Now Roger's Garhwal expedition re-ignited that footloose spirit.

What if I organised a Himalayan expedition, of six weeks duration say, and at the end of it bought a motorbike and travelled home on it, solo? Asia to Europe. Now that would be a trip. The more I thought about it, the more I warmed to it and wanted to do it. I did some preliminary research and came to the view that to do both, an exploratory mountaineering expedition followed by a bike trip, was possible. It would entail a good deal of organising and paperwork, and a few months off work, but I felt I could live with all that.

2008 would be the year to do it. Naturally, for the expedition a team needed to be formed. Ideally a party of four. Four was a big enough group to absorb expedition costs without it being too expensive. It was a small enough number for quick planning and easy decision-making. Plus it meant two ropes of two for efficient climbing. I was keenly aware that whoever I invited needed to have four attributes: motivation, fitness, alpine experience and most importantly, compatibility with other team members. Everyone had to get along. There could be no room for disruptive types such as egotists, know-alls, mavericks and whingers.

I approached people I had climbed with. People I knew well. Darach O'Murchu was the first to sign-up. He had been thinking of heading to the Himalaya, so the idea was an easy sell. At 31 years of age, he was an electronics engineer who, a few years earlier, gave up this work to pursue a life outdoors. We first met in Dalkey quarry on a warm April evening in 2005. He was getting by as a cycle courier around Dublin. That evening I found him still in his courier outfit and holding a spare wheel. He had no rack or rope but was looking up at the routes with longing. I was without partner but I had a rack and rope. We hooked up and climbed well together, with both of us leading the same grade. It was the start of a partnership that saw us meeting regularly to tackle many of the quarry's standard VS routes. Our techniques developed, our focus and fitness grew. So much so that three months after meeting, we climbed the Matterhorn's Hornli Ridge together.

He moved to Kerry at the end of that summer and spent his winters in Scotland, living out of a battered van and getting the odd guiding job to supplement his mountain training. We continued to climb together afterwards, spending a few weeks each summer in the Alps, and winters didn't slip by without us putting in a week or two on mixed routes in the Scottish Highlands. I admired Darach's toughness and the dedication he showed for his craft. I reckoned any man who spent three winter months in the wilds of Scotland alone, in a tiny Suzuki van with no heat, electricity, water or toilet would be well qualified to put up with any hardship the Himalaya had to offer. I wasn't to be proved wrong.

Another character keen to join was Paul Mitchell. I knew Paulie from the quarry. Although I hadn't shared a rope with him there, I knew he was a talented climber. He had a lot going for him. He was young, fit, determined and also, being of sturdy Westmeath farming stock, I knew he would have the fortitude to overcome Himalayan discomforts. Paulie is a quiet, intelligent bloke, rarely in a bad mood and slow to anger. As a result most people have no problem being in his company. It was these particular qualities that stood out for me. He would make an ideal expedition companion, I put the idea to him. He barely gave it a second thought.

'I'm definitely on,' he exclaimed, his eyes brightening. 'Where have you got in mind? When are we going? Who else is coming? How do we organise it? How much will it cost?'

It took over a year to get someone to fill the fourth spot. We racked our brains and came up with a list of a dozen or so people in the Dublin and Wicklow climbing scene who we thought would meet our requirements of competence and compatibility and who, like us, were keen to share the adventure. One by one we approached people. But to our surprise no one was willing to commit. Work, family obligations and the inability to take time off were the main reasons. Eventually I asked a friend of mine, Craig Scarlett, would he be interested? Although limited as a technical climber, Craig is a strong scrambler and I felt he had enough alpine knowledge and experience for what we wanted to do. Moreover he was known to all of us. The idea appealed to him. He mulled over it for a few days, checked his bank balance, negotiated with his employer, spoke with his girlfriend and then said yes.

A good deal of research had to be done and we all had many questions. I spent hours in the company of Roger and Sara, picking their brains on how they organised and managed their expedition; from permits and logistics, to agents, inventories and financing. Old hands in the Irish Mountaineering Club (IMC),

Joss Lynam, Paddy O'Leary and Sé O'Hanlon, were also approached. But where would we go? Then once there, what would we attempt? The Indian Himalaya was the obvious choice, as Roger and Sara had the latest Garhwal knowledge. The other boys had done several expeditions in the Spiti region of Himachal Pradesh. Paulie and I set to task, weighing up both areas. We knew both places had many unclimbed peaks, so choosing objectives in either wouldn't be much of a problem. Both places had their pros and cons. Garhwal has easy access, being only a day away from Delhi, but climbing permits were expensive. Spiti was cheaper for permits, but natural hazards such as high, unfordable rivers, were common. Debate followed. However the decision was made for us by the monsoon. An expedition to Garhwal needed to be outside the monsoon period of June to early September. However as Spiti lies further west in a region known as the Trans-Himalaya, it isn't affected by monsoon. Hence an expedition there was feasible any time over the summer. Thus with June and July being the only months available to all of us, Garhwal was ruled out. Spiti it would be.

In 2000 an IMC expedition led by Paddy O'Leary made the first ascent of Kangla Tarbo, a 6,315-metre ice-capped dome in Western Spiti. In 1961 Joss Lynam, as part of joint British and Irish team, made the first ascent of Shigri Parbat, an inspiring 6,526-metre peak 9 kilometres to the north of Kangla Tarbo. Over the years both men had explored unknown valleys in the general area. Their photographs showed a landscape of desolate glacial valleys bordered by sheer ice walls and winding ridges, all dominated by sharp, irregular peaks — some menacing, others magnificent. The names of some of these valleys were enticing: Khamengar, Ratang, Gyundi, Bara Shigri. I asked Paddy for the name of any valley he knew that remained largely unexplored.

'Try the Debsa,' he said.

A few nights later I was in Joss's attic, poring over photographs and book references of Spiti.

'Does the Debsa valley ring any bells with you, Joss?' I casually asked. He paused for a moment before answering.

'It does. But I've no idea what it looks like.'

In the 1990s the best maps that Paddy or any other explorer could find were small scale 1:200,000 types, where summit positions and heights are vague and blunt ridges meander all over the page like strings of spaghetti. These are rudimentary documents that are often wrong. In the '50s and '60s when Joss explored Spiti, no maps had been made. With such paucity of knowledge, Joss took it upon himself to draw his own. Using a plane table and photographs he had taken, he painstakingly drew a clear and concise map not just of the many mountains and features of the region, but included information of all expeditions that had been there. Details such as leader's names, exploration dates, the list of first and second ascents, and identified peak spot heights. It covered an area of 3,500 square kilometres. In time it was to prove remarkably accurate, being of value to various international mountaineers and turning up in their expedition reports and books. He rolled it out.

'The Debsa's about here,' he said, his fingers circling a white space where all geographical indications had faded out.

'So it's unexplored then?'

'Quite likely.'

This was looking good. The investigation continued. These days there is a wealth of information to be found on any topic in libraries and on the internet. For topographical research there are powerful tools, like Google Earth. In no time Darach and I were using this application, in a virtual Debsa, gliding over glaciers and peaks. I could see a few attractive six-thousanders all right, but Google Earth couldn't tell me if they had been climbed. Further web trawling and research of numerous books and journals indicated this area was largely unexplored. Luckily, I was able to get an accurate military map of the area on a 1:50,000 scale. I picked out a handful of peaks as potential objectives. Confirmation that they were all virgin came from Harish Kapadia, a pioneering Mumbai-based climber and scholar on Indian Himalayan mountaineering. Needless to say the prospect of entering a little known valley system high in the Himalaya with a choice of several unclimbed six-thousanders excited all of us. Here we were, four lads who had never been to India before let alone the Himalaya, embarking on an adventure with the chance of being pioneers and making a bit of history.

A lot of work was done in the twelve months leading to departure. Responsibilities and tasks were evenly shared. Darach took charge of climbing gear and hill food requirements. Paulie looked after all flight arrangements and medicines. Craig did the book-keeping, organised insurance and, being the most familiar with electronics, managed the power and communication equipment. I took care of fundraising, visas, peak permission and all dealings with Rimo our agent, charged with arranging hotel accommodation, transport, porters, cooks, base camp tents and food.

Raising the money wasn't easy. Over €14,000 was needed. Half of this came from our own pockets. The remainder from a Mountaineering Council of Ireland grant, club sponsorship and a welcome few thousand from Lowe Alpine.

Physical preparations weren't overlooked. With Darach in Scotland most of the winter and spring, Craig, Paulie and I organised weekend training sessions in Wicklow. Friday nights we would camp in forests. Saturdays were spent hiking up and down hills with heavy rucksacks to build up endurance and fitness. Those nights saw us bivvying again in forests. And Sunday morning hikes were spurred on by the thought of a large fry-up in Roundwood. In Kerry the four of us practised river crossings and alpine climbing in The Reeks. In Scotland, Easter was spent climbing in Glencoe and snow-holing in the Grey Corries.

Time passed quickly and plans fell into place. A six week expedition schedule was teased out, with four weeks to be spent in the mountains. A target peak was agreed and permission to climb it obtained from the Indian Mountaineering Foundation (IMF). Funding was completed with four weeks to go. All equipment, medicines and clothing were sourced and leave of absence obtained from our employers. Six months in my case, giving plenty of time for the expedition and the overland trip home.

On 31 May 2008, armed with our rucksacks and four large army bags containing everything we needed, we left Dublin for India. An air of relief flowed through us now that the arduous preparations were over and a sense of excitement was felt for the unknown journey that lay ahead. Our Himalayan adventure had begun.

TWO

Culture Shock

We landed in Delhi in the dead of night and were shuttled to the IMF head-quarters in the quiet outskirts of town. We could have slept for days after the flight and would have, only for a family of peacocks crowing for attention all day outside. It was three in the afternoon, hot and uncomfortable. Nonetheless we were hungry and keen to get a first look at Delhi in daylight. A bumpy taxi ride into the city centre woke us up. The strong sun revealed the city's characteristics. Wealth and poverty exist side by side; wide green parkland with grand colonial mansions next to broken dusty roads and hills of congested shanties. People seemed to be everywhere: on the streets driving all manner of smoky vehicles; riding bikes laden with gas and water bottles; on cracked pavements selling cigarettes, fruit, haircuts and shaves; peddling corn cobs from open grilles; squatting on corners in ones and twos, spitting and chewing; or lying in the shade, sleeping. On the whole, the city was a mass of chaotic humanity, surviving, hustling for trade.

The traffic as we had imagined was appalling. Delhi is one big free-for-all. Contraptions of all size and type vie for every available inch of road. Lurid green and yellow auto-rickshaws dart about like hunting piranhas. Taxis and cars muscle each other about at junctions and swarms of low-powered motorcycles, if not sandwiched between trucks, get shunted into gutters and on-coming vehicles. Horns blow incessantly, not to signal danger but to announce a driver's intent to overtake. Danger is ever-present, obligating a heightened sense of alertness. Yet despite the heat, fumes, noise, chaos and congestion, people seldom get agitated. As we were to see in the weeks and months ahead, Indians are surprisingly tolerant of disorder. They manage it, as they inimitably manage other disorders, such as regular power failures, monsoon flooding and the lack of personal space. Unlike us Western Europeans, they put up with such inconveniences, accepting them as normal. Obviously, while here, our attitudes would need to change.

The city is a mix of the old, decrepit and new. There are many clusters of roadside hovels, made of crude brick, bits of wood and plastic. Miserable habitations with no running water or sanitation, and yet these places have an abundance of satellite dishes, considered necessary for proper modern living. Stroll around Connaught Place and you'll fall into potholes and craters in the pavements. Look up and you'll see jumbles of telephone wires wrapped around poles, impossible to maintain. Some hang limply on the ground and you know they'll remain there. Buildings suffer similar neglect, with cracked plaster, broken doors and crumbling pillars. And yet in the same streets you'll find spotless Western-style shops selling the latest gadgets, mobile phones and expensive clothes.

But despite such contrasts, the many people of Delhi compensate for the city's shortcomings. People are friendly. They smile easily and are colourful. Men go about in light cotton clothes and sandals. Sikhs can be easily recognised by their bright, bulbous turbans, and women grace the eye with their striking saris and kurtas. We didn't meet any bad characters during our stay in Delhi. Plenty of hawkers and half-chancers looking to relieve us of a few rupees all right, but no one that managed to sour our view of India and its people.

A meal was had in Connaught Place, followed by a stroll around the circus. It was hot and we needed to buy bottles of water. An easy job to do, you might think. Not quite. Normally it just takes a seller, a buyer, a price, the exchange of cash and a makeshift fridge. But Indians have other ideas. We found a water wallah easily enough. But no sooner had we gathered around his stall when three of his mates appeared out of the crowd, strengthening the customer proposition. Four bottles of water were shuffled around. One lad worked the fridge. Another wiped the bottles with a rag. A third, the stall-holder, engaged Darach for the money and the fourth presented both change and bottles. As it turned out, an attempt was made to short-change Darach who wasn't yet familiar with the currency conversion, and struggled with the mental arithmetic. The result — confusion among us all. Argument with the wallah and his crew was limited as we had no Hindi and they had very little English. What had started out as a simple transaction had developed into a complex debate involving eight varying opinions, much fingering of loose coins and grubby notes, and pointing at four bottles which were steadily warming in the baking heat. It wasn't as if we felt we were being robbed of our life savings, it was only water, after all. But eventually we settled on a price, completed the deal and walked off, scratching our heads. The wallah's men disbanded, vanishing into the crowd as quickly as they had formed. What had we learned here? For one, Indians are a curious lot, drawn to any commercial activity like magpies to shiny objects. It doesn't matter if they're not employees or part of the business. If there's a hint of money and goods changing hands they perk up. And why not? A rupee or two might fall their way. And if not, then at least they were entertained.

As a country of 1.1 billion people, India has no shortage of people to allow businesses to get over-staffed and for the services they give to customers to be unnecessarily elaborate. We needed a lift back to the IMF, so we came upon two black and amber taxis parked on the inside ring of the circus, with several wallahs hanging around them. The cars were Hindustan Ambassadors; old-fashioned curvaceous vehicles modeled on the 1950s Morris Oxford. A throwback to the days of British influence. Anyhow, it took the efforts of five of these lads to get us on the road. The first was the boss, the eldest, who haggled a price. The second was our driver, who ushered us into one of the cars. He hopped into the front and tried starting it. It wouldn't budge. A third, the ignition expert was summoned, and after some fiddling under the bonnet and tweaking of wires along the steering column, the engine cranked up. The driver hopped back in. A flurry of words followed and a fourth chap appeared to place a cushion behind the driver's back in order to give him support. This same lad scampered off but returned sharply as he had forgotten his most critical task — removing the two sticks of incense which had been burning either side of the statuette of Shiva on the dashboard. A fifth remained on stand-by to deal with any other matters that might have delayed us. Thankfully though, that was it. As we crept out into the mayhem of Connaught Place, a half-dozen pairs of attentive brown eyes were trained on us. Sometime later at a T-junction, having steered our way through hazardous suburban traffic, the Ambassador conked out. It was dark. What's more, driver had lost his way. More ignition tricks were performed, with the four of us outside pushing the boot in order to get the car moving again. Pot luck and guess work saw us home.

We were beginning to see that life in India is anything but straight-forward. Simple activities such as buying water or getting from A to B can develop into complex, colourful exercises. In India it seemed anything goes.

❋ ❋ ❋ ❋

On our second day we met our Liaison Officer. Officially, the LO's job is to keep an eye on us; to ensure us foreigners don't become spies in the mountains, photographing roads, bridges or military installations. They also help by getting teams through police checkpoints and assisting with inner-line permits which are needed for access to politically sensitive areas close to the Tibetan border.

Finally, they confirm success or failure on a chosen peak. Our designated LO was a tall, lean 27 year-old from Bangalore. Masthi had a law degree and came from a comfortable farming background. He was also a keen mountaineer and was eager to know as much as possible about us, our climbing style, our gear and our plans. He was a bit too eager for our liking. Earlier from Roger and Paddy, we learned the IMF had assigned LO's who had little or no mountaineering experience and had little interest in gaining any either. We were hoping we would get a character like that — someone just willing to tag along and who wasn't bothered about what we did or how we did it. Energetic, enthusiastic mountaineers who wanted to be an integral part of our climbing team was not what we had bargained for. We were a self-reliant unit of four.

We also met Nima, our man from Rimo. A likeable lad, responsible for the logistics of getting us and our supplies into the hills.

We visited several bazaars in the afternoon to buy batteries, toiletries and camera accessories. The searing sun sapped our energy as the day wore on. Little relief was found in the shade of merchants' stalls, nor was it helped by the persistence of market children trying to sell us sunglasses we didn't want. Mangy, pariah dogs loped around and mendicants abounded. The four of us stood out everywhere we went. Half of Delhi insisted on selling us something, anything. As the sun set we retired to Connaught Place, to overcome a day's sweat and dust, and rejuvenate with a meal of dosa and glasses of cool lime soda.

Next morning Nima visited us at the IMF, bringing canisters of gas for our stay in the hills and an approach schedule. A day's bus journey would take us to Shimla. Two nights there would allow us time to get inner-line permits for passage through Spiti as we would be close to the Tibetan border. Shimla's markets would also provide us with stocks of fruit and vegetables. Then a two-day jeep trip north through Kinnaur would bring us to Spiti and the village of Sagnam. From there, with porters carrying our loads, we would make a three day march up the Parahio and Debsa valleys to reach our planned base camp at Thwak Debsa. After that we would be on our own for a month. Just the four of us: two cooks, our LO and the mountains. We were looking forward to it. It would be cooler and infinitely more peaceful in the mountains, far from the heat and noise of the city. A briefing with the IMF's Director on what we could or couldn't do in the mountains followed our chat with Nima. Later that afternoon, after checking our inventory and packing our kit, we headed into town for something to eat.

In Hinduism cows are sacred. Since Vedic times over 3,000 years ago, they have been associated with Providence and earthly compassion because of their milk, their dung which is used for fertiliser and fuel, and their leather for clothing and goods. Their meat is not to be eaten and neither are they to be harmed. They occupy a privileged place in Indian society and as such, their security and well-being is practically guaranteed. Cows all over the world are not known for any exceptional intelligence. However I believe most of the ones I came across during my time in India are well aware of their special status, and they do a good job exploiting it. So it was funny to see for the first time a small herd of six that night, on the busy road outside the IMF compound. As we made for a taxi, their leader casually wandered onto the main road and halted on the centre line. His mates followed slowly, lining up haphazardly behind him. Once stopped they wouldn't budge. They weren't your standard Friesian or Angus, timidly going from one field to another, but a team of grey, bony-shouldered hulks with sagging necks and ugly heads, caring little about anything going on around them. Car horns blared as drivers swerved manically to avoid them. Trucks jammed and small vehicles such as motorcycles and auto-rickshaws screeched to slow down before cautiously weaving past. Interestingly, no harsh words were to be heard. Ten full minutes of obstruction followed before the leader nonchalantly urinated on the line. Then he looked back at his herd, decided enough was enough, and led them back to the side in the same casual manner. This incident, typical of the way in which cows roam freely, is a fact of life all Indians seem to accept and one they do not try to change. In India, over-riding all authority, be it police, government or Brahmin priests, one thing is clear: cattle rule.

❊ ❊ ❊ ❊

Wednesday 4 June. At 6 a.m. we loaded our bus and set out north, up the Grand Trunk road — a historical route between Calcutta and Peshawar — towards Shimla. A large movement of people was heading the same way, forming a jumble of multifarious vehicles travelling at different speeds. There were ox-carts and auto-rickshaws, horses, motorbikes, lumbering Tata trucks, tractors and trailers, battered cars and vans and dinged, overloaded buses. A maelstrom of choking fumes, blaring horns, speed and raised dust. It was as if Delhi had been plunged into war and all of its inhabitants shared a collective urge to evacuate suddenly, scrambling on the first vehicle they could find. We spotted several dilapidated Suzuki vans, operating as taxis, stuffed with dark bodies. Deathtraps in motion. I couldn't resist a jibe:

'Hey Darach, look over there,' I said pointing to one. 'Does it remind you of Scotland? People live in Suzukis here too.'

We were swept along, absorbed by the tide.

The billboards along the road advertise luxurious city apartments, flashy mobile phones and stylish Japanese cars for the discerning professional, but behind them you can find decaying brick factories, ox-drawn carts and ragged road dwellers who could well be from the Middle Ages.

The road was a hive of commercial activity. From the comfort of our seats we watched hundreds of people plying a trade of one sort or another in the ditches and side roads. Bare-backed men toiled in metal fabricating shops. Women attended fruit stalls. Potters spun jugs and urns. Mechanics beavered about skeletal cars and motorcycles jacked up on blocks. There was much more: tailors, timber merchants, clothes washers, barbers, chai wallahs and so on. All of them pitching their products and services out of makeshift huts and tumbledown shops. Everyone seemed to be busy and have something to sell. You could be forgiven for thinking the many ragged beggars had a sought-after trade.

Despite the roughness of the Grand Trunk road, with its shanties, wood-smoke, clamour and dirt, a great sense of life is present. Compared to our high Western living standards, most people here are poor. But their urge for survival and strength to turn a few rupees any way they can is great. Moreover, from the calm expression on their faces it is clear no one complains about their lot. This is the natural order of things in their world and they accept it. Their dignity is commendable. The realisation of how lucky and easy we have it at home in comparison wasn't lost on us.

We made our way through the flat farmlands of Haryana, passing wheat fields and haystacks and rice sprouting in wet paddies. Women dressed in saris were bent over crops. It rained heavily as we approached the wooded hills of Shimla.

Masthi irritated us at dinner. In his eagerness to impose ideas and a measure of authority, he insisted we have briefing sessions each night to review what we had done each day and to plan for future days.

'We're all part of one team, working together, with one objective,' became his recurring mantra. Assuming the role of a drill sergeant, he declared what time we should all get up at and have breakfast. Now none of us wanted to listen or put up with any of this nonsense. We all knew one another well, we worked effectively together and we solved problems democratically and so far, without dissent. His muscling in like this only unsettled us. We were still only getting to know him. Our collective view was if he didn't change his tune quickly, he might jeopardise the expedition, if not the spirit of it.

Quietly after dinner, Craig, Paulie, Darach and I agreed we'd put up with him until we reached base camp. After that, everything would be dictated on our terms.

In addition to the four of us, Masthi and Nima, our party was completed by the arrival of our kitchen staff, Raj Kumar and his nephew Manbahadur. Both lads hail from the Khumbu region of Nepal. Their genial nature, their willingness to please and their smiling faces made a good impression on us. They also brought pedigree to the team. Raj had been chief cook on six Chris Bonington expeditions. We had heard good reports about him and he was much in demand. These two didn't have to be motivated or told what to do, the following day or any other. We didn't have to worry about them. No sooner had Nima handed them a shopping list when they disappeared into the labyrinth of Shimla's market, hunting out the best fruit and vegetables to last us in the back of beyond.

Getting inner-line permits wasn't easy. They were necessary to allow us get through police checkpoints near the Indo-Tibetan border. Nima had arranged a fixer to get our papers processed in the office of the District Commissioner at the top end of the town. Masthi was actually meant to do this. But Nima seemed to know what he was doing so we let him and the fixer get on with it.

Meanwhile the market became our morning's distraction. It is a jumble of hundreds of stalls perched on a steep hill, with everything you can imagine on sale: silks, woollen clothes, carpets, electrical goods, tools and furniture, books, belts, bags, pictures, leather goods and so on. Tantalising spices flavoured the air as we moved by large hessian sacks of clove, cinnamon and ginger. Our taste buds were stirred on seeing stacks of sweet red jalebi, or a cook prodding hot cauldrons of bubbling samosa. Balti-looking porters lugged heavy chests of grain and vegetables on their backs up the rain-soaked hill, and two bare-footed sadhus ringing handbells, padded from shop to shop seeking alms. Above our heads, acrobatic grey monkeys clambered over walls and telephone wires, stopping occasionally to look down and size up potential food raids. Enviously we watched them, their effortless climbing agility and balance.

We were pleasantly surprised by the atmosphere of the place. The streets were crowded, and it didn't help they were all narrow and winding. Nonetheless a sense of relaxation was felt. Business was colourful and enjoyable and, unlike the bazaars of Delhi, we didn't encounter any hard sellers.

Shimla was put on the map by the British in the 19th century. Desperate to escape the stifling heat of the Indian plains, they effectively governed their sub-continental empire from here during the summer months. The town's climate of cool mountain air, grey cloud and frequent rain must have given them a reassuring sense of home. But this was not what we wanted. Our hope was for clear skies and dry weather, not so much in Shimla, but to where we were headed in Spiti. Inevitably we were going to get rain showers in the Debsa. So with this in mind Craig and Masthi took the task of buying umbrellas for all of us. Many dreary wet days spent on campsites in the Alps taught us the importance of umbrellas. I had thought we would get conservative, black ones, appropriate for the weather. Instead the lads returned with large multi-coloured ones, the kind favoured by the golfing fraternity. Huddled under these brollies we must have looked a strange sight to the locals and monkeys; four glum-looking white blokes and a tall, shivering Indian. Mountaineers we weren't. More like neglected caddies at a second-rate Pro-Am tournament in rain-soaked Ballybunion.

By midday there was no sign of the permits. After lunch, still no sign. We needed them before five as we were leaving the next day. Nima's fixer was showing no sign of urgency. What's more we had learned that the District Commissioner, who had been in the job years, was retiring this day and a new man was taking over. On hearing this and having listened to Roger and his stories of tediously slow Indian bureaucracy, I started to worry. I could picture what might happen. Our papers would languish in a junior clerk's in-tray to be forgotten about. The new DC would be busy dealing with the old one all day and handling fussy subordinates desperate to make good first impressions. Our papers wouldn't see a middle level manager's desk for days, perhaps weeks. Meanwhile we would be hanging around Shimla an extra day, Friday, followed by the weekend, watching our schedule slipping. Our porters, who Nima had arranged to meet us in Sagnam, would be waiting, getting bored, perhaps wandering off, convinced we had abandoned them.

Three o'clock and still no movement. We stood in the main corridor of the DC's building, with low and mid-ranking officials buzzing about. Plenty of activity but nothing happening. Just the fixer trying to placate me by explaining the chain of command and who needed to do what to get our permits issued. Nima innocently went along with it. It was great, but when Masthi joined in and started lecturing me on the machinations of Indian bureaucracy and the virtues of waiting, I came close to losing it.

'Masthi, I know all about bureaucracy and how it strangles you. I don't need excuses and I don't need delays. Now get out of my way!'

We managed to get the permits that evening. A little charm and diplomacy on my part to a quiet, middle-aged woman in a side office did the trick.

That woman was the DC's personal assistant. In my view the PA is the second most important person in any organisation. Just after five we were handed our papers. I could have kissed her before leaving.

The rain continued the following morning. A 280-kilometre journey over twisting mountain roads into Kinnaur meant an early start. All hands loaded the two jeeps and we set off, grinding up through the misty Shimla hills. The road a mixture of gravel and potholes. Dhabas — dark, pokey grub shops — dotted the route. Around ten we stopped at one of these places for the drivers to have breakfast. It was on a bend, overlooking a valley of rich green farmland. Not wishing to risk belly-ache by eating, Craig and I opted to hang around outside, admiring the view. We were all very conscious of the risk of food sickness which could be detrimental to any expedition, particularly at the start of one. We chose our eating houses carefully. We only drank bottled water and wiped our hands with alcohol before any meal. The other lads, the cooks, drivers, Masthi and Nima, with stronger constitutions, could take their chances in the dhabas. Not us.

Anyway, Craig and myself walked to the back of the building, down a stairway and into a field. Stretched into the distance were lush terraces filled with drills of potatoes, peas, apples and cherrys. Homesteads stood between allotments. It was all quite pretty and well organised. Some moments went by as we took it all in. There was nothing unusual in all this. It was only when I looked down next to my feet, at a familiar looking plant with narrow serrated leaves and a pale stalk, did my eyes open. I bent down, tore off a strip and smelled it. Musty weed. There was no mistake, it was cannabis. And not just at my feet. It was growing all around me, in patches here and there, down the field and mixed in with the crops. Thick, bushy stuff everywhere. I had never seen so much grass growing so freely. And it wasn't being farmed, it was wild and thriving. Acres of it.

Right, start harvesting, I thought. I picked some leaves and held them in a bundle, thinking they would make for a good distraction the odd night at base camp. What a gift. It was all so easy — so convenient. Then came the recoil of doubt. A few spliffs wouldn't do any harm but if it became a routine every night and possibly every day, then we might not get much climbing done. Our expedition would be wasted as we would be wasted. This presented a tough choice. Twenty years earlier a free-spirited Gerry would have harvested the entire crop. But here I was now, showing signs of responsibility and maturity that can only come about by wisdom and the onset of middle age. A decision was needed, one which I did not want to make.

'What do you think Craig, will we bring a bagful?' I asked, hoping he might decide for me.

No such luck.

'I dunno, Gerry. Whatever you think, it's up to yourself.'

Wonderful.

I looked around. The ganja was everywhere. Meanwhile above, the other boys were emerging from the dhaba. Jeep doors swung open and slammed shut. Engines started up. Shouts went out and we had to get moving again. I hesitated some more. Eventually, reluctantly, maturity won out. The weed stayed in the ground. I thought, God, how I've changed.

THREE

With Gods on our Side

The clouds parted and the temperature rose as the day wore on. Our drivers, two young Shimla lads, were skillful, continually dodging potholes and wayward vehicles. We passed many gangs of workers repairing the road from damage wreaked by the harsh Himalayan winter. Men and women toiling with picks and shovels, shifting loads and filling holes. The reek of hot asphalt. Clouds of dust billowing in the air. There were souls breaking piles of rock with lump-hammers, swinging and smashing, like prisoners in a chain-gang. It was a miserable sight. Not far from each gang we noticed clusters of makeshift tents; dirty plastic sheeting crudely held together with sticks and randomly placed stones. These were the worker's homes. These crews, often whole families, live out each summer in these forlorn spots, eking a wage before the encroachment of winter and a return to villages and towns. None of us envied them. Their lives are hard and, as low castes, their chances of progress in Indian society is slim, if not impossible. According to Masthi, the barriers in India's caste system today are slowly diminishing, but looking at these unfortunates, it was hard to believe it. Nevertheless, just like those of the Grand Trunk road, these people were unperturbed. Their work was rotten, their living conditions primitive by anyone's standard, but they accepted both with great equanimity.

From Shimla there's only one route to Spiti. This is the modern road that runs parallel to the old Hindustan-Tibet trading route. It winds its way along the Satluj river, passing through gorges, steep cliffs and formidable man-made rocky overhangs. The Satluj is one strand of a major river system; the source of life and power for millions on the Indian sub-continent. It rises at Lake Manasarovar in Western Tibet, an area of deep spiritual importance to Buddhists and Hindus alike. From here it flows west, carving valleys through the Himalaya, gaining strength. In Himachal Pradesh it is fed by the Spiti and Baspa rivers, the increased power of which is enough to drive the turbines of the state's hydro-electric plants. Continuing west, it merges with the Beas at Amritsar, irrigating the expansive rice and wheat fields of the Punjab. Then it veers south to join the Indus before entry to the Arabian Sea.

On the road, our spirits were high. We were all glad to be out of the city, above the plains and looking forward to the weeks ahead. Talk flowed freely. Indians, Nepalese and Irish got to know each other and a relaxed atmosphere prevailed. Relations with Masthi were softening. Our first impressions of him in Delhi may have been harsh; I knew he meant well for the team. I for one was starting to like his company. It was good to be able to chat freely on any subject, to hear his opinions and to increase my knowledge on all things Indian. Our conversations were lengthy, fluid affairs, touching many different subjects: mountaineering, politics, law, corruption, religion and the caste system. On religion, Hinduism particularly interested me, with its multitude of colourful gods and stories. We spent the night at Kalpa, and shortly after leaving the following morning, we stopped by the roadside temple of Durga. Durga is an avatar of Shiva's wife Parvati. Like some other Hindu gods, she has several arms and legs to help her fight off demons. To the devout she is considered a warrior and, when angered, takes the form of Kali, a dark-skinned grotesque creature with a bloody cleaver, a belt of severed limbs and a garland of human skulls. Her colourful temple overlooking the Satluj is popular among travellers seeking protection from all hazards of the roads, rivers and peaks of the region. As Christians, lapsed or otherwise, we looked on as people conducted solemn pujas — offerings of prayer and money — in front of the doll-like statue. Hanging bells were rung by visitors on arrival and departure to ward off unwanted spirits and each of the faithful received a sprinkling of rice from a priest to cast on the altar. The priest also daubed tilaks — red marks on the forehead — which is a symbol of the inner, spiritual eye and part of the ritual of paying homage to the divine. All of us except Nima, being the sole Buddhist, participated in puja.

Everything was going well for us so far. We were making good progress. No one was sick. All permits had been obtained. Porters had been arranged and not a sour word was to be heard among us. The only worry left was the weather, some-thing out of our control. Thinking a prayer might help, I took Masthi to one side.

'Masthi, when you're up there with Durga, do us a favour and ask her to have a word with Indra, the weather god. We could do with dry, settled weather for the next four weeks. You know what I mean?'

'OK Gerry. I cannot promise you anything. But I will ask her for you.'

'Good man.'

We continued along the road through Kinnaur, criss-crossing the brown, racing Satluj at various points. Rugged mountains of a similar hue stood all around us. After the many months of speculation and preparation, it finally felt good to be in the Trans-Himalaya. Gradually the verdant orchards and pastures of Kinnaur gave way to the barren, open mountains of Spiti. Spiti is a land of sharp contrasts. From vast blue skies to wide upland devoid of vegetation. Arid brown earth overwhelms tiny patches of farmland centred around villages. Small green fields are lovingly tended. The whole effect looks like emeralds on the surface of the moon. Wheat, rice, peas, apples, barley and mustard seed are grown in these fields. Surrounding them, dry stone walls are capped with thorn bushes to keep foraging bharals and ibex out.

Moving from Kinnaur deeper into Spiti, the landscape isn't the only thing that changes. Hinduism gives way to Buddhism. The signs of which are plentiful. Prayer flags are threaded along bridges. *Mani* walls stand by the roadside and *chortens* sit by the outskirts of villages. Physically, Spitians differ from their Kinnauri neighbours by their Tibetan features; flat round faces and almond-shaped eyes. Their language is separate also, Spitian having evolved from a Tibetan dialect over a thousand years ago.

We got through police checkpoints unhindered in the afternoon. At tea-time our convoy pulled into Tabo — a fort-like monastery complex, founded in 996 AD. In the millennium since, Tabo has been a centre of Tibetan scripture and learning, and a hub of trade between India, Tibet and Central Asia. As dinner was cooking we took a look around. Few monks were about. Through the courtyard, past thick clay walls, Nima led us into the main temple. A red statue of Buddha, seated on a throne of lotus and flanked by lions, made up the inner temple. Around it, painted on the walls, were powerful images of Bodhisattvas and other deities, as well as some fiendish types. The enclosure, the darkness and the sense of forced self-examination was unsettling, but not new. As a Catholic, albeit a recalcitrant one, I was used to such challenges. It reminded me of familiar lessons of living a good life and being rewarded with entry to heaven, or leading a bad life and being relegated to hell. On the face of it, this was all relatively acceptable to me, and acceptable to most Buddhists, who profess similar views.

The word Spiti means 'Middle Land'. Middle because it lies across the main range of the Himalaya, known as the Trans-Himalaya; a dry, barren place. Spiti has been of huge political and strategic significance for many centuries. It is surrounded on all sides by former competitive empires: Ladakh to the north, Kinnaur to the south, Tibet to the east and Kulu to the west. Records of foreign invasions stretch back a thousand years, with Tibetan chieftains having dominated for much of the 11th to 19th centuries. However their rule was interrupted, although temporarily, by successive invasions of Ladakhis, Kulus, Baltis and Sikhs until the British, by the Treaty of Amritsar, wrested control in 1821. It is interesting to note that throughout these times the Spitians themselves never sought to fight any aggressor, or mount any serious resistance. Instead they cleverly exploited their environment, preferring to flee to shelter at high ground as their villages were plundered, allowing the harsh Spitian winter to decimate the invaders.

After 1821 the British marked the boundaries of Spiti and in 1860, the Trigonometrical Survey of India started mapping the area. However British rule, like that of every invader, didn't last. Spiti automatically became part of the Indian republic upon independence in 1947. Slowly some public services were introduced to the region: policing, banks, teachers and schools. Ironically the Indo-Sinai war of 1962 was of benefit to Spiti. Although it wasn't involved in the conflict, its border location meant a large influx of military. As a result, two main roads were built; one on the old Hindustan trade route from Shimla to Kaja in the east, the other to the northwest, linking Kaja and Manali in Kulu. Both routes opened up the entire region and are used today. Apart from the roads and basic public services, a hydro-power plant was constructed near Kaja, providing electricity to the main villages. Other than that, life in Spiti has changed little since the days of Tibetan and Ladakhi rule.

Night fell by the time we reached Sagnam. The day had been a long dusty haul up the Spiti valley with the constant rattle of a diesel engine in our ears. Now it was a relief to breathe fresh mountain air and to hear silence. Nima got us billeted in a guesthouse for the night, the only one in the village.

Sometime during the night our porters arrived from Kaja and Manali. We didn't hear a thing. But when we woke up, all twenty-two of them were waiting outside to carry our loads on the three-day march to our planned base camp in the Debsa valley. Nima took charge of loading. All our provisions and equipment were put into white nylon sacks and distributed among them, twenty-five kilos a man. We soon discovered we had too many loads and not enough porters. Several of the men took to carrying extra loads, up to forty kilos. More weight meant more money. But Darach and I didn't like the look of this. Twenty-five kilos was the norm.

'They'll break their backs, Nima,' I said. 'We can't allow this. Tell the head porter to reduce the loads and find more men — village men.'

With some reluctance the head porter agreed, so he and Nima went off to round up more help.

Meanwhile we wandered around Sagnam, taking it in. It is a typical Spitian hamlet of small square houses, all clustered together, with rough stone walls and flat dark roofs. Dry muddy lanes form rudimentary streets, and open channels of water weave around each dwelling. It is a spartan place, having no telephones, electricity, cars, or any of the other conveniences associated with modern life. A peaceful, appealing place lost in time. It is also a very active one. Brightly-shawled women were to be seen washing clothes or tending the fields. Men were busy building a shop and guesthouse, and small children amused themselves playing on an incongruous tractor. From the roof of the guesthouse I could see two older children, baskets in hand, laying out yak dung to dry in a courtyard. Prayer flags, blackened and tattered by the winds, sagged above rooftops. An inquisitive goat was nosing bundles of sticks and the awkward bray of a donkey could be heard in the distance. Everyone it seemed, regardless of age, appeared occupied.

There is something very attractive and unassuming about these hardy mountain people, I thought. Smiles come easily to them and no one is rushed. Some have a little English, and anyone we spoke to had enough time and interest to stop, chat and ask questions. Where were we from, and where were we going to? Did we like Sagnam? And would we be coming back this way? We must have appeared odd to them. Four white-skinned strangers in bright modern clothes, swamping their village with our hoard of equipment and twenty-two loitering porters. I had to admire them. Like mountain people the world over, they are completely dependent on their own energy, skills and the benevolence of nature for their survival. No EU grants or dependence on commercial food supply here. Theirs is a fully self-reliant existence. Their fields produce vegetables and grains. Their sheep, goats and yaks provide milk, meat and wool for clothing. Also, in a land devoid of trees, animal dung is their principle source of fuel. Needless to say, life isn't all easy. Crop failure brings hardship and the ravages of winter can destroy roads, isolating them for much of the year. And yet they survive, happily and successfully. Unlike their ill-fated invaders of old, it is their ability to work closely with nature that keeps them thriving in such a sparse, unforgiving environment.

The head porter returned with no extra hands. All the village men were busy building. However Nima managed to procure five donkeys and a donkeyman. Loads were then evenly distributed and we set out, westward up the Parahio valley, towards the small settlement of Kaho Dogri. The day was bright and windy, and it felt good to be finally exercising.

Curiously all our porters were Nepalese. They migrate west to Himachal Pradesh and Ladakh each summer in order to make some money during the

Nepalese monsoon. Raj and Manbahadur do likewise, only as cooks and camp managers on climbing and trekking expeditions. Quite unexpectedly these two lads took charge of the porters, helping them with their loads and directing them. As expedition leader I was anticipating having to deal with all this and having to get around the language barrier. But the lads beat me to it. I was impressed.

Later, one by one we filed through Dogri and set up camp at the edge of the village. Like Sagnam, the few locals were welcoming, greeting us with the customary 'Jule,' pronounced Ju-lay. Small children waved and watched us with interest. On passing a dwelling, my eye caught the glint of shining objects. Looking over I spotted three women hidden in a doorway with large gold rings in their noses.

Our camp was on a bank, two hundred metres above the Parahio. It offered a fine view up this meandering river — otherwise known as a nala — continuing into the V-shaped Debsa valley. Triangular peaks, familiar to us only from map observations, stood around us. To the north in a tributary valley, stood the tantalising pinnacle of Ratang Dru, a snow-tipped arrowhead just shy of six thousand metres, lancing skywards. Although several kilometres from us, the higher altitude and clear air made us believe it was only a short distance away. As camp was being assembled, Craig and I did a recce up the valley for the following day. We came to a feeder river north of the Parahio which our caravan would have to cross. This nala was seven metres wide and its water was swift and waist high. The one metal bridge that forded it had been seriously damaged by flooding. I weighed things up. We humans could scramble over the boulders, onto the bridge and get to the other side before relaying the loads. It wouldn't be easy but we would manage it, however the donkeys couldn't. A nala crossing was the only option for them. But I was worried that given their light weights and small size — they were only one metre high to the shoulder — they might get washed away or worse, drown.

That night Raj cooked our first meal. An extravagant affair by our alpine standards: spicy soup, salad, rice, ladybeans, dal, potatoes and spinach, with pears for dessert, plus coffee. It was served in a comfortable, gas-lit dining tent. Bellies full, we slept a peaceful first night under canvas.

At breakfast we watched the donkeys being loaded by their handler. They were docile little chaps, unfazed by their cargo and quite content to chew on tufts of grass or on our leftover vegetables. I have always had a soft spot for animals and I have to say the prospect of them struggling across that nala with the strong current and heavy loads bothered me. I didn't want anyone, man or beast, to suffer needlessly on this trip.

But the animals surprised me. I was last to break camp. Darach was one of the first. When I caught up with him at the nala I asked him about the donkeys. I couldn't see them.

'Where are they?'

'They're well ahead.'

'You mean they've already crossed?'

'Yeah, no problem. Look, they're up there.'

And sure enough, they were ambling along, a good stretch up the valley, without a care in the world. Untroubled by the forty kilo loads and the water, they calmly crossed, half swimming and half scrambling, with their heads bobbing above the surface.

It took longer for the rest of us. Some waded through the river but most, as I anticipated, formed a human chain and passed loads to one another between the boulders and bridge.

I could see snow-capped mountains up ahead. There are many mountains in the Himalaya higher than those in Spiti, but to us, these were impressive. I reflected on this. It is incredible to think that this landmass was once a flat sea bed around 70 million years ago. That was before the collision of two of the earth's plates, the north-moving Indo-Australian and the Eurasian. In the process the Tethys Sea disappeared and the crushing motion thrust giant, crumpled peaks upwards. Thus a 2,500-kilometre Himalayan chain was formed. Those geological forces are still at work, pushing the mountains higher at a rate of 5 millimetres a year and the whole chain north 67 millimetres per year. Today, mountains with summits over 6,000 metres above sea level and over 600 kilometres from the nearest ocean are home to the fossils of sea creatures that once swam in the depths millions of years ago.

Close to the nala we came by an isolated black boulder with a table-like top. On it was a prayer stone, the size of a plate, placed there by locals. The mantra *Om Ma-Ni Pa-dme Hum* was artfully carved on it in Tibetan script. Next to the boulder I found another rock, a piece of red limestone the size and weight of a brick, smoothed by the continual rolling action of the river. It held a fossil on one of its sides, a perfect spherical ammonite at least 50 million years old. I placed both stones side by side on top of the boulder for all to see and reflected on their significance. They had one thing in common — their age, and yet both held very different meanings. The fossil stone represented an ancient geological past, when neither human life nor the Himalaya had formed. The prayer stone represented another existence beyond earth — the eternal one of the afterlife. I found this contrast staggering. They were just two stones, side by side in the same valley but symbolically they were aeons apart.

Our caravan stretched out in a long line up the flat bank of the Parahio. The white sacks stood out on the porter's backs, held firm by a belt pressing around each man's forehead. The sun beat down. Dark, stratified peaks towered either side of us. We looked like ants on the march.

By lunchtime we made Thidim, an area of pasture with four stone huts at the confluence of the East Debsa and Parahio rivers. Two women were tending a field. Earlier in both Sagnam and Kaho Dogri, Darach and I had studied the irrigation systems used by the Spitians to bring water to their villages and to cultivate their fields. It is ingenious. It starts with a water source, a nala at a higher point above the village. This leads to a network of channels going around each homestead and street. By simple gravity, water flows into and around the village, serving cooking and cleaning needs. A parallel duct from the flow serves clean drinking water needs. The water is then directed to the fields where it is cleverly managed. Shallow trenches run along the perimeter of each field, continuing in parallel tracks across them. These also demarcate areas of different crops in the same field. Small mud dykes are built up in these trenches at strategic points. Whenever a particular section of field requires water, the appropriate dykes are opened by hoe, allowing the water in to spread. After enough in-take the dykes are rebuilt and the water directed elsewhere. Water naturally drains downhill to the lowest point in any field. It is here that the remainder is channeled to another, lower field, where the process repeats itself. No water is wasted and no part of any field is deprived of it. The best thing about the whole system is that it is carefully regulated. Such capable engineering reminded us of the Romans and how they skillfully harnessed water for their cities by the construction of vast aqueducts. Here the Spitian method is similar and, though of a smaller scale, it has a great advantage over the Roman system. It is far more flexible and easy to manage.

We progressed up the Parahio and crossed the adjoining Khamengar river without difficulty, mid-afternoon. This marked our entry to the Debsa valley. It had been a good day. Everyone performed well carrying their loads. Our donkeys fared particularly well and, having seen them in action, I now had a huge respect for them. These lightweights could not only carry heavy loads over dangerous rivers but, like goats, were nimble on narrow crumbling tracks on steep ground.

Every man and animal earned a rest that night. We made camp on a small flat pasture. A strong, cold wind whipped up from the west; it was an effort to put the tents up. The more we headed west the more we had the wilderness to ourselves. Civilisation was disappearing. Ironically this invoked a comfortable, safe feeling.

Another sumptuous meal was created by Raj, with every attention to detail. The delph and cutlery were spotless. A tablecloth and candles were laid out. The dishes were varied and plentiful and the timing and service impeccable. As alpinists we weren't used to these high standards. We were more familiar with heading into the mountains in pairs and having to cook and clean for ourselves; to carry our own loads and arrange our own shelter. Also, having heard and read enough expedition horror stories about unscrupulous cooks, abysmal food and crooked agents, we were pleasantly surprised by our luck. Everything was running smoothly and we were chuffed. Also we couldn't help thinking our expedition had an old-fashioned quality about it, like the early Alpine explorers or the Duke of Abruzzi on one of his grand campaigns. These were lavish affairs with armies of porters and servants catering for every need, from wines and cigars to writing desks, libraries and armchairs. OK, our needs were much simpler, but we had put a lot of time and effort in to getting things right, such as finding a good agent, itemising food, organising a schedule, detailing logistics, estimating porter numbers and so on. However we hadn't anticipated having no trouble at all and on having everything done for us so carefully and well. Here we found our lives easy. We didn't have to lift any loads or clean any item, or even erect a tent. We barely had to think. Our only obligation was to wake up in the morning, eat, confirm our day's route and stroll behind the porters and animals like gentleman aristocrats. It felt odd, indulgent even. And yet we acknowledged it was a feeling we could easily get used to.

Our final day's march was the hardest, up and down ravines and awkward scree slopes. The sun beat down. The altitude was 4,000 metres. Our pace slowed as our heads and lungs adapted to the thinner air. We weren't the only ones flagging. Around three we reached a nala, the Bauli Khad, which forced us to stop. We had to cross it, but doing so was tricky. It was the fastest we had yet seen and the banks were steep and littered with unstable rocks. There was no easy place to cross and a slip at any point meant certain injury. The noise drowned any conversation. We humans could manage a crossing, although slowly and carefully, but only one of the donkeys was prepared to have a go. Two others shied away and two more lay on the ground, unwilling to budge. What with the hours they had put in, the heat and the loads, they had decided enough was enough. Moreover, their handler refused to lead them on any further. I couldn't blame him, it was too risky. But I had to hand it to the animals; they had done Trojan work. Instead loads were man-hauled across. While this was going on, Darach, Raj and myself crossed and pushed ahead to find base camp. Not far from the Bauli we came to a flat green pasture at the confluence of the East and West Upper Debsa nalas. This was Thwak Debsa, which translated means 'flat place on a glacier.' It would be base camp — our home for the next few weeks. Despite tiredness, Darach and I couldn't help being excited by what we saw. Thwak Debsa was beautiful — a wide park of lush grass and gentle slopes, carved by lost glaciers. Torrential rivers abounded now. Several formidable peaks stood around us. Most of them six thousanders, a few quite technical. To the south we got our first view of our target; a bulky massif, 48 square kilometres with rough walls and irregular peaks. It had a classic cone summit, a glacier on its shoulder and a long, inviting Southwest Ridge. Marked with a spot height of 6,135 metres on our map, it seemed to us magnificent.

FOUR

First Exploration.
Let's Not Go There Again

One by one the rest of the crew rolled in. Raj picked a flat spot for our tents and got to work. It was great to get a sense of space again, particularly after the walled confines of the Parahio.

The next day we organised ourselves. A cook's tent and dining tent were erected and a toilet tent a hundred metres away, over a hole Raj dug in the earth. To avoid conflict and provide space, each man had his own tent. A spring was found trickling from a bank at the confluence. This became our water source. By piling up rocks, Manbahadur channeled its flow with a simple diversion, creating a pool which allowed us draw upon it easily.

That first morning, Nima and the porters left early. The previous night before dinner, I asked Nima to assemble them so the four of us could thank them for their work. Everyone crowded around. Not wanting the porters to lose out, I made a short speech and in full view of everyone, handed the head porter a wad of notes.

'There's two hundred rupees for every one of you here,' I announced. 'Make sure this man gives it to you when you get back to Sagnam.'

They laughed on Nima's translation.

Another feast was dished up by Raj which put us all in fine form. Plans for the coming weeks were discussed. But for now we would spend time around base camp acclimatising. At 4,250 metres our bodies needed a couple of days to adjust to the lower oxygen level before attempting any objectives.

It was a beautiful first night. The sky, clear, black as pitch, hosted a waxing moon and a million stars. Silhouettes of grand peaks and ridges loomed around us. The roar of funneling nalas could be heard below. Other than ourselves not a soul stirred for miles. We were just where we wanted to be; ensconced in a little-known mountain wilderness with bundles of hope, energy and ideas. The many months at home thinking and preparing was yielding a result and the hard work of getting to base camp in one piece was over. Thankfully we were all getting on OK. The weather was good, our peak stood proudly in front of us and an unexplored valley system surrounded us. Things were looking up.

At 6 a.m. Raj and Manbahadur woke us up with bed-tea. Conveniently a bowl of water was left outside each of our tents for washing. Luxury. This may have been normal service for them but it was new and strange for us. That said, it would be a routine observed each day in base camp and, much like the fine meals Raj kept conjuring up, we couldn't complain. With this kind of excellent service it was no wonder Bonington kept choosing him for his expeditions.

Breakfast over, I washed some clothes at the nala. Craig, Paulie and Masthi kept themselves busy while Darach, feeling unwell, remained in bed. Later I rigged up a field shower at the confluence. Nothing complicated, just a plastic bag with an attached tube and sprinkler. The sun heated the water in the bag and gravity provided the flow. As domestic shower units go, the view was second to none: overlooking converging nalas, a desolate, glacial basin and beyond that, untouched peaks. While behind me, scattered on the pasture, were large boulders standing nobly like figures on a chessboard.

That afternoon I took a walk up this boulder field to get a better view of our surroundings and a sense of what we were taking on in the coming weeks. On the way I passed a small, dry-stone enclosure of rocks piled into four low walls: a seasonal shepherd — *gaddi* — shelter. Venturing up a slope I got a partial view of the East and West tributaries that make up the Upper Debsa. These two glacial valleys encircle a broad massif. Their heads meet at a col, south of it, while here at Thwak Debsa, their mouths converge as meltwater to form the main Debsa river. From then on the Debsa flows east, to be joined by the Khamengar and Pin rivers, forming the Parahio nala. The Parahio flows into the Spiti, which eventually meets the Satluj river. As I looked at the massif and these twin valleys I reminded myself what, according to Nima's translation, Debsa meant: a rocky, mountain summit surrounded by glaciers. This made perfect sense. The Spitians couldn't have chosen a more appropriate name.

I looked to the south, halfway up the East Upper Debsa and studied our intended objective, Peak 6135. Its conical summit was more pronounced than when seen from base camp. A subsidiary summit stands to its north, emerging from a snow-bound saddle. The outline of both peaks contrasted sharply with the clear blue sky. I waited and watched as a half-moon arched over both and took a photograph as it hung momentarily above the summit cone. I can't wait to get up there, I thought, and get a view over the whole area. Fingers crossed.

A cool, katabatic wind blew down from the western valley which made me shiver. I pulled up my hood, took a few more photographs and headed back to base camp.

Darach was up. Before dinner, with Raj and Masthi helping, we laid out hill food for the coming weeks and then packed it in an orderly way into two steel chests. There was no shortage of stuff: ready-made meals, tinned meat, cakes, porridge, nuts and chocolate bars.

The next day, Paul, Craig, Masthi and I did a recce up the East Upper valley. In the preceding months we had decided we would make an attempt on Peak 6135 by its Southwest Ridge. To our minds it was the mountain's most attractive and feasible route. A recce of it and its access from the valley floor was needed to verify our knowledge and confirm a plan. Darach was still feeling sick and decided to remain in camp. The recce was also a chance to move two tents up the valley in preparation of an Advanced Base Camp.

Crossing the nala was hard. We picked the widest point of the confluence, formed a diamond-shaped scrum and tentatively edged sideways across. The water was freezing and the current strong. Our feet kept stumbling over unseen boulders. It was vital none of us fell otherwise the likelihood was we would all be swept away. Paulie stood at the front, leaning against the torrent, balanced on walking poles. With each step he made, we synchronised as best we could. Shouts went out. The roar of the nala whipped them away. Danger was etched on our faces and our arms and leg muscles strained. The deeper we went, the harder we worked. Feet slipped and rocks tumbled below. It was touch and go. But luckily our balance and nerve held. We stepped onto the far side, shaking with cold and relieved it was over.

We dried off and pressed on. A 4-kilometre hike over talus and grass slopes saw us at the foot of the peak. It looked enticing. We weighed it up. Firstly we would face a slog up the side of a waterfall to reach a hanging valley — a potential Advanced Base Camp site, then a scramble over a boulder-field to the flank leading up to the ridge crest, then another scramble over loose rock and tors to get to its technical piece: a triangular tower, 100 metres high. This marked a halfway point. Using binoculars, Paulie and I studied this section carefully. Going straight over it wasn't likely, as a fair chunk of it was vertical and would take too much time. Taking a route left, around it by the Northwest Face looked dangerous. It was exposed, possibly overhanging in places and the rock looked unstable. The best line seemed to be a traverse to the right, up a broken snow couloir and over a rib at the top.

'What do you reckon, Paulie? A running belay up the right and we pitch it where we have to?'

'Yeah, I'd say that's about right.'

Beyond the tower it was anyone's guess. But from our view back at base camp the rest of the ridge seemed possible.

Past the mountain, the view up the valley wasn't so favourable. A mass of mountain waste covered the place. Heaps of mud, boulder and broken glacier; all horrible underfoot. Beyond that, an array of brooding peaks formed the valley's head. These intimidating peaks are part of a mountain chain demarcating two regions: the Kulu-Spiti divide. No one had been much further up this valley than the point we were now standing. Furthermore, given what we were looking at, we could have forgiven anyone for not wanting to. We stashed the tents under a rock, marked it with a cairn and headed back to base camp.

It was after four when we got back to the confluence. Crossing it by foot this time was impossible. With the sun melting the glacier all day, the water level rose, covering our waists and the current had strengthened. We made two attempts, using a rope which Darach had anchored on the far side, but it was no use. Paulie was first to try. He made two metres, got knocked down and was lucky to hang on for his life. The idea was scrapped. Having to bivvy the night a mere 50 metres from base camp was now a possibility, leaving another attempt for morning when the water level would be low. However there were still two other options. One was a slog up the West Upper valley to search for a snow bridge to cross. The other, a Tyrolean traverse. We chose the traverse, thinking it might save time. Moving upriver, we found a narrow section, flanked high on either side by boulders. From the far side, Darach and Raj threw a rope across. Setting up the traverse took time. A first rope got snagged in the rapids, refusing to budge, and a second rope kept falling short. Meanwhile the roar of the nala drowned our shouts, hampering communication. Rocks with messages attached were thrown back and forth. Eventually we got rigged up, with a taut rope tied to slings, wrapped around boulders. One by one we clipped on and monkeyed across. It wasn't easy. It had been a long, tiring day and the act of hauling yourself upside-down across the rope with your arms and legs aching is exhausting. Psychologically it was no small matter either, what with the deafening rapids below, waiting to swallow us. The exercise took longer than expected. Nevertheless, we made it back into camp just as it got dark. We were tired. But more importantly we were glad we were safe and thankful the day was over.

Friday 13th came next — a convenient day for a rest. After a leisurely breakfast the four of us had a meeting by the river to plan the days ahead. Our main objective was to attempt the peak but we also wanted to explore the valleys around us, as no one else had. Additionally we needed to acclimatise, which meant spending time at greater height. The maps came out.

In my research of mountaineering history of Spiti, I found only two parties that had done any exploration in the Debsa valley system. One was Paddy O'Leary's expedition to the neighbouring Khamengar valley in 2000 where his team made the first ascent of Kangla Tarbo. After that he led his team into the East Upper Debsa where they searched for a pass they thought might link the Debsa to another valley, the Killung — not far from our intended peak. Without accurate maps or the advantage of Google Earth, they weren't to know no pass exists. However the team had other success when two members, Sé O'Hanlon and Hugh Reynolds, ventured up the West Upper Debsa and crossed the Kulu-Spiti divide by way of a high pass into the known Parvati valley. However theirs wasn't the first crossing of the Debsa to Parvati. That honour went to a small British and South African expedition in 1952. Kenneth Snelson, along with scientists J. de. V. Graaff and E. A. Schelpe were the first explorers of the West Upper Debsa, having crossed from the adjacent Dibibokri and Ratiruni valleys, west of the divide. These men marched across the head of the Debsa, ascending the only col linking both West and East Upper valleys on the south side of a massif, 8.5 kilometres direct from Thwak Debsa. Critically though, Snelson never crossed this col, preferring to retrace his steps back across the West Upper Debsa and return to the Dibibokri for further exploration and climbs. Thus no one had yet made a crossing between both valleys of the Debsa's head. Likewise, no one had set foot on the head of the East Upper valley. Given these facts, we reckoned we might be able to kill three birds with the one stone, by attempting a first crossing of this col. Success here meant being the first to penetrate the head of the East Upper valley. It also meant good acclimatisation, with the col at 5,600 metres, putting us in state for a peak attempt. The third advantage, if we took the west-east route, was being able to stock more gear — ropes, fuel, crampons and any leftover food — at the base of Peak 6135 before returning to base camp. Thus considering the distances, the weight and terrain, we estimated such a mini-expedition would take four to five days. It was an idea that galvanised all our thoughts and aims into a plan. But more importantly, it was an idea that excited us. We would prepare ourselves in the afternoon and set out the next day.

Saturday started off well. The weather was good. We retrieved the rope that had snagged in the nala and we were on the trail up the West Upper valley by 9 a.m. Masthi by his own choice remained in base camp. Unavoidably our bags were heavy, what with all the stuff we had to carry: climbing gear, sleeping bags, shelter and enough food and fuel for five days. We traipsed up the banks of the nala. It was slow going. Undulating grass pasture promptly gave way to slopes of mountain rubble, a mix of reddish-brown limestone and shale. It all made for hard work. We reached an ice-bridge the size of a tennis court which was peppered with mud and stones. Deep cracks ran along its length. Given the summer heat and the melting of such structures, we made sure we crossed it carefully. After several hours plodding uphill we came to the mouth of the glacier. The valley had opened up now and a cold, katabatic wind struck up to greet us. Grey nimbostratus cloud had built up throughout the day. It descended and started to rain, lightly. We had to find a camp spot for the night. It was either the glacier or a lateral moraine. We chose the moraine. The rocks kept us up off the ice but their sharpness and irregular shapes gave little comfort when lying down. Enough time was spent shifting them around to make acceptable beds. The rain persisted. We sourced water from glacial channels and just managed to cook and eat dinner before the heavens opened. Heavy rain, thunder and lightening took over. All metalwork got thrown to one side as each of us took cover.

In our eagerness to reduce weight we had agreed before setting out to carry bivvy bags instead of tents. This idea was all very well in good weather, but as we were soon to learn, such a decision came at a price. Splashes of rain managed to seep in through the opening of the drawcords, and the condensation from our breaths covered the lining. Very soon dampness crept into our sleeping bags and our heads, necks and shoulders became wet. In cramped boredom we waited for the rain to stop. There was little we could do other than lie there timing the flashes of lightning against the peals of thunder and listen to the patter of rain on our bags. Thankfully after a couple of hours it stopped, upon which we emerged from our shells in darkness. The clouds had broken up and a full moon and blanket of stars came out. Quickly we fixed a brew. We felt better with our new-found freedom and chatted in the silvery light. All was calm again, only the sound of our voices, a gentle breeze on our hoods and the occasional rumble of rockfall on an unseen valley wall.

There was no urgency among us to get moving in the morning. We strung our gear out on the rocks to let it all dry as much as possible. Not that it did. The weather hadn't improved much. It was cold and there was no sun. It wasn't raining but portentous cloud enveloped the mountains, hanging on faces, drifting slowly over ridges and instilling a sense of loneliness and bleakness. These peaks, grey sentinels that make up the Kulu-Spiti divide, were uninviting, not just to look at but also to climb. All vertiginous wet slab, ominous precipices, shattered rock and broken ice pillars. I was glad we weren't touching them. The glacier had more appeal. It was largely flat, a kilometre wide, more in places and 12 kilometres long, bending at the valley's head. Our aim for the day was to make 6.5 kilometres along it, to a camp at a height of 5,200 metres, within striking distance for the col the next day.

Gear packed, we donned crampons, roped up and trudged on. Marching for hours in a straight line on a featureless glacier can be tedious, but we were glad of the firm snow and ice underfoot which compared well against the unsteady rubble of the previous day. Up we went, the Debsa massif on our left, the triangular peaks of the divide on our right. Our calls for better weather went unheard. Clouds built up throughout the morning, lumbering across the valley, threatening rain. It began to drizzle. Heads bent, we pushed on but the signs weren't good. The drizzle got worse. Around two we got within half a kilometre of our target and were looking about for a water source when the rain started. Slowly at first and then heavier. There was little time for preparation — each man made a dash for his bivvy. A rush ensued; to roll out Thermarests, cover up rucksacks, put on down jackets and off-load crampons. Once inside the bivvy, the prisoner effect kicked in. There are few things worse than being stuck in a narrow cocoon on an isolated glacier in the rain. For a start it can be cold, damn cold, especially when you've had no time to unravel sleeping bags. There's not much space for movement and precious little comfort in lying on a half-inch thick mat with half a kilometre of solid ice beneath you. Also the solitary nature of the bag makes talking to others difficult. Each man is left to his own thoughts, and with the cold and discomfort it's impossible to focus the mind on anything positive. There are only two ponderables: when is the rain going to stop, and what do we do if it doesn't? The chances were it would drag on for hours, possibly even days. As we were to find out, with such thoughts a man can easily get dispirited. The boredom doesn't help either. Here it was frustrating being curled up in a ball listening to the spits of rain, trying to establish a pattern to it in vain hope of it moving away. The irritating thing was it was consistent, not light enough to entice you out of the bag, not heavy enough to be a passing shower. Just a steady quality that seemed interminable. The torment didn't end there. We had made 5,100 metres and our lungs were still adapting to the thinner air. Frequently the confines of the bag had a suffocating effect, half real, half imaginary. Every so often the body would panic for oxygen.

You would have to twist upwards and set your mouth against the drawcord to take in air. A few gulps brought instant relief. However this peep hole created another problem: water ingress. King Canute and his effort with tide was about as futile as our attempts to keep water outside our bivvies. It collects in seams and folds and works its way down to the entrance hole. Drip by drip your head gets wet, followed by your neck and arms. Then the top of your sleeping bag becomes a sponge. Condensation from your breath only adds to the misery. The longer it goes on, the worse it gets. This gloom then reaches a low when you feel the need to urinate. I won't go into detail here, but let's just say this procedure is rarely a dry affair. Therefore it doesn't take long before you're cursing yourself for not having packed a tent.

For four hours we endured this state. Then I thought I heard fewer drops hitting the bag. Peering out of the opening, I noticed the clouds had parted, slightly. I sensed a respite.

'Come on lads, get up. It's stopped raining.'

Like rising polar bears, three stiff beasts emerged from their lairs, groaning and swearing. Stoves were lit and packet dinners prepared. Fortunately we just had enough time to eat and organise ourselves. Water bottles were filled, bivvies shaken down, wet clothing removed and damp socks stuffed beneath layers, next to our skins. It was going to be another long, hard night. Then just before the brew was ready, the rain returned.

It was a struggle to get any sleep. Inside, the dampness kept building up and the cold permeated our bones, causing endless shifting. The rain spat down, mocking us. Our heads struggled with dreary thoughts only broken by the odd clatter of ice, sliding down the massif. Paulie suffered the worst. A leaking bivvy had him shivering all night. Improvising with a torn survival bag was of little help. Around four, the rain eased. Around five it stopped and we crawled out of our shells. Paulie looked as pale as a ghost. There was no question of him continuing now, running the risk of hypothermia. He had to get back to base camp. Disappointed, he packed up. And with a bowl of porridge and a mug of tea inside him, he started back down the glacier. The rest of us considered our options. The weather remained unpredictable, with thick cloud rolling about. Crossing the col would be difficult work. But the prospect of a third rough night on the ice in bad weather, and the dangers it posed, put us off. It simply made no sense to go on. Nevertheless, I at least wanted to get a look at the col. From where we stood it was 2.5 kilometres up the glacier, hidden around the bend. Darach and Craig agreed. But as soon as we began marching a mist came down, obscuring the whole area. That was enough. We gave up.

Disappointed, we turned on our tails and followed Paulie's trail down the glacier towards base camp. It was a weary trudge back, given the lack of sleep and our tiredness from the weight we were carrying. Back we went, revisiting our earlier footprints, past the snout and over the cumbersome moraine to meet the flurry of the nala. We were amazed to find no trace of the large ice-bridge that had spanned the nala on our ascent. Triggered by the rains, it capitulated, its payload of boulders and mud washed down the Debsa. It was a good example of how rapidly great changes take place in the mountain environment.

Looking back on our venture, it was bad weather and inferior shelter that had let us down. It was unfortunate we didn't even get to see the col, never mind cross it. But we did manage to gain some height, leaving us better acclimatised. However the exploration wasn't all lost. We got a consolation prize. On our way back that third day we came across a line of paw prints traversing the glacier. It was difficult to tell what animal they belonged to. However given the altitude, the inhospitable landscape and the complete lack of any vegetation, there was only one animal we were aware it might be. A snow leopard. If so, we wondered what he was up to. Most likely he had been hunting during the night. His track wasn't far from where we had camped. He would have smelled us. Perhaps saw us. Would he have considered us fair game? Probably not. Given our miserable state I'd say if anything, he took pity on us and padded away. He would have been right.

Returning to base camp was like re-entering a holiday camp. It was good to be back to familiar comforts like a tent and a dry sleeping bag. And it was great to be back with the other boys. Raj and Manbahadur ran a first rate camp. Of their own volition they were always doing things to make our lives easy, such as collecting washing we might have left out in the rain, securing our tents in advance of rough weather, or repairing them whenever they were damaged. Their quiet, empathic natures and smiling faces made for a happy atmosphere among us all. The thought often crossed my mind that if all of us Westerners had the same qualities of selflessness and care as these two men, then the world we all live in would be a much better place.

They didn't drop their standards when it came to cooking either. Their meals were the highlights of occasional rest days. Such lazy days began with bed-tea, served to us individually in our tents at 6 a.m. A leisurely wash, followed by a 20-metre stroll saw us in the dining tent for breakfast at 7 a.m. There the feasting began: fried eggs, French bread or omelette, a choice of chapattis or pancakes, porridge, peanut butter, jam, cereal and tea. It was hard to work this off. The best we could do was some washing or shower down at the river, followed by sun-bathing or checking gear. This took us to lunch. Room was made for the likes of spiced coleslaw, ghobi, aloo, roast vegetables, dal, occasional tinned meat, beans, potato cakes, rice, pasta and freshly baked bread. Getting through lunch always took time. Little was said during it and afterwards, more often than not, the most we could do was stumble to our tents and rest. Around four, Raj made tea. One afternoon he made masala chai, a spiced concoction of Indian tea, milk, cloves, ginger and cinnamon. We liked it so much that normal afternoon tea wasn't entertained from then on. Meanwhile the lounging continued. The idle afternoons were spent reading or writing diaries, resting limbs, watching pecking choughs outside or simply dozing in the tents. Dinner was served at seven. This was usually a heavier, more elaborate version of lunch, always with soup, but never were the same two dishes served in one day. Tinned fruit, biscuits and custard made up dessert. Naturally, coffee and tea were never forgotten. As you can guess, we were then ready for bed. It has to be said, after such rest days we needed to get out climbing mountains, if not merely to justify our presence in the Himalaya, but to simply lose weight.

Our days spent in Thwak Debsa couldn't have been better. The slow pace, the purposeful rest and the fact that we all got along made life easy. It was a privilege just to be here, in a beautiful remote valley, far away from the noise of the city — any city — and the stresses and cares of our lives back home. Here there was no traffic, no meetings to attend, no deadlines, no radios, tel-evisions or phones. Neither were there artificial lights, mechanical noises, bills, bad news, electric pylons, buildings or crime. Just the warm sun, the sounds of the wind flapping the tents, the nalas, the nightly arc of the moon over the peaks and a multitude of stars; the daily gathering of cloud expanding in an azure sky. Freed of all cares and urban anxieties, our minds and moods were allowed to wander happily with the elements of nature and the rhythms of the earth. Days such as these we didn't want to end.

From base camp we could see 5 kilometres up the East Upper Debsa to our peak on the left-hand side. Its Southwest Ridge, clean and straight save for the bulge of the tower midway, was like a siren call. Our eyes were continually drawn to it. To climb it as a round trip from base camp would take about a week. The question was, would we get a few days good weather for it? Granted, its condition had improved since our valley exploration but only time would tell. I often wondered as I lay in my tent looking up at it, what the view was like from its summit. Would we see lots of intimidating iced peaks?

What about the big unnamed and unclimbed peaks of the Kulu-Spiti divide? Would we look down on new, unknown valleys? And what about directly north, would we spot the mountains first ascended by Paddy O'Leary's team and Joss Lynam — Kangla Tarbo and Shigri Parbat? Possibly. It was an exciting prospect and one that required a bit of luck. Nevertheless it was within our capacity to at least attempt it. After all, here we were, four lads in the Himalaya for the first time, chasing a dream of exploring and making a first ascent. Our view was, if we were successful, great. If not, then no bother. But at least we wanted to give it a fair go.

It was also interesting to see ourselves operating in isolation. We were focused. Cut off from the outside world, everything else in our lives such as our jobs, our families, our girlfriends seemed very far away. Almost non-existent.

Regarding Paddy and Joss, it was encouraging to know we were following their example. Ireland hasn't produced many pioneering Himalayan mountaineers, but their achievements, particularly what they did in Spiti, have been among the most prominent. It is interesting, there are many well known mountains and regions on the planet which, through exploration, are associated with particular nationalities. Take the French and Annapurna for example. The Germans and Nanga Parbat. The Russians in Central Asia. The British in the Alps and the Norwegians at the Poles. There are others. But when it comes to Ireland and pioneering exploration, the exploits of these two men forged an affiliation between our country and India. By our expedition we hoped to follow and expand that history and tradition.

But another kind of tradition was important to us, one that Paddy and Joss observed, and that was climbing ethics and style. For example, we weren't carrying an Irish tricolour to plant on any summit. To me, the thought of doing this on another nation's mountains is repugnant. Thankfully gone are the days when people climbed mountains as an expression of imperial pride. However I think those who do this today are usually unaware of their arrogance and disrespect to the lands and people of which they are guests. It is narcissistic nationalism. After all, how many of us Irish would like to see the Union Jack or Star-spangled Banner waved in our faces from the top of Carrauntoohil or Lugnaquillia? I for one was having none of it and the other lads felt the same. Also, we weren't doing this expedition for attention, vanity or money. We were doing it for ourselves. Finally our other principle was to explore and climb with the utmost consideration for the environment. We would have nothing to do with that other disease of modern climbing, imposing yourself on a mountain route by fixed protection and the use of bolts. We would try and leave the mountains and valleys as we had found them — untouched.

A cold wind blew through Thwak Debsa from the west. It was familiar to us now, being a daily occurrence, always stirring up around lunch. We rested. There was little movement around camp, just the flapping of flysheets and the choughs pecking around the stones on the grass. Paulie and I lingered in the dining tent. Our conversation drifted around several things: the failed col exploration, the rock routes familiar to us at home and the peak attempt ahead. A quiet, apprehensive air came over us. It has to be said, a lot of what makes up mountaineering is failure and what you make of it. A raft of problems can hinder or prevent any type of climb: bad weather, poor conditions, inaccessibility, sickness, injured partners, the lack of money or time. To date I've had my share of plans thwarted by all of these factors, but that's mountaineering. There's not much you can do only accept it, and I do. Yet when all aspects of a climb are in order and the climb itself is successful, invariably the satisfaction felt negates all earlier failures. Otherwise we would hardly keep doing it. However, to add another dimension, the possibility of being jinxed is something quite different. Now Paulie and I were beginning to wonder if this was the case with the pair of us, given our misfortune of the past few days. We had both been on climbing trips at home and in the Alps when part of a club or group. But whenever we shared a rope it seemed things rarely went right. Two examples stood out. One was when we attempted some little-known rock climbs in Luggala, Wicklow, as part-preparation for an ambitious attempt on the Piz Badile later the same summer. No sooner had we started the first pitch of *Highway* when we were attacked by midges. Swarms of them, their mission to eat us alive and not let us climb. We were forced to run for cover, back to our cars and home. Then months later, when we went to do the Piz Badile, our plans were scuppered by bad weather. We had one week for it and a range of ambitious options on it: up the North Ridge on the Swiss side, over the top and down the Italian side; a drive back around to the Swiss side for a crack at the Cassin route on the Northeast Face if we felt up to it, or an attempt on the Molteni route on the South Face if not. It was a tricky project that involved complicated car splits, multiple hut bookings and clever storage of gear. Nevertheless we thought it out and came up with a good, logical plan. Everything seemed fine. We were both in good shape, climbing at the right grade and mentally very prepared. Paulie had spent the summer in the Alps and we arranged to meet up in the campsite in the village of Bondo at the base of the mountain on a Saturday in late August. However no sooner had we met when it started to rain. It rained and rained, non-stop for five days. In all that time we didn't so much as get a glimpse of the Piz Badile. Climbing it was impossible.

When the sky finally opened the following Thursday, a foot of snow covered the North face and ridge. It would take another three or four days for that to clear. This was too late for us, we were out of time and luck. The project was scrapped. … Luggala … the Piz Badile … and now the Debsa col debacle; the failures with Paulie were mounting up.

'Our luck's got to turn soon, Paulie,' I said, trying to enthuse.

'I hope you're right,' he groaned.

FIVE

The Climb

Wednesday 18 June. Preparation for Peak 6,135 metres began. The first task was to ferry loads of food, fuel and gear up the East Upper Debsa to stock an Advanced Base Camp (ABC). The four of us set out early. The river crossing was dodgy, given the heavy loads and strong current. But we managed again, holding our nerve and operating a tight diamond formation. The biting cold of the water penetrated our bones and it took the best part of an hour's march up the valley before we felt right. We collected the tent stash, continued up the valley and crossed the nala over an ice-bridge. The peak stood in front of us. To its side was the hanging valley which we planned to use as a site for an ABC. Reaching it was an arduous slog up the side of a waterfall, chock-full of boulders and scree. We only made it halfway though, a combination of sluggishness and rain put paid to the effort. The weather had been unpredictable since we had started exploring, being a mix of rain, wind and sun most days, while erratic cloud movement made forecasting difficult. We hoped a few settled days would give us a chance on the peak. We tipped the loads next to a boulder, marked the spot and began the return trek to base camp. I took a second look at the East Upper valley head. Those portentous peaks of the divide seemed worse than before; all hanging glaciers and vicious, curling cornices. Rain clouds drifting from the Parvati only accentuated their threat. They were forlorn mountains, not to be touched.

Four weary bodies made it back to the confluence in the late afternoon. Higher water levels forced a return to the Tyrolean traverse. With Masthi assisting on the opposite bank, the rope was tensioned and we monkeyed across. It had been a slow day. None of us had fully recovered from the earlier valley exploration and there was no objection when I proposed another rest day.

❄ ❄ ❄ ❄

Friday 20 June. Off we went with the last of our food and equipment for ABC and the peak attempt. Across the icy river once more, with Raj, Masthi and Manbahadur seeing us off, waving as if we were soldiers heading off to war. The weather looked promising. We plodded up the valley, crossed the blue ice-bridge and reached the gear stash halfway up the waterfall. In retrospect we were glad of the rest day, otherwise we would not have been able to carry gear any further. It was a struggle to get it all to the top of the waterfall but we managed it with two relays. Tired and with night approaching, we erected two tents at 4,800 metres to form an ABC and collected clean water from snow-melt feeding the river. Binoculars were passed around as we sized up the ridge and a discussion took place over dinner as to what style we would use: Alpine or Himalayan. To climb Alpine-style is to make a single push to the summit, carrying everything you need on your back and making camps en-route. Himalayan style involves a gradual ascent to the summit where all camps, food and equipment gets stocked by people moving up and down the mountain first, much like a conveyor. We agreed to go Alpine, with Camp 1 proposed past the tower at around 5,600 metres. The test was if we felt OK at this height, we would push for the summit the following day. If not, we would adopt Himalayan tactics and retreat to ABC for an extra day.

❄ ❄ ❄ ❄

Saturday 21 June, 6.20 a.m. We left camp and trudged over rocks to the nala, to approach the base of the peak. It was a fine morning with little wind, a broad blue sky, a full moon in the west and streaks of cirrus in the north. It augured well. The nala had no easy crossing point. By now river crossings had become a ritual with us. Little was said. Each man chose a spot where he thought the depth was lowest and the current weakest, before hopping across and exploiting as many protruding rocks as possible. Our choices weren't always correct, this morning being no exception. Our clumsiness was evident. In mild shock on the far side each of us nursed knocks, numbed feet and toes.

We traversed over the boulderfield, indirectly towards the Southwest Ridge. Tons of loose, multi-hued, limestone, shale and slate was scattered around us — iron red, purple, grey, green-grey — some of it rounded by river action, others jagged from glacial exertion. We forged up a gully and onto a rib. Scrambling on the rib was a struggle, what with the loads and the thin air. Movement slowed and seldom were any of us able to haul ourselves over a feature or ledge without stopping briefly for breath and to muster strength. By now it was clear to us that Himalayan climbing is a slow slog, largely pack animal work demanding strength, determination and purpose. There is little grace or speed involved, and definitely no artistry.

One by one we made the ridge crest, with each man collapsing on a pile of rocks. Our pains were rewarded by fine views in the morning sun. Looking down to the north we could make out the tiny yellow flecks of our base camp tents, 5 kilometres away, with the East Debsa nala going by. Further on we could clearly make out the broad icy dome of Paddy O'Leary's Kangla Tarbo. And beyond that, to the northwest, the imposing pyramid wall of an unclimbed six and a half thousander, dominating the divide.

The ridge was in poor state. The quality of its rock was dreadful, mostly shattered slate and shale, all loose and sharp, layered and brittle. Each step had to be thoughtfully placed. A careless foot meant a certain slip and a bruising fall. God, how we pined for the firm granite of Wicklow. Our ears became accustomed to the constant clatter of rock underneath us, falling like delph off a kitchen table. It was hot, slow work. The only respite was the clear view and settled weather. Several tors had to be tackled as we progressed, usually by scrambling over or around them. Here the rock was more stable. However it was sometimes sharp and thin, and often cracked when loaded. At this height and so far from camp, nothing could be trusted.

A casual glance up the ridge, I spotted a lammergeyer lifting off the peak. I had read of these birds with their huge wingspan and effortless flight. A member of the vulture family, similar to the Andean condor. He soared elegantly past us, smooth and controlled, never once flapping a wing or turning its head — the embodiment of grace and calm. He glided down over ABC, wheeled right into the Debsa and gently pirouetted before vanishing in the distance. Perhaps he was a sign, I thought, an avatar of a powerful god sent to guard this mountain, only for us to disturb him. Would the gods approve of us trespassing on this untouched, hallowed space? One way or another we would soon find out.

We edged closer to the crux — a bulwark, 100 metres high of unknown technical difficulty, halfway up the ridge. The tower. Our plan had been to climb it or traverse it by the right-hand side before making camp above it. But it was getting late, mid-afternoon and our bodies were tired. Instead we decided to make Camp 1 on a saddle below it. It was just as well we did, as within the hour the weather had turned. Grey cumulus cloud which had been building all day in the west, closed in. A wind struck up and it started to snow. Nothing major, but conditions that would have made an attempt on the tower dangerous given our physical states and the time of day. Quickly we erected the tent, secured it with rocks and began melting snow. A quick dinner was eaten.

We scampered for cover as the wind picked up and the temperature dropped. Into the tent we crammed like sardines. Limbs and backs ached from the loads. Gear, boots and bags were shuffled awkwardly about before we lay down and reflected. Earlier from the comfort and distance of base camp, the ridge looked straightforward. Nothing too onerous, just a long linear structure with one relatively small technical piece. But it's one thing studying a mountain from afar, quite another when you're up close to it. Problems and obstacles are magnified. Small snow patches become large fields. Gullies grow longer and deeper. Seemingly direct routes transform into long, winding affairs. This we had anticipated, but now that we had put in a hard day experiencing poor chossy rock, we realised this mountain was a lot tougher than we thought it would be.

Sunday 22 June, Camp 1. We awoke at 3 a.m., with the usual reluctance to stir out of warm sleeping bags and into the cold. The sky was clear and starry with a moon in the west. A good sign. Torchlights flashed. Outside, Paulie and Darach fumbled with pots and stoves to heat up porridge. Inside, Craig was not for stirring. He was too exhausted from the previous day and elected not to carry on. Three of us only would make a summit attempt. Decisions were quickly made. One rope and a light rack to be taken, as opposed to double that for four men.

Quietly in the cold, grey dawn we trudged up to the base of the tower. A layer of snow covered much of the scree. Trainloads of scree. We roped up and Paulie took the lead. Darach took coils at the back and I clipped into the middle, video camera in hand. Our packs, though lighter than yesterday, were still a burden, especially now that we were higher. Paulie chose an intricate line to the right of the tower. Up onto crumbling ledges and down snowy breaches. Slings were cast around spikes and attached to the rope with cold, tinkling karabiners. We moved together. As he progressed placing each piece of gear, I unclipped when I reached his earlier pieces, only to clip on again beyond them, for Darach to follow and collect. We came to a chimney. Awkward moments were felt as each man ascended, boots slipping on either side, sending cascades of loose rock down on the next man. 'Below' became the refrain as helmets and shoulders were showered. Paulie, free of such hazard, looked on as Darach and I ducked for cover as best we could. Wires were slotted into cracks, hexes were placed and everything clipped to the rope by extenders. Gingerly we crept up over steps and awkward ledges to the back of the tower. 140 metres of this saw Paulie anchor onto a large flake and belay us. We had overcome the tower.

Stepping out of its shadow we could see the continuation of the ridge. It formed a gentle angle, curving left and then right for a distance of 450 metres, before fading out at the base of a summit ramp which was a wide snowfield. The door was unlocked. All that remained now was the energy and courage to open it and reach the top.

Slowly we pressed on. We clambered over more tors and sharp rock, stopping every so often for a brief rest, a sip of water and a nibble of chocolate and nuts. The mountain was demanding a price. So far Darach was holding up OK, though I noticed Paulie was weakening. His lead had not come cheaply and his pace now slowed. He wasn't alone. If truth be told, I too felt I was running out of steam.

This thing is purgatory, I thought at one stage. The terrain, the thin air, the loads. What crime did we commit for all this? More importantly, what penance must we do to overcome it?

We made the end of the ridge and faced the snowfield. At an incline of 45 to 50 degrees, shovel-shaped, it appeared to have the height and width of a football field. Needless to say, none of us were champing at the bit to get at it. We were dog-tired. I eyed up the slope. The time was 10.15 a.m. Earlier we had agreed a turnaround time of 1 p.m., latest. This last section I knew would be a psychological battle. To ascend it would demand mental strength and stamina. We donned crampons and I thought for a second. Here going lightweight was key. 'Lads, I'm off-loading everything I don't need here. I'll take the rope, some water, the camera and that's it. No spare clothes, food or anything else.'

It was a risk, but a small one as I saw it, given the good cloud and wind conditions. But it was a necessary one if I had any chance of getting to the top. Paulie considered it, agreed and we both dumped our gear under rocks at the head of the ridge. Darach kept his. I also needed food, sustenance. Quickly I devoured a handful of nuts and a half bar of chocolate.

'Right. Lets go.'

Slowly we began our duck-walk up the slope. Axe in one hand, pole in the other. Luckily the snow was relatively firm and we only sank a few inches. After a few minutes I could feel power returning to me. The food had kicked in. As with a lot of climbs, most people have their bouts of strength and weakness. They also have phases of leadership and periods in which they need to be led. I felt stronger now and considered it my time to lead. Up the slope I went, alternating style in accordance to the angle of snow: duck-walking, side-stepping, half and full front-pointing. A rhythm set in. Axe, pole, left foot, right foot … thirty steps and then stop. A couple of breaths then continue. One third of the way up I turned to look at the boys, who were thirty metres behind.

They stopped when I stopped.

'Come on lads, we can nail this,' I called, thinking this might encourage them. I was certain if we persisted we would do it. However a niggling thought bothered me. What if we weren't on the summit slope but a false one and we had more work cut out for us beyond it? A demoralising prospect.

Put that notion aside, I heard myself say. Just keep bashing on.

Halfway up, my step count reduced to twenty, followed by a rest and deep breaths. Shortly after, I was down to twelve. I could feel the sun's reflection from the snow stinging my lips and the rims of my nostrils.

Don't let this thing beat you, I commanded myself.

I looked back. The boys were gaining ground. I took a line rightwards, aiming for a gap between rocks at the top. I was determined I wasn't going to fail. Not now.

Finally I made it; stepping onto a knife-edge crest and looked over the side to find a sweeping drop down the Northeast Face. We did it, we made the top. There was no more mountain. Instant feelings of joy and relief coursed through me. I called the boys up.

'Look at this lads, we've made it.'

There was no doubt. A ridge line running northwest to southeast marked the top and a rock pillar beside us, 7 metres high, was the mountain's true summit. We were delighted. Eighteen months hard work researching, fundraising, planning and perseverance had paid off. It was time for cursory jubilation. What's more, we did it in good time and in good style. It was 12.10 p.m. Moments later we climbed the pillar and placed our hands on its uppermost stone simultaneously. Whoops of joy cried out. Each of us kissed the uppermost stone to mark the achievement. Undeniably it was a special feeling knowing we were first to set foot on this mountain and reach its summit.

We lingered here for twenty minutes, taking photographs of everything. It was important to get evidence of having reached the top. I panned the video camera. Only the magnificent sight of the Himalayas surrounded us now. All kinds of peaks and formations abounded: snow domes, serpentine ridges, pyramids, jagged teeth and crumpled layers. Constructions of all shapes and sizes. I looked down at our massif and took in its subsidiary summits to the north and southeast, with ridges snaking off in the same directions for 5 kilometres. Further north in the distance stood the iced slopes of Paddy O'Leary's Kangla Tarbo (6,315m). And beyond that, the burly form of Shigri Parbat (6,526m), first ascended by Joss Lynam in 1961. To the west and south were spectacular technical peaks, still awaiting a first ascent. All told it was a glorious sight, one I'll never forget.

Celebrations over, we scrambled back onto the snow and started back down. Our happiness had instilled a renewed sense of energy as we made our way daggering down the slope. It had taken two hours to ascend it but less than thirty minutes to descend it. We retrieved our belongings on the ridge and tentatively scrambled back over the tors. Each man was conscious of not making a rash step or a mistake at this stage, the consequences of which would be serious. By 3 p.m. we made the tower. Oddly, since leaving the summit, I had a strange feeling of detachment. As if all my thoughts, words and actions were being conducted outside of my body by someone else — as if I was stoned. Later, Darach mentioned the same sensations were felt by him the first time he went to high altitude. I can only put it down to the lower level of oxygen reaching the brain. It forced me into a tunnel-like operational mode on the technical part of the tower. I couldn't think to any depth as to what I was doing, just manage the gear and move as if I was a robot. *Feed out, slack, unclip, remove gear, clip gear onto harness and downclimb.* In that order. *Don't look around. Don't question or improve anything, just wait for the next move and repeat.*

It was a slow progression down the chimneys with a couple of errant rock-falls en route. Paulie took a hit on the helmet this time, but overall everything worked. We made Camp 1 by 5 p.m, stumbling the final few metres. Craig was waiting, fixing a brew. The three of us collapsed in heaps, like spent salmon, tired but exceptionally content.

❄ ❄ ❄ ❄

Monday 23 June, Camp 1. We woke up late to another clear blue day and to the luxury of not having to do anything quickly. We just had to remove ourselves from the mountain at our leisure. We melted a gallon of snow, cooked breakfast, broke camp and descended. Again, hauling heavy loads over loose rock proved tricky. Nevertheless, we made it over the rock stacks and rubble quicker than expected. In just over two hours we were in the hanging valley by the river. Minutes later we were back at ABC. Nothing would do us now other than sunbathe for the whole afternoon. It was quite a contrast to the exertions of the previous days. Now four pale-skinned Micks prostrated themselves on the warm rocks of the Upper Debsa like the geckos on the Galapagos. An odd sight. The most strenuous activities carried out were flipping onto our backs and stomachs, applying sun crème and taking sips from our water bottles. But hey, we had earned it. That evening I took the camera and wandered higher up the valley. I scrambled up a lateral moraine and followed it a distance. When it ran out I recorded some footage of our mountain.

I wanted to capture it from the south and get some shots of the route we took: the ridge, the tower, the ridge again, the snowfield and summit. On return to camp, the four of us examined the film. We were happy with it. But our bodies weren't so pleased. Torsos and limbs tingled with sunburn.

Tuesday 24 June. We dismantled ABC and packed everything for the return to base camp. The thought of two trips on the valley to retrieve gear wasn't appealing, so we chose to move it all back in one push. Or try to anyhow. This meant, what felt like, a 40-kilo load per man. It was slow, back-breaking work, stepping down the edge of the waterfall, across the icy water and down the boulder-strewn banks of the East Upper nala. Several lengthy stops were needed in order to keep going. The baking sun didn't help. We made the confluence after 5 p.m. and dumped the loads on a rock for collection later. We were exhausted. Taking essentials, we crossed the river by the Tyrolean for the last time. Masthi and Raj assisted on the far side and congratulated us when we got over. Job done.

In base camp we shook hands and celebrated with cold drinks. Before dark, I looked up at the mountain from the door of my tent and reflected. We had been fortunate. The weather had been kind and the conditions favourable. The mountain had allowed us to dance with it. Quietly I saluted the lammergeyer.

Masthi was full of energy from hanging about base camp all week. Over dinner he regaled us with an assortment of mountain horror stories and tragedies; descriptions of multiple deaths on vertical faces, serac falls and crevasse casualties. All of it was highly uplifting, especially after what we had just done. But as he spoke, each of us slipped into our own reverie; our thoughts drifting back to the mountain.

Wednesday 25 June. We had earned a couple of days' rest, and over the coming days we awoke to late bed-teas and breakfasts. Strange noises stirred the first morning. Looking out of our tents, we witnessed an impressive sight. Four hundred animals — sheep and goats — rolled up the Debsa. They were led by two gaddis and a pair of dogs, part of an annual migration to summer pastures in the mountains. Bonanza — Indian style. They filed into camp, a mass of white wool and spindly legs, bleating and chewing as they milled around our tents. We weren't alone any more. It was strange seeing our quiet mountain home suddenly transformed into a crowded farm. But it was good to see them.

This was mountain culture after all, and a distraction for us to talk about. No inconvenience, Thwak Debsa had plenty of room for us all.

Later the gaddis brought the flock back down to the Bauli Khad where they set up camp. The next day, Masthi, Darach and I paid them a visit. I was curious to learn about them and their lives. We found them sitting barefoot in a tiny dry-stone hut, with a canvas tarpaulin stretched over their heads serving as a roof. Outside, the hut was surrounded by the flock. Both men seemed perfectly at peace with themselves. What struck me was their civility and their willingness to talk. Gopichand, the younger of the pair, told us of their lives. Theirs is a rugged one. Both came from a town in the south, Rampur, and every summer they travel north to the Debsa with their flock. This is a journey of twenty-five days, crossing high mountain passes and treacherous glaciers. Once in the Debsa, they remain for two months, moving the animals about in order to avoid overgrazing in any one spot. After that, they retrace their steps home. Their absence from Rampur allows the cultivation of crops in the spring and summer months. The whole exercise is part of a farming tradition carried out by their kind, going back centuries. It is not the only migration they make. Trading trips and travel to other grazing grounds can keep them away from their families and homes for up to nine months of the year. Considering the hardships we mountaineers face, I couldn't help thinking these men and their animals endure far more discomfort. They have to overcome many mountain hazards on their long march. They have to fend off predators. They have to live rough and they have to constantly deal with the elements. Yet Gopichand's smile and dancing eyes told otherwise. This was their accepted way of life after all.

Masthi translated as he spoke. Their hermitic life-style was a revelation. Both men were in excellent health and lived on a simple diet of grains, milk and vegetables. They had never been sick in their lives and had never seen the inside of a hospital. Both had full sets of teeth and neither had ever worn glasses. Gopichand looked a youthful forty, but was actually fifty. More incredibly the elder, Dilbar, looked around sixty but was apparently closer to eighty. What's more, both men expected to live well beyond eighty.

'This is quite normal for them,' Masthi explained. 'Gaddis in this part of the world live long, healthy lives.'

The animals looked on as we talked, bunched together around the hut for protection. Already the surrounding grass had been eaten and the bare earth unsettled by hundreds of small hooves. The sheep resembled thin Wicklow cheviots; limited in mind, roman-nosed and carriers of dense, matted fleece.

The goats were far more elegant. All were of a Kashmir breed, with sharp horns, lithe bodies and fine, long wool. Every few minutes a young pretender would clamber onto a rock, casting a regal eye out over the flock. I thought of King Puck. Meanwhile the dogs stood guard, ever watchful of opportunistic snow leopards.

A curious thing about the gaddis was how well they dressed. You would think a nomadic shepherd in the mountains for months would be clad in dirty rags. Not these boys. They wore cream woollen suits, heavy and warm, of well crafted serge spun from their flock. The kind of high-quality garments that wouldn't look out of place in any well-heeled social club. Ignoring their shoes and flat caps, the pair could be mistaken for wealthy types.

The gaddis were also highly resourceful. A carpet of cut grass lay on the hut floor, with more piled up on long flat stones for their beds. But it was the bundle of firewood outside that amazed us. We were at a loss to know how they were able to find any wood in such a barren place. The nearest trees were in the villages, at least a day's hike away. Yet foraging among the rocks, they had gathered a sizeable pile that morning.

The longer we spent in the company of these men, the more I could see a few basic truths. For one, they were living proof on how to live a healthy, productive life with very little means. By working with nature and not wasting anything, they were able to feed, clothe and shelter themselves, as well as look after their flock and their distant families. More pertinently, they were showing us the folly of many of the things we aspire to. The desire for money, status, power, a flash car and a castle of a house. Often we fool ourselves into thinking such things make for quality, worthwhile lives. Of course, they don't. After all, what's the point in working yourself or others to death in trying to attain them? Often irritating and distancing those around you when you do. Not to mention the damage you can inflict on the environment in the process. Many of us with modern ills and urban lives have lost touch with our past. A lot of Westerners — us Irish particularly — are only one, two or three generations away from the simple agrarian communities known to our predecessors. These communities, though imperfect, espoused wholesome life-styles far removed from what we experience today. These gaddis, by their simple ways, their values and expectations, are an accurate reflection of how our recent ancestors were. Sadly, they also show just how far we have chosen to become estranged from them.

We were delighted at having done the peak. The burden of expectation around it had been lifted and now we could relax. Anything further we attempted would be viewed as bonus as the expedition's primary objective had been met. We had enough time, ten days, before the schedule ran out and our sojourn in the mountains came to an end. What would we do next? There was a choice. The first was to tackle another unclimbed peak. The second was to attempt another valley exploration. Given we had just spent a week slogging up and down a mountain, the collective mood was for something different and possibly less laborious. So back to the valleys it was agreed. A different valley this time, moving away from the Debsa.

On the march in we had crossed a nala, the Bauli Khad. This nala flows from the north, from a long glaciated valley into the Debsa. At its head is a col on the Kulu-Spiti divide, and over this col lies an extensive valley system, the Dibibokri. In my research I found only a few parties had been in the Dibibokri, mainly attempting first ascents like us. In 1961 an Italian team made the first ascent of a 6,349-metre peak on the divide. In 1956 a young British party, Peter Holmes, Garry and Judy Walker, together with their porters, made an epic descent into this valley from the divide. They had been exploring and climbing in the Ratang valley further east, having made several first ascents there. However the first major Dibibokri exploration was made by Kenneth Snelson's party in 1952. Snelson made the first ascent of Rubal Kang (6,187m) near the Kulu-Spiti divide before succeeding in making the only ascent of the Dibibokri-Bauli col. But critically, like the col in the Debsa, he never crossed it to enter the Bauli Khad. One can only assume his aim was merely to see what lay on the far side. Mindful of this, I could find no evidence of anyone having been in the upper Bauli Khad valley. So here three exciting prospects emerged. By venturing northwest we could be the first to explore the upper Bauli Khad. We might also make the first crossing of the col into the Dibibokri. And if we kept going, we might reach the Parvati valley, thereby establishing a new route from the Debsa to the Parvati across the Kulu-Spiti divide. All these prospects were tantalising as well as pioneering. With the maps spread out in front of us, we hatched a plan that afternoon over tea.

We would only know if a Debsa-Dibibokri-Parvati traverse was feasible by getting a look at the col. Hence, a two-day recce up the Bauli was called for. If the col was feasible we could return to base camp and prepare a lightweight expedition back over it and then west, out of the Dibibokri and down the Parvati to the village of Pulga, where we would reach a road-head. If the col was impassable or the Bauli Khad problematic, we could retreat to base camp and exit the Debsa by the way we came in; namely back down the Parahio to Sagnam. Alternatively, we could revisit the West Upper Debsa and enter the Parvati by the same route Sé O'Hanlon and Hugh Reynolds did as part of Paddy O'Leary's expedition of 2000. Arrival at Pulga would then mark the end of our Spiti expedition. But the col was the prize. Darach and I decided to set out on a recce the following morning. Paulie chose not to. He had been eyeing the many boulders around base camp and was itching to climb them. Craig opted to remain around camp also, nursing a swollen toe.

'Have you chosen a name for your peak, gentlemen?' Masthi asked that night over dinner.

It was a good question. In exploration and mountaineering there is a tradition that whoever makes the first ascent of an unnamed mountain or discovers a significant geographic feature such as a valley or col gets the first chance to name it. This freedom applies to all areas of the Himalaya and consequently it is considered a privilege. A chosen name is not guaranteed and cultural conditions must prevail. The main one being any proposed name must reflect the local language and culture as much as possible and not be something alien or vain. I had put some thought into this, weeks earlier. Given we were in Spiti, a Buddhist land, I was hoping to come across a name or title within Buddhism or something local to the region that would be suitable. But I hadn't been long enough in Spiti to get familiar with its language and people and any words I learned at the monastery in Tabo seemed too long and inappropriate. However Hinduism offered possibility. I was reluctant at first to consider anything Hindu, given Peak 6135's location. But then I was aware the one major valley adjacent to the head of the Debsa was named after a Hindu god, Shiva's wife, Parvati. What's more, Hinduism and Buddhism share many characteristics. So I thought, if nothing else, why not a Hindu name? Why not something connected to The Ramayana?

This ancient text is venerated by all Hindus. It is the story of the young prince Rama and the trials and tribulations he went through for his beautiful wife Sita. It is a classic tale of good and evil, with moral lessons on the importance of sacrifice, of doing the right thing and of giving service to others. My consideration was, Rama assembled an army and embarked on a project to reclaim his kidnapped bride from the evil King Ravana. He overcame many obstacles to achieve this — making sea crossings, venturing into unknown lands and fighting great battles with Ravana's forces. It was a formidable undertaking that demanded individual and team strength, focus, resources and determination. And he succeeded. We, on the other hand, may not have had to fight wars, or organise ourselves on such a large scale, but we needed similar attributes and resources for us to succeed in our endeavours. And we did. Therefore a connection of a kind could be made.

Earlier in my research, I could find no mountain in the Himalayas associated with Rama. There are mountains named after other gods, the best known being Shivling. So I put it to the lads:

'How about we name it Ramabang, lads? Where Rama is the God and "bang" in Hindi means "place of"? Ramabang: place of Rama?'

Ramabang. It had a good ring to it. The boys liked it. But I was conscious of what Masthi might think. He was the only Indian among us, a Hindu and a representative of the IMF. To me it was important he like and accept it.

'Well Masthi, what do you think? Do you consider it a worthy name? Worthy of Lord Rama?'

Masthi nodded. 'Yes, Gerry. I think it is a very good name.'

'Excellent. Ramabang it is then,' I said to affirmations and nods all round. And with this small but significant matter addressed, we adjourned happily to our tents.

SIX

Crossing the Divide

Friday 27 June. Bauli Khad recce day. At 6 a.m. Raj's voice woke me from a deep sleep.

'Tea Sir?'

I unzipped the tent door and looked out. The sky was overcast and the air chilly.

'Bad weather, Sir,' said Raj. This was his polite way of telling me the forecast was terrible and any notions we had of heading up the valley were foolish. I brushed his comment aside.

'Not at all, Raj. Sure it's only a regular grey day like what we have at home.'

He remained silent. Darach and I got up, washed, dressed and had breakfast. As we were packing our bags the sky darkened further. Moments later the wind picked up and the heavens opened. Thunder rolled. The rain came bucketing down. Torrential stuff. Into the tents we scurried, where we were forced to remain for most of the day. The recce was abandoned. This was no loss as we would try again the next day. But I learned one thing: my judgment on weather forecasting wasn't always right; people in the Himalaya knew better.

The following morning, though still grey, held more promise. Darach and I set out. Paulie took to the boulders and Craig took care of his toe. Two kilometres out, it started to rain. We took cover under the tent flysheet. The rain fell lightly and, curiously enough, it made us think of the mountains and crags of home: Kerry, Clare, Connemara, Gola. Grand recollections of days spent climbing and hiking in these evocative places came to mind. We mulled over routes we did and others we had yet to do, imagining the feel and shape of the rock and the critical moves. Names came and went: *Howling Ridge; Bonnán Buí; Seventh Heaven; Run of the Arrow.* Silence fell as we slipped into reverie. 'They're not going anywhere, Darach,' I said minutes later. 'They'll still be there when we get home.'

The rain lasted two hours. It remained grey but we pressed on. Moving away from the Debsa, we trekked up the Bauli's lower, western end, keeping a high direct line, until we reached a cliff, which made it impossible to continue up the valley at this height. Grumbling, we dropped into a gully and cautiously zigzagged to the Bauli floor. The view looking down was uninspiring: a terminal moraine, the product of widespread destruction. Piles of broken rock lay strewn about; a geological ransacking. It reminded me of photographs of London during the blitz. We picked our way through and stepped onto the glacier proper. It was late afternoon. We continued until we found meltwater channels, and decided to set camp on a bed of stones nearby. Meanwhile the weather had improved. Clouds had lifted and better views were to be had to the south. Darach pointed something out to me. I had been too busy plodding up the glacier and erecting the tent to notice anything. There, in the distant south, stood a fine conical summit protruding from a massif. It was snow tinged, with clean ridge lines on either side. Bright, deep snowfields layered its shoulders which rolled onto subsidiary peaks, while thin banks of cloud streamed gracefully over its tip. It was Ramabang — our mountain, standing tall and proud, spearing the heavens. It was a fine peak, well named and fit for a king. We were chuffed with ourselves.

A biting cold wind had us in the tent before dark, wearing every bit of clothing we had. We slept well throughout the night, just the dull cracking of the glacier interrupting our dreams as it shifted deep below us.

The morning was perfect. No wind, no cloud and a crystal blue sky. Every feature around us appeared close and sharp. The col, though 4.5 kilometres in the distance, felt like a short stone's throw away. It was clear now, a mix of snow slopes and scree ramps. We had our porridge and set out at 5 a.m., anxious to make as much ground as possible before the sun brought a thaw to the glacier. Everything was calm. There was no wind and any running water had shrunk to trickles. Just the sound of our breaths and our crampons crunching the ice. All morning we trudged deeper into the valley. It was hot, slow going, with regular stops for water and rest.

The col is a chink in the armour of the Kulu-Spiti divide. To its right stands a huge 6,507-metre unclimbed tower of serrated ridges and snow-filled gullies. The most impressive part is its massive South Face which we had spied from Ramabang. A shining, uncompromising wall — the cathedral of the region. Left of the col stands a smaller peak, part of another wall of treacherous hanging glaciers and crumbling rock buttresses. The whole lot forms an impressive amphitheatre. Like Ramabang, it was exciting just being here; to know you're the first humans to venture into this pristine place and set eyes on its secrets. I thought about this afterwards and came to the conclusion that exploration, in any field, is really an attempt to satisfy one's curiosity and hope to be surprised by the new.

In our case, the mystery of not knowing what a valley or mountain looks and feels like, what obstacles or problems it presents and whether you'll be successful investigating it or not. This is the essence of mountaineering and exploration. There's a purity to it. Usually there are no guidebooks or detailed maps to follow, you're the one writing and drawing them.

On a deeper level, I tend to think many of us venture into the mountains to free ourselves of the cares and constraints of our everyday lives and to get a sense of peace. We also long for natural beauty, perhaps hoping to find the nearest thing to paradise on earth. Sometimes, whether climbing, scrambling, walking or camping, we do.

We plodded on, avoiding a convex section broken by crevasses and seracs. By eleven we made the foot of the col. Our original intention had been to check its viability as a mountain pass before returning to base camp, but now we were here and making good time, we couldn't resist the urge to climb it and get a look over the far side. So up we went. Axe and pole in hand, side-stepping with the crampons, over a mix of melting snow and scree. It only took a few minutes to get to the top, placing us at an altitude of about 5,600 metres.

A fine sweeping view of the Dibibokri opened up to us. With one foot in Kulu, the other in Spiti, we took it all in. Looking down, a descent into the Dibibokri was possible; not simple but not technical. An axe, a pole and the comfort of a rope would do. Quietly we looked at one another and grinned. We had unlocked the mystery of the col and knew a first crossing from the Debsa to the Dibibokri was on. Metaphysically, we now stood eyeball to eyeball with Snelson.

Satisfied, we retraced our steps back down the Bauli. As I moved along the glacier I thought about what we had just done. A first exploration of an unknown valley and the first ascent of a mountain pass on one side. I couldn't contain the satisfaction I felt. Looking over towards Ramabang, I jumped, punching the air with my fist and issuing a howl of delight. The cry echoed around the valley.

We arrived back at base camp later that afternoon and reported our findings to the boys. We were dog-tired. Two full days' rest were called for to prepare ourselves for the hard march back to the divide and down the Dibibokri and Parvati. However three of us only would be attempting this: Darach, Paulie and I. It was unfortunate Craig's toe hadn't improved enough to take on another exploration. Because of this, he decided to accompany Masthi who was heading back to Manali.

Our last night together was one of celebration. In a thoughtful gesture, Raj baked a cake to mark our achievements. It was a sponge cake, iced on top, with a stick drawing of a mountain and the words *HAPPY SUMMIT PEAK 6135* scribed on it. A small bottle of Jameson came out. The celebratory mood lasted well into the night. Although our expedition was still far from over, it summed up quite simply what we were all about: a few mates doing interesting things in the mountains, enjoying the craic.

At dawn the next morning Craig and Masthi left for Sagnam. In their place the gaddi's flock rolled into camp. I awoke to hear animals bleating and munching around the tent porch — possibly a hint for the rest of us to move out.

Breakfast was a quieter affair with just the three of us now. The atmosphere was changing. Thoughts and conversation turned towards packing up and moving out. A reluctance to accept the expedition winding down was palpable. This shift was felt all the more by the arrival of the first of our porters. They had ridden on buses from Manali and Kaja and had trekked up the Parahio from Sagnam. It was strange seeing them; a raggle-taggle lot in short wellingtons, wearing bright gypsy headscarves and grey blankets draped over their shoulders like capes. They looked more like groupies from the Jimi Hendrix Experience than Nepalese mountain men. In twos and threes their numbers grew. They gravitated towards Raj's tent, ate some food and sprawled on the grass, sunning themselves.

Paulie, Darach and I packed for the days ahead. Everything was laid on the ground and divided up into three loads of equal weight: food, fuel, tent, climbing gear. Paulie was anxious to move on. Over the previous days he had solved most of the boulder problems around camp and was now experiencing a touch of cabin fever. I felt different though. A bit sad to be leaving base camp. I had grown comfortable with the routine of life here, of the quiet pleasant days and nights, the absence of all cares and worries, and the banter with the lads. I was particularly sad to be leaving Raj and Manbahadur who, not only had been exemplary cooks and camp managers, but had become great friends.

Wednesday 2 July. A calm, chill morning. The sun emerged from the lower Debsa, casting shadows over Ramabang's sides. We broke camp. It was a hive of activity as Raj, Manbahadur and the porters shuffled about, stuffing tents, cooking equipment and steel chests into nylon sacks. All the gear would be carried back to Sagnam. It would be placed on a jeep and transported to an agent in Manali where we would collect what belonged to us a week later. Pauli, Darach, and I would travel light, with five days' provision. The remaining expedition food, of which there was much, would be distributed among the porters at Sagnam. Hoisting our packs, we shook hands with Raj and Manbahadur and said farewell to the men. Then we marched out in the direction of Bauli Khad.

For two hours we tramped over rocks and dried river beds, uphill and onto the Bauli ridge. Here we stopped for a rest and a last look back at Thwak Debsa. A sadness came over me. Base camp was no more. We watched Raj and the last band of men march off like ants with the loads on their backs. An excited gaddi dog skirted among them, all tiny moving flecks in a magnificent wilderness, with Ramabang towering over them. I knew I would never forget the happy times spent in this idyllic spot; the trials crossing the nala, the friendships forged, the afternoon winds and bending grass, the warm sun, the lazy rest days and the black, peaceful nights. Beyond, the rest of the world could be forgotten.

Fittingly, a lone griffon circled above, seeing us off. The more I reflected, the more maudlin I became. I could feel a lump in my throat developing and could take it no longer. We turned our backs and moved on, leaving the Debsa to its rightful owners: the afternoon winds and running nalas, the flora, the nomadic gaddis and their flock, and the wheeling lammergeyers and griffons — custodians of paradise.

We retraced our route up the Bauli Khad and camped at the same spot on the glacier as before. We were looking forward to a good night's rest. Given it was the first day out, we had carried a lot of weight and were tired. Five days' food and fuel would run down with each day, which in theory, would make for easier going.

It wasn't a great first night. In our effort to minimise weight we carried one two-man tent. This was more comfortable than bivvies, but with three of us in it, plus pieces of gear, it was a bit of a squash. None of us got much rest.

❄ ❄ ❄ ❄

Thursday 3 July. We made the col in two hours, panting up the glacier. A short rest was had at its base before ascending it easily. We spotted a plane. A commercial jet heading north to Leh. It was the only blemish on an otherwise spectacular day.

We lounged on the crest of the col for half an hour, admiring the view back to Spiti and Ramabang. Towers loomed to the left and right of us, while up ahead, stood the challenging but alluring white mountains of Kulu. In a few moments we would make history. The significance of this, though profound in our heads, remained unspoken. Darach led off with Paulie behind, carefully front-pointing their way down. I lingered a while, unwilling to shift my gaze from Ramabang and the pristine Bauli. A final look over the shoulder and it was down the crest, revisiting the ghostly steps made by Snelson, fifty-six years earlier.

Descent led us into a semi-circular glacial basin: a blind off-shoot of the Dibibokri. To get onto the Dibibokri proper we had to weave around a heavily-crevassed convex section. We roped up. As the lightest, I took up the front.

Steering clear of the yawning ice, I led down a couloir, in shadow of the vertiginous Kulu-Spiti wall to the right. It was hard going. Once free of the ice, we scrambled down a pile of boulders and emerged from the shadow for a rest on rocks to soak up the sun. Bodies prostrated, we drifted in and out of sleep. The break and the warmth was bliss. But the respite was short-lived. A rock the size of a television set tumbled off the wall and bounded towards us. It shot through like a cannon ball, narrowly missing Paulie. I never saw him move so quickly.

We continued, tracking a snow passage beside a moraine, leading into the belly of the main valley. The Dibibokri is a huge amphitheatre of large impressive peaks and sweeping glaciated valleys with dark moraines the length and breadth of airport runways. We were mere specks on it. I couldn't get over the scale. As we marched I made a rough mental calculation, estimating the main Dibibokri and its tributaries to cover a space of 72 square kilometres. The deeper we went, the more the divide stood out. For the most part it is an impenetrable wall with a couple of meaty six and a half-thousanders. I recalled the plight of another, British, party to the area in 1956. Then, two young lads, Peter Holmes and Garry Walker, together with Garry's sister Judy and three porters, found themselves marooned on this wall. They had been climbing and exploring the Ratang valley further east and were hoping to follow Snelson's exit from the Debsa to the Parvati but little did they know with their crude map they were well off target. Two valleys off, a direct distance of 15 kilometres. Blindly they headed west, crossing the Khamengar and ascending the divide, assuming a short descent would find them in the benign Parvati. Instead and to their horror, they stared down a 700-metre precipice to the Dibibokri. Retreat was not an option. They had run out of food days earlier and had neither the time nor strength to make it back to the mouth of the Ratang. They had to go on. Forced to jettison most of their loads, they cautiously down-climbed the wall in the teeth of a storm, and it is to their credit they did so without injury or fatality. On some modern maps their crossing is shown by a pass marked 'Holmes Col' but this is wildly inaccurate. Plainly from what we could see, no col or pass exists. The only way off the divide is an unenviable steep descent to the glacier. In their lost, weakened state, it must have been a dreadful experience, yet they survived and somehow managed to get down the Dibibokri and then into the Parvati. The fortuitous trapping and butchering of two goats helped. Looking up at this wall from the comfort of our location, we had to hand it to them; they were pioneers all right. Facing such unknowns and a desperate situation, they succeeded with remarkable skill and tenacity.

Digressing for a moment, just six months earlier and out of the blue, the Irish Mountaineering Club Secretary, Sé O Hanlon, received an email from a Garry Walker — the same Garry Walker that was with Holmes on that trip in '56. He had just come across Paddy O'Leary's expedition report of Kangla Tarbo on the club's website and just wanted to say hello. Sé told the rest of us. Garry recalled having come back from Spiti and being contacted by Joss Lynam in 1957 for some information, as Joss and Garry's former maths teacher at Sherborne College, John Stephenson, were planning their own expedition to Spiti in 1958. Garry also spoke of his adventure and of the 'frightening rockwall' he, Holmes and company had to descend; the one we were now just looking at. Shortly after, when I contacted Garry, telling him of our plans, he wished me luck and joked that I might pick up some of the gear they had to throw away in order to get off the wall.

'Who knows? We might be glad of it,' I said.

Dog-tired, we made camp on the medial moraine, late afternoon. The usual routine followed of boiling meltwater for a meal and a mug of tea. The temperature dropped. Clouds formed up the valley and cloaked the tall peaks of the divide. Conspiring with the light they manufactured eerie shapes on the faces and ridges. We felt a profound sense of loneliness. There wasn't another soul around for 20 kilometres. What's more, it wasn't likely another soul had entered this valley in ten or twenty years.

Fatigue overcame discomfort and a better night's sleep was had in the tent. A clear frosty morning brought sublime views of the Dibibokri's naked giants. We headed west, down the moraine, cautious in our step. Millions of red rocks littered the place and a misjudged move could have had alarming consequences.

By mid morning we reached the mouth of the glacier: a chaotic maze of broken rock, haphazard ice and powerful converging nalas. Assuming ourselves to be on the wrong side of the main river, we considered island-hopping to cross. But the perilous strength and depth of the water prevented us. A lengthy circumnavigation involving heading back up the glacier wasn't appealing, not with our heavy packs and the many hours that would be lost. So we maintained a course on its southern side, progressing southwest to the lower reaches of the Dibibokri. It was a step into the unknown. It wasn't clear from our map if we could cross at any stage, or if further rivers or cliffs would pose greater obstacles, leaving us stranded. We continued in hope. As we descended, we started to find clumps of vegetation.

We reached the confluence of the Dibibokri and Ratiruni nalas with the intention of crossing the latter — it being tamer. It would be slow, possibly risky and we would still be on the wrong side, but there didn't seem to be an alternative. Luckily Darach spotted an innocuous single steel cable spanning the Dibibokri. A gaddi crossing. First thoughts on using it weren't favourable. It was rusty and held in place by the weight of pillars of rock on either bank. But it held firm under my weight so we gave it a go. Paulie led off, monkeying across, trailing a rope behind him. The bags went next by way of the rope, with Paulie hauling in on the far side. Darach followed and then I clambered across, taking the end of the rope. While doing all this, two gaddis with horses appeared out of the scrub on the far side. They were bemused by us and our style of crossing and were curious about the strange equipment we employed: harnesses, karabiners and nylon rope. Our clothing and boots would have been a novelty also. Similarly, we wondered how they managed to cross. Clearly they would use less precaution. They busied themselves unloading the horses of sacks of grain and firewood, piling them next to the pillar. As they showed no inclination to cross while we were there, we pressed on.

A narrow gaddi track snaked its way along the river-bank now. It felt strange underfoot. Given the rough terrain we had covered over the past month it felt too easy, as if we were cheating. A mist came down and it started to rain.

Down the track we spotted a large boulder, rectangular in shape, standing upright. Nothing strange there, I thought, apart from its size and shape. But a second glance revealed more. A young gaddi was squatting beside it. He appeared to be talking to himself. Not so. A hole had been dug at the boulder base and one corner built up with earth and rocks leading into a small room. Smoke plumed out of the hole. Through the blackness we could make out a second gaddi tending the fire inside. It was the oddest gaddi shelter we had yet seen. With the diffusion of smoke and mist it looked more like a forbidding burial chamber.

Our contact with people and the green alpine environment heralded a change. The cold harshness of the glaciers with their absence of life and colour was behind us. The dangers and strains were receding as we emerged from isolation. Movement was simpler and our packs lighter. Ahead the Parvati beckoned.

We had a comfortable night's camp on a pasture high above the nala. No cold winds or icy surroundings now. It was a treat to be able to sit on a rock alone, away from the tent after dinner, nursing a brew and gazing around, reflecting. Above, clouds billowed playfully up the valley. Below, the grey nala roared south. Around us thick grasses carpeted the valley, lapping up to the base of the high granite walls, and horses munched sorrel nearby. In the distance, alpen glow painted the peaks of the Parvati and the odd cry of a high-spirited gaddi echoed out. Tranquility descended on us. In a couple of days the expedition would be over.

The divide had been crossed and the hazards overcome. It was downhill most of the way now, over a trail to the villages of Khirganga and Pulga. Part of me wanted to continue on, but a bigger part of me wanted to remain on the rock, mulling over the expedition and not wanting it to end. Paradise is after all, a difficult place to leave.

❄ ❄ ❄ ❄

Saturday 5 July. The march went on. Over the ridges a brilliant sun appeared. The shadows of the valley retracted and as the morning wore on, the night's dew disappeared. It was another fine day. Two gaddi dogs eyed us as we ate breakfast and tailed us when we broke camp. We came to a small river and carefully crossed, barefoot over slippy rocks, feet numbed by the cold. The dogs, pawing the icy current, thought better and remained put. Further on, the valley widened and our senses were assailed by a sea of colour and scented air. Alpine flowers in full bloom covered the entire valley floor, a bewildering array of buttercups, irises, potentillas, forget-me-nots, king-cups, azaleas, poppies and eidelweiss. There were shrubs of dwarf juniper and scatterings of wild strawberry. This extraordinary, unexpected vista stopped us in our tracks. We found ourselves bending down to admire, smell and photograph them frequently. Other than as drugs, I never thought flora could have such a profound influence. As we had spent the best part of a month in a desolated area of bare rock, ice, greyness and lifelessness, this was a sharp, overwhelming experience.

We passed several dry-stone huts. Gaddi shelters. They reminded me of the hermitic beehive shelters of the Skellig islands. Unlike their Kerry equivalents, these huts served a seasonal purpose only, as no hardened ascetic or shepherd could endure a Himalayan winter in them without considerable suffering. Then we came upon two Kulu gaddis and their flock. The animals were bunched around a shelter, eyeing us enigmatically. The biggest goat among them was ensconced on the roof, nosing the air. With a vigorous shake of the horns he commanded attention. Nearby, behind a boulder and hidden from the herd, the gaddis were butchering a sheep that had been killed in a fall. Thousands of flies swarmed around them. It was a grisly sight. Blood stained their arms and clothes. Chunks of red flesh got thrown to one side. The animal's matted fleece lay on a bush, while its severed head sat clotting on the grass. Strangely, despite the flies, the activity and the smell, the herd didn't seem to notice. Ignorance is bliss. We looked at them, wondering, which one would be next?

Late morning we reached the junction with the wide Parvati where we stopped on an outcrop for a rest. The day was still fine and a penetrating sun heated our bones. Eastward across the valley, the pyramid form of Kulu Eiger stood out. Much like its Swiss namesake, its dark North Face offered an ambivalent invitation; one we were happy to decline. Kulu Eiger had only been climbed twice by this face, but anyone interested in it can be assured of better rock than its Swiss counterpart. Firm granite as opposed to crumbling limestone.

Moving on we dropped down to the Parvati floor, crossing its river by way of a cable and cage to its southern bank, before continuing west. At first the track was good, winding its way over easy slopes of bush and rhododendron, but after two kilometres it deteriorated, petering out in places and veering dangerously over sloping slabs above the nala in others. The nala was turbulent. Delicate footwork and balance was called for on the slabs, which wasn't easy given the pendulum effect of our packs. We were well aware a slip in the wrong spot would make certain disaster. In compensation, the Parvati offered stunning scenery: thousand-metre cliffs on the far side, cleaved by thunderous waterfalls.

The further we descended, the richer the vegetation. Bushes gave way to small silver birch trees and later, lush pine forests and ferns. The air was heavier too. Slowly we marched back into civilisation. We passed a couple of gaddi shelters, bigger ones this time, and saluted their occupants. No rotund Tibetan faces any more, all dusky Hindi countenances now. The Kulu-Spiti divide is also a racial demarcation.

We hopped over stones in a marshy creek and made for the coolness of a forest and its sheltering canopy. Two slim figures in bright clothes came out of the woods, carrying bundles of sticks on their heads. We stepped off the track to allow them pass.

'Namaste,' we greeted.

'Namaste,' they replied, gracefully filing by.

Both were epitome of purpose and poise. We watched them in curious silence for a few moments as they walked towards the creek and then out of view. There was something unusual here, we thought. Hardly surprising given they were the first women we had seen in weeks.

At around four we made camp in a meadow where dozens of buffalo grazed. They were all sleek beasts with shiny grey hides. While we were making a brew their owner and a helper came by and sat with us. The owner had broken English. We got talking. A slim gent in his early thirties, he had the odd habit of casually laughing at every comment he or any of us said. Not that this bothered us, the tone of our chat was jovial and the content simple. Initially I put it down to shyness. It transpired both men were from Chandigarh in Punjab, and each spring they travel to the Parvati's high pasture to graze the herd for the summer months.

A transhumance, much like the gaddis of Debsa. Only these two and their animals make a longer journey, forty-five days through valleys and mountain passes, each way. We weren't chatting to them for long when the clouds grew thick and it started to rain, forcing us to break for cover. Before doing so, we learned the buffalo man made a good living from his herd. He sold the animals' milk in the valley and the cheese in the markets of Kulu. What's more, he told us a good, full-sized animal could fetch 20,000 rupees in any of the markets of Punjab or Himachal Pradesh. This fella owned 70 buffalo and they cost next to nothing to keep. As we lay in the tent we did the sums. One thing was clear. By Indian standards this buffalo wallah was a very rich man. Small wonder he couldn't stop laughing.

❄ ❄ ❄ ❄

Sunday 6 July. The morning broke, misty and warm. Oddly this was a novelty to us as every other morning we had braced ourselves for cold starts. We ate breakfast and left the tent out to dry on the grass. Thankfully our loads were much lighter now. We had worked our way through all of the food and most of the gas. Personally I was glad we had run out. I couldn't face any more boil-in-the-bag stuff. I was prepared to go hungry.

We continued west. It was our fifth day and our bodies and clothes smelled, but we didn't care. We were high above the river now and we worked our way down a rocky track of forest and ferns. The monsoon downpour came and after some hours trudging through mud and roots, we reached Khirganga village. It was the first sense of settlement since Sagnam. Khirganga is a small place of rough wooden houses, dirt tracks and a bar. Hungry and thirsty, we padded into the latter for pancakes and juice. It was a weird place, a cross between a temple and a junkie's squat. It was decked out in prayer flags, hanging lamps and bunting, with a large mural of the goddess Parvati on the wall and voluminous worn mattresses covering an earth floor. Scattered on the ground were a group of long-haired Israeli's, half of them stoned. Someone produced a guitar, another a set of bongos and a dark langorous girl started singing Yiddish folk songs. Notably, unlike the rest of India, none of this crowd seemed remotely interested in us. However we noticed the enterprising merchants of Khirganga were interested enough in them. The bar's menu had schnitzel, falfafel, hummus and pita bread heading the fare, with local and Indian dishes relegated to the end. Looking around, this was all we needed after weeks alone in a mountain wilderness; a shock return to a civilisation of drugged Israelis in a flaky den with a cold atmosphere and alien sounds. Sourly we decamped to Khirganga's sulphur baths.

Flowing from the mountains and uphill from the village, thermal green water is diverted to fill a square concrete pool and allowed to drain off. Here we mingled with the locals; our thin frames immersed in aquatic pleasure. We didn't know ourselves. Within minutes the bath had purged all recollection of mountain hardship. The warmth and feel of the water, the steam rising from it, the mist and rain on the wooded hills and the fraternity of smiling locals, initiated a sense of mental and spiritual well-being. It was ecstasy. As to our physical states — aching limbs and tired backs thought they had died and gone to heaven. Also, it felt unusual being clean again. No more dirt. No more smell. We were tempted to remain in the pool all day.

Back on the trail it was hard going in the rain. We marched through more dense forest, over fallen trees and slippy, muddy rocks. Wooden bridges were crossed on the outskirts of small settlements. Our only aim now was to reach Pulga, a sizeable village with a road which marked the end of our expedition. Now the alpine upland lent part of itself for domestic use. Sporadic vegetable patches dotted the route. Around stone houses were small paddocks of apple trees laden with fruit. The thick smell of cannabis permeated the air.

Pulga drew close. We passed people and horses headed both ways. Children with pidgin English assertively begged for money — a strong reminder we were back in tourist-land. Shortly after, the track diverged into different paths but we were too weary to work out the right way. At a junction Darach met an old woman and asked her for directions. She was seventy-five if she was a day, thin, wizened and shawled, and no more interested in giving us help. Instead she took a large block of hash from her shawl and waved it at us with considerable insistence.

'You buy good hashish? Very, very good.'

'No thanks.' We weren't in the mood. To us this encounter was unexpected and strange. We weren't used to classifying pensioners as dope peddlers.

We staggered up the last hill into Pulga, made it through its cluster of mud lanes and found a resthouse just as the afternoon rain fell. Relief at last. We felt great to be rid of our back-breaking loads. It was a luxury experiencing a hot shower and carpeted floor, and it was a joy to be able to lie on a soft bed. Here the simple things in life weren't lost on us. The new-found comfort allowed us to reflect on what we had achieved. It had been a tough five days: 46 kilometres through the mountains, overcoming obstacles and harsh terrain, but it had been worth it. We had made the first crossing of a mountain pass, establishing a new route connecting three major valleys: the Debsa, Dibibokri and Parvati. Granted the exploration had taken its toll in terms of body weight and fatigue, but these inconveniences could be put right. The main thing was we had done it safely, without injury or disagreement and in good style. Between that and the first ascent of Ramabang, all our objectives had been met. We were delighted with ourselves.

We made up for the lack of food that night, eating everything we could from the resthouse kitchen: kofta, thali, chapattis, pizza, omelette, chips, chocolate balls, masala chai … the list went on. Extras were ordered and little was spared. The quantities would have put Raj to shame, but it all tasted great. Then we slept like kings.

Next morning after breakfast we hopped on a local bus that would bring us the rest of the way down the Parvati to Kulu town, changing there for another to take us up the Kulu valley to Manali. A one-day trip. It was a jolt back to civilisation. With our bags outside on the roof, we were confined inside with half the population of Kulu crammed around us. The noise of the engine, the fumes and the constant blasts of the horn were unsettling. We passed through crowded towns and dusty villages. Regular stops ensued. Hordes got off and hordes got on. Stick thin men and wide, saried women with babes in tow, scrambled for seats. The bus took off and the clamour continued. What with the din and the dust, the fumes, the litter and the deluge of human activity, it was all too much. Silently each of us screamed escape — back to the mountains.

SEVEN

A Strange Thing, Civilisation

In Manali we hoped to rejoin Craig. We had arranged to meet at a hotel in the old part of town. I was looking forward to hanging around with him, possibly exploring the surrounding area on motorbikes, but when we arrived there was no sign of him. He had stayed in the hotel all right and left a note at reception. Unfortunately the death of a close relative forced him to return home two days earlier. Masthi also had returned to Delhi.

We planned to spend nine days in and around Manali, resting and recuperating, with possibly some rock climbing and anything else that took our fancy. There was work to be done also: gear to be sent home, presents to be bought and the writing of the expedition report. Things didn't start well. The boys fell foul of a suspect pizza in a dubious café. Darach was laid up for a day and a half, but Paulie fared the worst. Weakened and pale, he was consigned to his bed for three days, sweating, shivering and vomiting. I was spared, not having touched it. Nevertheless, things were done. Our gear was collected from Rimo's agent, hauled back to the hotel, itemised and packed into four army bags for shipment home. Hours were spent in an internet café crafting the report and emails were sent home.

There's a buzz about Manali. It is a medium-sized hill town clustered among deodar forests, next to the formidable Beas river. It is the last place of significant business activity before giving way to lonely Himalayan peaks to the north. Thus it is a lively spot, full of shops and markets selling everything domestic and industrial you can think of, as well as goods specific to the region: mainly apples and woollens. There's an atmosphere of indolence and energy. The Mall, its main street, is a magnet for idle men to while away the hours, sitting on the pavement chatting and smoking beedees. Around them shoe-shine boys work the crowds in an animated way, insisting on repairing and cleaning any kind of footwear for a few rupees. I thought this odd as most people seemed to wear sandals, so their market must be limited, still they prevail.

Their cries ring out over the heads of the men and into the muddle of backstreet shops and markets; convivial places full of aromatic spices, steaming pots, vegetable hawkers, barbers and custom tailors. There is little sense of frenzy here. Buy something at your leisure, no pressure. If not, come back another day. Away from the Mall, scores of auto-rickshaws ply the streets, ferrying locals and tourists between the bus station and surrounding hotels. Weaving among them, Israelis on Enfield Bullet motorcycles, thumping their way up and down Banon's Hill to the charas and coffee shops and budget dosshouses of Old Manali. The grey streets of both new and old town are often caked in mud, dust and grime. Summer monsoon rains provide them with a regular and effective washdown.

To us, Indian life in all its colour and strangeness returned. Certain scenes remain in my head. The elephant with flowers painted on its ears, plodding up the Mall with a payload of tourists couched on its back. The tiny acrobatic children performing a high-wire balancing act with bicycles and poles; their enterprising parents simultaneously issuing orders and rattling coin jars in front of a large bemused crowd. Or the sight of a woman bringing her milch cow for a walk over the bridge of Old Manali with the animal tethered like a pet dog. Oddities aside, the best thing about Manali were its people. Mostly Hindu, we found them a genial lot; helpful and polite, happy to share a joke. Like many other Indians we met, Manali's people are keen traders, always ready to make a few bob with their goods and services, even if what's on offer isn't exactly what you want. And why wouldn't they? With little or no state help, their lives depend on it. That said, we found them honest in all exchanges. In several shops I was made to feel very welcome, offered a stool, plied with questions as to my origins, salary, profession, martial status, reasons for being in Manali and so on, and then promptly offered a hot glass of chai, which was always difficult to refuse.

Back to the oddities. India has some strange practices that the locals accept as normal but the rest of us find bewildering. Take the Post Office, an institution you would think would run smoothly, given they are in every town throughout the sub-continent. But not in Manali. We learned this the morning when we went to post our kit bags home. We cantered into the building in an upbeat mood. A throng of eager customers were already present. There were a half-dozen counters open. One counter for stamps, another for parcels, a third for registered letters and money orders and so on. The thing was, demand was strongest at the parcel counter, and after this, the demand for stamps. We thought an orderly queue might form at parcels but we were wrong. Very wrong.

Instead a scrum of impatient bodies jockeyed for position and the attention of the teller. Combat ensued. Elbows jabbed like lances, shoulders acted as rams and parcels morphed into shields. Hands went up for attention and cries went out as the clerk's every move was zealously watched. Into this mill we went, a three man team: Darach at the front, me struggling in the middle and Paulie at the rear on bag watch. We jostled and ploughed, trying desperately to keep some form of order and not let ourselves get shoved out or shouted down. But we had to be quick, bodies nipped in and around us. Heads sprung out of nowhere and gaps between limbs got instantly filled. We lacked the native guile, speed and all important Hindi, but we made up for this in height. After twenty minutes mauling and a flurry of failed attempts, Darach managed to lunge to the front of the counter. More pushing followed but he managed to hold position. A few requests fell on deaf ears before assertion drew the clerk's attention. Yet for all that hassle, the clerk refused to deal with us. Instead he handed Darach a list of instructions before dismissing him with a casual wave and a wobble of the head. Soon we learned it is not enough to simply walk into an Indian post office, hand over your money and bags and expect the bags to be processed. A strict embalming and lettering ritual must be observed. This involves visiting a tailor and getting him to wrap your goods in a white cotton loincloth, stitching it fully and sealing it with wax at the seams. Then with a marker you write the forwarding name and address on the cloth, along with your return details. It doesn't end there. No clerk will accept it until he sees the owner's visa number on it, together with his passport number, passport expiry date, nationality and the name of the embassy that granted his visa. What is the purpose of all this? Well, no one really knows. It was done in an earlier century and the practice has continued since. The rules just fell short of demanding our bank account numbers, salaries, blood types and next of kin. All this we did, leaving four green army sacks with the tailor and returning to the office hours later with four white, scripted body bags. Back to the scrum, this time confronting different locals and a bunch of Israelis with their white sacks full of souvenirs and who knows what else, bound for Tel Aviv. Again, only one clerk on parcels. What with the heat, the mal-functioning air-conditioning, the pushing, the harsh-sounding Hebrew and the shrill, impatient Hindi, it was unbearable. Everyone wanted that clerk immediately. The thing was there was no need for any of this trouble. Apart from the parcel clerk and the bloke on stamps, all the other clerks were idle. Nonchalantly they sat around, oblivious to the bottleneck, with no inclination to share the workload. To us this was infuriating. To the clerks, it was the norm. Eventually we got the teller's attention where, surprisingly, we were marshaled to the other side of counter to join the clerks. Progress at last. Sacks got weighed, passports were examined, more notes made and the words 'By Sea' scrawled on the loincloths in large red letters. Next, the sacks were hauled into an adjoining room, a prison-like cell with thick steel bars and padlocks and more clerks. There stood a mass of other white sacks with similar markings and the hopes and agitations of a hundred other exasperated souls.

That was just parcels. Letters and postcards exacted their own form of torture. Granted there was less of a scrum for service. Peddling stamps is, after all, an easier and speedier operation and if you're only looking to post one item there's no drama. However if you've got a dozen letters to post, or twenty-five postcards to family and friends like I had, then you're in trouble. You see, the Indian postal service sells stamps that don't stick. There is no adhesive on them. To overcome this, each office provides a bottle of glue and a brush for customers to do the necessary themselves. One bottle and brush per office. You can see where this is going. It costs seven rupees to send a postcard from Manali to Ireland. This means two stamps per card and the obligatory Par Avion label which, unsurprisingly, also has no adhesive. You hand over your cash and the clerk gives you three sheafs of perforated stamps, upon which you withdraw to the bench. Then the ordeal begins. Twenty-five postcards requiring three stamps each amounts to a tearing and smearing operation that has to be repeated seventy-five times. Inevitably things get messy. The glue drips everywhere, the stamp skates about and the card gets soggy, resembling paper mache. Meanwhile, you've to fend off other punters circling for control of the glue. Thus, a job that would take five minutes at home takes an hour and a half here. This got me thinking. I came to the view that if Manali's post office typifies others, then the entire Indian Postal Service is dogged by vast inefficiency. Huge savings in time and money could be made by making simple improvements. Take the number of clerks, for example. They don't need as many, particularly if half of them do next to nothing. Some could be dispensed and the workload spread evenly among those that remain. Futile, time-wasting demands like the loincloths and the excessive details should be cut out. A proper queue system should be established. And the stamps should be self-adhesive. If those few simple changes were made, everything would run better. Tasks would be done quicker, workloads distributed fairly and customers would be a lot happier. These are all sensible ideas. But when I thought about it further I realised I was thinking like a Westerner too familiar with the corporate, capitalist world of ruthless cost savings and efficiencies. This model didn't seem right either. Moreover, it has never appealed to my Socialist, co-operative nature.

Taking the broader view, India has an enormous population of 1.1 billion. It is well known there aren't enough businesses providing enough jobs for such numbers. If my ideas were to be implemented it would mean the loss of thousands of postal jobs and the redundancy of innumerable others: gluemakers, tailors, wax merchants and loincloth-makers. Countless individuals and communities would suffer. This led to my conclusion that despite the pain the postal system inflicts, it appears it is only us non-Indians who have a problem with it. Everyone else knows it is a mess and they seem to accept it. It somehow works and is good enough. Therefore it is safe to say that unlike us, the Indian Postal Service will never change.

Eventually I gathered my postcards, a bundle of wet paper and smudged ink, and handed them to the clerk for franking. I was weary now and only too glad to get rid of them. Tentatively he shuffled them out on the table in front of him. I took a swig of a drink and wiped my brow. That was when I discovered another postal anomaly. The glue didn't work.

❄ ❄ ❄ ❄

Mark Twain once said of India: 'So far as I am able to judge, nothing has been left undone, either by man or nature, to make India the most extraordinary country that the sun visits on his rounds. Nothing seems to have been forgotten, nothing overlooked.' He was right. India is extraordinary. He might also have called it strange and full of the unexpected. Unlike the developed West where life in both urban and rural areas is organised and predictable, the opposite is the case in India. Here a traveller must expect the unusual and unexpected at all times. I was reminded of this one afternoon on a trip to the village of Vashisht in the nearby hills. The boys remained in Old Manali. Darach was drawing maps and Paulie was dying in bed. My aim was to explore two old temples, one dedicated to Rama, the other his teacher Vashisht, from whom the village got its name. Given the mountain we had climbed, I was particularly curious to see Rama's temple.

The village is small, one hilly street of stone shops and houses. A row of trinket and shawl shops line either side, with a couple of cafés and massage parlours thrown in. Beyond that lie verdant woods and a commanding view of the Beas valley below. A few Western longhairs in tie-dyed garb ambled about. They blended in well with some of the locals, who could have been their Eastern equivalent. These fellas lounged outside a dhaba, smoking beedees. The ever-present smell of charas drifted in the air and monsoon clouds gathered overhead. From what I could sense, the village could have been lost in time. Woodstock and hippy counter-culture came to mind.

I moseyed up to the end of the street, turned right, walked up the steps to Rama's temple and took off my shoes. The temple is small and square, neatly constructed with dark wooden struts and thick stone walls, evenly lined and painted an auspicious sanguine. At its rear stands a carved column of weathered granite, said to be 500 years old. Inside, a quiet aromatic chamber leads to an enclosed altar where the small triumvirate figures of Rama, Sita and Lakshmana reside. Red and orange silk robes adorn them, strings of wooden beads drape around their necks and intricate silver tiaras sit on their heads. Their solemn expressions exude a remote, virtuous air. As I was studying them three young, gregarious Hindu girls walked in. They immediately fell silent on seeing their deities, bowing their heads in quiet supplication. In this dark place a distinct aura of peace and tranquility could be felt.

Next door stands Vashisht Rishi's temple. Here an ancient black statue with arresting silver eyes is the centre of attention. The building is 1,900 years old and made of skillfully carved pine. A Brahmin priest guarded the entrance while I was there, rhythmically applying red tilaks to the foreheads of visiting worshippers. According to Hindu texts, the sage Vashisht is the son of the god Brahma, creator of the universe. He was the enlightened teacher of Rama. But as I learned from the priest, perhaps the most notable thing about him is the claim that he meditated in this spot for 88,000 years. Vashisht may have had a lot of time on his hands, but in today's world his pilgrims don't. Nevertheless they use their visiting time wisely. Of the ones I saw they remained solemn and resolute, exhibiting unwavering devotion when doing puja and prayer.

Overall, while in both temples I could sense a deep level of veneration and calm. It seemed to rub off on me. I left both places in a serene, almost meditative state. But that was set to change. Out in the street, just yards from the temples, an assortment of indiscreet junk sellers peddled their wares. Over their heads wrapped on a pole, a tannoy blared loud rock music, drowning their cries. The din could be heard all over the place, yet nobody seemed to mind. The odd thing was the song that was belting out: *Californication*, by the Red Hot Chili Peppers.

West Coast hedonism meets transcendental Hinduism. Yes, a strange place this India, I thought.

❄ ❄ ❄ ❄

The days drifted by. The lads recovered from their illness, and when they felt ready to eat again I led them to a restaurant I considered hygienic and safe. Mom's Kitchen on the edge of Old Manali was a clean and reputable place owned and run by Rajan, a retired surgeon and his wife Neena. They came to

Manali from Delhi fourteen years earlier in the hope of living a quiet, healthy life in the Kulu hills. But after some time they realised their new life was a bit too quiet so, putting their operational and culinary skills into practise, they opened the restaurant. The business quickly grew. So much so that they soon found themselves working fourteen hours a day, seven days a week; but that was all right, they weren't complaining.

We enjoyed chatting with Rajan and were impressed by him. He was neat, well-spoken, affable, and a man of substantial intelligence. Here our education on local culture and other matters Indian continued. Rajan told us how Manali got its name. To Christians, this story will be familiar. According to Hindu lore, Brahma created the earth and on it placed Manu, the first human. One day Manu found a fish in a pool. Unknown to him it was an avatar of the god Vishnu. Instead of eating it, he fed and looked after it, putting it into containers as it grew. When the fish grew large enough he released it into the ocean and then forgot about it. But years later the fish returned and warned Manu of an imminent flood. Manu was instructed to build a wooden boat and fill it with all the animals, fruit and vegetable seeds he could find, which he did. The flood came. Vishnu's fish returned and with the boat attached to its tail, he towed it to safety. Manu then became the progenitor of humankind. Manali was named after him and a temple dedicated to him stands on a hill at the top of the old town.

Then I asked him if he knew why there were so many young Israelis in the valley. They outnumbered all other foreigners; it was hard to miss them. He told us India is a popular destination for them, once they are discharged from military service. Often they stay a year, spending winters in Goa, summers in Himachal Pradesh, before returning home to university or a career.

'India is very tolerant of different religions, you see. It doesn't matter if you're a Christian, Hindu, Buddhist, Jew or anything else. So Israelis feel comfortable here.' We nodded. He went on. 'And look around you … there is plenty of grass to smoke here in Manali, and also because India is cheap.'

Many places in India have deities unique to an area whom the locals worship. Manali is no different. Rajan went on to tell us about another local immortal, Hadimba, who commands the respect and attention of the town's faithful. A female, Hadimba was once a feared demon who thrived on blood sacrifices. In the Mahabharata, an epic on the wars between two rival families, the god-like Pandavas and demon-like Kauravas, her marriage to one of the Pandavas transformed her from a demon to a noble god, though her power remained undiminished. Rajan went on to tell us of the mythology around her and how she had affected him. Years earlier when he first came to Manali he couldn't find a place to live. He lost a lot of money in a crooked land deal and spent a futile year in the courts seeking compensation. Everything he did seemed to go wrong.

'I had nothing but bad luck in those days.'

But he did have an open mind. In desperation he turned to Hadimba for help.

'I said, why not pray to the local god, as the locals here in Manali do? What have I got to lose? I was at the point of giving up and returning to Delhi, to look for another job.'

But things turned. A chance meeting with a friend in a Delhi club led to a conversation with a wealthy liquor baron. The baron had property all over India, including a fine house in Manali that had been idle for years. When the baron learned of Rajan's plight he empathised with him. With no plans for the house, he magnanimously offered it to him. Rajan was to pay whatever he could afford. Shortly after, all of Rajan's other problems were resolved.

'Think what you wish, call it a miracle, but all I can say is Hadimba must have done this. And other people have told me similar things. Many people come to Manali and they want to stay. But they experience all kinds of problems, for one reason or another, and are forced to leave. I have seen it. Those who pray and provide offerings, they are usually OK.'

Offerings involved the slaughter of an animal, usually a chicken, a goat or a sheep at her temple in the quiet woods of the old town. I listened intently as he told us of the hole in the ground where sacrifices are made. Blood flows down the hole and disappears. Over the years scientists have tested the earth to see where the blood goes. But apparently none of them have ever found traces of it. It vanishes mysteriously.

'You believe she still feeds on it?' I asked.

He shrugged. 'Who is to know? Go and see for yourself.'

It was intriguing to hear Rajan's story. Here was a man of scientific background and rational thought, yet he had an open mind on the possibilities of the supernatural.

The next day I visited Hadimba's temple. Her importance and popularity was clear. There were many people, mostly Hindu, milling about doing puja. Her demonic associations were also in evidence by animal skulls and antlers hanging on the temple walls and carvings of evil, saber-toothed monsters all over the entrance porch. I found the spot of animal sacrifice — a hole the size of a bucket between old flagstones. There was nothing being sacrificed while I was there but flecks of congealed blood on the ground were evidence enough. A Brahmin accepted food offerings inside the temple, hacking up coconuts and pineapple with a machete and placing them on top of a natural rock altar.

The place was dark and cavernous. Burning torches and flickering candles around the walls evoked a forlorn, hopeless, underworld. Still, I didn't get any sense of fear in the place. But what I found fascinating were Hadimba's footprints on a slab beneath the altar. OK they weren't real but the outline of two bare feet symmetrically carved in relief on grey limestone. According to Rajan, everyone wanted to believe they were real. The extraordinary thing about them was they were big. So big that if they were a true reflection of Hadimba's feet she would have worn size 15 shoes at least. Extrapolating further, if shoe size can be associated with height, she would have been over eight feet tall. Now that was something to fear. I left the place with one over-riding thought. That regardless of whether you believed in her or not, Hadimba was not the kind of woman to mess with.

Following Rajan's other recommendation, I visited Manu's temple. I was full of expectation, imagining an ancient stone structure of thick grey walls and giant wooden beams, all of it elaborately carved by craftsmen, dead thousands of years. Something like the Rama or Vashisht temples. But what I found was something quite different. A narrow, pot-holed lane led to a square, and beside that, a walled compound. At the latter, a steel gate and series of steps led to the temple. It couldn't have been more than thirty years old, constructed of grey, industrial-grade brick and glass. Inside was little better, with no pilgrims, no Brahmins and no atmosphere. As for Manu himself, he was a small, insignificant black statue, flanked by decaying flowers and the usual scattering of coins and rice. To me it was a disappointing place, too modern and bland, the opposite of what I was hoping for and completely at odds with the ancient allegory I expected it to represent.

I didn't stay long. For me the real attraction was what I saw outside, across the lane. Three blokes sat together in the shade of a door, facing the temple. At first I took them for sadhus, or quasi-sadhus, what with their facial hair and orange garb. One wore a turban. Moving closer I could see they were no holy men, but beggars of an unusual type. Snake-charmers. They had a cobra and a python — evil looking things — and as people came by the cobra was allowed raise itself out of its basket, while the python was given free rein to coil itself around the necks and shoulders of the three men. No need for any flute-playing or enticement, these serpents were more than keen to ominously slither about. They were all scales and muscle, with flat heads, whipping tongues and black, beady eyes full of dangerous intent. A shivering unease went through me just watching them. But the odd thing was, the state of their handlers. Or more appropriately, the state of their heads. All three had the dozy, delayed look of habitual drug use about them. Moreover, the snakes didn't faze them in the least. This all became clear when Turbanhead produced a chillum of smouldering grass and passed it among them. They inhaled slowly and deeply, a smoke-cloud engulfed them and their expressions remained unchanged. Then Turbanhead arose, lifted the cobra from its basket and held it towards me.

'You want to touch?'

'Eh, no thanks.' I withdrew. Now I couldn't speak for these boys, but to me, the idea of being stoned and handling snakes doesn't mix. It is a strange way to make a living and a further example of the unpredictable nature of India. Manu's temple may have failed to live up to my expectations in the same way Manu's peers, Adam and Eve, disappointed someone else a long time ago. But co-incidentally, like those early days of creation, it was the snakes who stole the show in this Hindu garden of Eden. I tossed a few coins into the bucket, took a photograph and cautiously side-stepped away.

Later I thought about these snake wallahs and I compared them to myself. We actually had a lot in common. All of us were risk managers of a sort. Me as suit in an office in corporate-land, poring over contracts and projects, analysing risks and protecting GP. This can be a demanding job at times: the larger the deal the higher the stakes. The snake wallahs had their own set of concerns, namely to keep the snakes well fed, ensure a plentiful drug supply and avoid jerky hand movements at all times. The difference was that they could enjoy benefits I don't have: no boss, no deadlines and no stress. They had an outdoor job in the sun and were able to get high any time they liked. The more I thought about this, the more attractive the life of a snake-charmer seemed to be. Those fellas had it sussed. The key question now was: did I have the guts to make that career change?

❉ ❉ ❉ ❉

Saturday 12 July. Our time in Manali was up and we were ready to move on. The expedition report was finished and the remaining expedition funds divided evenly between us. Plans had been made by each of us for when we broke up. We were going in different directions. Darach was heading to Pakistan. He had secured work with an agency to bring a group on a trek to K2 base camp. After this, he was going overland home. Paulie was heading back to Delhi to meet his girlfriend, Barbara. Their Indian adventure would continue with a six-week tour of various states by train. Meanwhile I was going east to Nepal, still with the idea of getting a motorbike and riding it home. Everything looked good.

Our six week mountain adventure had been great and we agreed it was something we had to do again in a few years. On the night before leaving we had a final meal in Mom's Kitchen. Rajan queried me on my visits to the temples.

'So you went to see Manu and Hadimba, how did you get on?'

'Grand. It wasn't what I expected though. Big feet, snakes and drugs.'

He laughed.

Next morning we saw Darach off on his bus. Paulie and I took a night bus to Delhi. We found a hotel in Connaught Place and delivered our expedition report to the IMF. Barbara arrived the following day. Back in Delhi, in many ways it felt a lifetime since I was here. But it confirmed one thing — our expedition was over. However another adventure was about to begin.

PART 2

Explorations in Ladakh

ONE

Nepal

I flew to Kathmandu. With the Spiti expedition over I felt satisfied and relieved. Satisfied that the many months of work, planning and fundraising were over, that the expedition was a success and everyone's expectations had been met. Relieved also in that it passed safely with only minor hitches. As leader, the sense of responsibility I felt for others had been lifted. I was on my own now and free to do as I pleased. Liberating though this was, it nevertheless felt strange to be suddenly in a new place without any of the boys. I would miss their company.

The plan was still to get a motorbike and ride it home. But to do this from India is almost impossible. Indian law doesn't permit motorcycles be sold to foreigners, even though in practice it is easy for any non-national to buy a bike there. In order to take it out of the country and cross multiple borders, a *carnet de passage* is required. These are obtained from the motoring authority in the traveller's home country. The thing is, no motoring authority anywhere wants to step on the toes of the Indian authorities and will not issue a carnet because of the law. The whole thing doesn't make much sense, but to get around it some people travel to Nepal where no such law applies. I learned of people buying bikes there, securing a carnet from their home place, and riding back to Europe through border controls and customs largely unhindered. So this seemed like a good idea to me and one worth trying. There was only one kind of bike I wanted: a classic Royal Enfield Bullet.

Enfields started out as bicycles, manufactured in Britain in the 1890s. They became motorcycles prior to the First World War and were used by the British army in both World Wars. Their simple, sturdy design and military use inspired the motto 'Made like a gun, goes like a bullet.' In 1955 the Indian government placed an order for 800 of these 'Bullets' for military and police use along the northern border. Demand grew and a factory was set up in Madras for state and civilian production. In a twist of fate all Enfield manufacturing in the UK ceased in 1970 but in India the Bullet's popularity spread and bikes of 1950s design are still being made today. This old-fashioned design is a world away from today's characterless, computer-designed bikes of high technology and hard lines. The single cylinder air-cooled engine, the naked, see-through look, the teardrop-shaped tank, the spokes and above all, the forthright growl, makes the Bullet a thing of beauty — an oddity in a contemporary world of transport where bikes and cars all look and feel the same.

I had come across a reputable Enfield dealer, an Englishman with a shop in Pokhara. The intention was to see him, source a mechanically sound Bullet, get it registered and equipped, secure the carnet and begin the journey home.

Thamel, the centre of Katmandu is a tourist trap. It is a congested quarter of narrow streets of junk shops selling everything from souvenirs and cheap jewellery to trekking equipment and tie-dyed clothing. By day it is difficult to move around with the crowds, the plethora of rickshaws and speeding motorcycles, while at night it a hard place to find a quiet spot, with rock music blaring from the many terraces and rooftop bars. Half Eastern, half Western, Thamel is an uncomfortable bastion of hassle and noise.

I found a guest house and got hold of a few English language newspapers to learn of the country's state. Economically, things weren't great. I noted inflation was running at 11.5 percent. Unemployment was rife. Mass demonstrations seemed to be commonplace, and fuel was in short supply. Moreover, with violence reported against some elements of the business community there was little incentive for foreign investment. These stories were indicative of Nepal's political and economic woes stemming from almost two decades of unrest. In 1991, on the back of popular protest, royal authority was restricted and democratic elections introduced. Parliamentary governments were formed but were ineffective and short-lived. In the following years the country experienced much instability. A Maoist movement — a form of Communism based on the ideology of Mao Tse-tung — emerged. Its members railed against government, demanding an end to the 250-year-old Hindu monarchy, a new constitution and an end to the repressive caste system. They also purported to champion the rights of the rural poor. In 1996 their campaign turned violent with attacks on police, public officials and civilians. For ten years, strife wrecked the country, leaving an estimated 12,000 people dead and 100,000 people dispossessed. A peace deal was brokered in 2006 and the Maoists entered the political mainstream. In 2008, after more protest and a strengthening of the Maoists hand, a new legislature was established and the monarchy abolished.

With the king gone, Nepal was declared a republic. A fragile peace and a delicate political situation exists. However, Nepal's problems remain. Attaining peace and political accord is one thing, eliminating hardship is another.

❄ ❄ ❄ ❄

I wandered around Kathmandu over subsequent days, to get a sense of it and to get away from the artificial Thamel. All the streets are potholed and, given the rains, became rinks of puddles and mud. They are dangerously plagued by darting rickshaws and motorcycles, so a heightened sense of awareness is vital. Still they are industrious places full of life and colour. The people are thin and elegant, the women particularly so in their cheerful saris and kurthas. Much commerce takes place, from the omni-present trinket sellers with their hoards of junk, to vegetable traders with baskets of organic riches: aubergine, onions, beansprouts, courgettes, lemons and ginger.

I moseyed up to Durbar Square, the old town, the former seat of Malla kings who ruled the Kathmandu valley from the 13th to the 15th century. Here their ancient palaces and ornate wood and adobe temples remain. The bustle of trade and moving people continued. Several images of the area remain in my head. The first, a pair of sculpted heads — gods Shiva and Parvati — both cosy together, looking down from the rafters of their temple, indifferent to the noise and activity below. The other, a ground-level statue of Shiva, this time in very different mood; fiery and destructive. He stands, war-like in red paint, with a necklace of skulls and a fearsome countenance. Legend has it during Malla times miscreants were hauled in front of it to confess alleged crimes. If they failed to do so they were threatened with the wrath of Shiva, followed by eternal damnation. Quite an effective form of medieval lie detection.

Then another sight, bordering on the macabre. The decapitated head of a goat, on a chopping block outside a butchers shop. Recently slain, it had been carefully skinned. Its eyes and horns were left intact and its front teeth stuck out. It looked like an altar sacrifice. Facing the street and passing crowds, it gazed morosely into the afterlife.

I passed sadhus — emaciated holy men in scruffy robes, with brightly painted faces, long, matted dreadlocks and jewellery on hands and feet. They held out their palms as I went by. But I was suspicious. These fellas weren't ascetics, more like charlatans cadging alms in return for a pose and a photograph.

On past the thanka and trinket sellers until an unusual thing happened. A friendly woman trader gave me a present. It was a small oval stone with Buddha's all-seeing third eye carved on it.

'Here, take it as a gift,' she insisted. 'Next time you come, you will buy something from me.'

How could I refuse? 'Thank you, I will,' I said, putting it around my neck. 'And this will be my good luck charm.'

I found Freak street. 'Freak' was the name given to thousands of Western hippies who flocked to India and Nepal in the '60s and '70s in a fashionable quest for spiritual enlightenment and cheap drugs. The street became their communal narcotic home. But the halcyon days were short-lived when in '73, President Nixon paid the newly crowned King Birendra a sum to ban marijuana use. Birendra took the money and by '75 all Freaks had been deported to India. Replacing them as municipal layabouts were the native sadhus. They brought their own form of counter-culture that never seems to go out of style. It was inevitable that once the hippies had gone the street would lose much of its allure and psychedelic purpose. A few of the old cafés I had read about still remain. But of the one I visited I could find little trace of free love, peace and pot. These days the street is just another warren lost to the trinket and rag sellers. Sadly, times move on.

I wandered the outskirts and eventually walked back into town. Along the way I passed small mounds of burning refuse scattered here and there. Clear signs of poor civic services. Crossing the bridge of the Vishnumati river I looked over the side and got a shock. On the Western bank were piles of rubbish. Acres of it, mostly domestic waste that had been tossed off the bridge over years and had formed unsightly mounds. A vile smelling, putrid mess. From where I stood I could make out several large grey pigs nosing their way through it by the waters edge. Judging by their size they thrived on it. But what disturbed me more was the presence of a handful of people rummaging through heaps in a similar way to salvage anything they could eat, use or sell. This was a pitiful sight. Standing there watching this forced me to examine myself and see how I compared. In terms of good fortune, the difference between myself and these people is enormous. By pure luck I was born in a wealthy country. One with good public services: clean water, sanitation, health, education and a welfare system. A relatively democratic country free of tyranny, with a rule of law, a functioning economy and stable government. Equally I am blessed I have never gone hungry or been without shelter. I have a good job with a pension and I earn more than enough to meet my needs and pay for my frivolous mountaineering activities. Compared to these people and to millions like them in Asia and elsewhere, my life is one of utter privilege. This realisation was nothing new to me but the view from the bridge was a stark reminder.

My conclusion was the same as it has always been — that this world is a deeply unfair place. It is allowed to be unfair by those with the power to change it; be it through the interests and actions of governments, investment banks, fund managers and corporations. And critically also by us individuals, in the kind of people we vote for, in the choices of what we buy, in the laws we accept or reject, the company strategies we abide by and in the political activism, if any, we engage in.

The riverbank scene was a reminder and a jolt for me. The kind of scene many more of us, particularly those of us in a cosseted group, would do well to see first-hand.

❄ ❄ ❄ ❄

Sunday 20 July. I took a morning bus to Pokhara to see the bikeman. On-board I met Sam, an English girl in her thirties who had lived most of her life in California. She was attractive and friendly, and was in the middle of a solo world trip. The bus filled up quickly, mostly with locals and with a few other travelling Europeans. Everyone got a seat. A few young Nepalese students with spiked hair, black Metallica T-shirts and silver chains were last to board. Our bags were chucked onto the roof. The bus chugged out of the city, through noisy, dusty streets, past unsightly grey factories and ramshackle brickworks, and off up the winding, wooded hills. Sam chatted away, recounting her Asian adventures to date. She had just spent three months in India, but as a white Western woman travelling alone, the experience wasn't great.

'I couldn't wait to get out of the place, because of Indian men! Every day I'd get propositioned for marriage or sex. They'd walk up to you, as complete strangers and ask you straight out. I got fed up with it. Honestly, I think most of them are very messed up.'

The poor girl. Trying to find refuge from lustful types wasn't easy, and Indian men weren't the only ones to blame. Often she met and travelled with other people, Westerners mainly, anticipating safety in numbers. In Jaipur she hooked up with a wealthy middle-aged American couple on holidays. Things went well for a while. They wined and dined her, brought her around the sights and encouraged her to stay with them in the best hotel.

'But then the old boy tried it on with you, didn't he?' I remarked.

She shook her head. 'No. Not quite. They both wanted to have sex with me.'

The bus rolled on. The students busied themselves rolling spliffs and teasing each other. At the first stop they abandoned their seats and made for the roof. It was cooler outside. They could lie on the bags, get stoned and listen to music with no one to bother them. Perfect. Inside, the rest of us drifted into the quiet

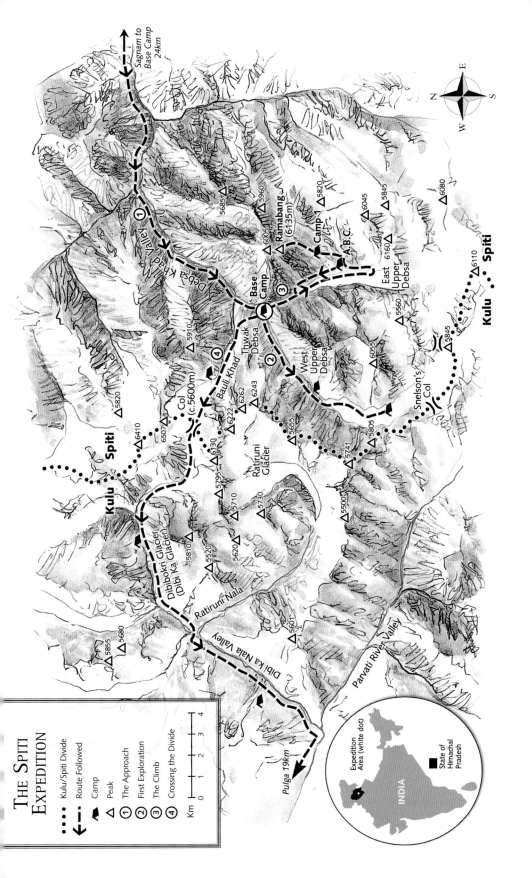

THE SPITI EXPEDITION

Legend

- ••••• Kulu/Spiti Divide
- ‒‒‒ Route Followed
- ▲ Camp
- △ Peak
- ① The Approach
- ② First Exploration
- ③ The Climb
- ④ Crossing the Divide

Km
0 1 2 3 4

Sagnam to Base Camp 24km

Debsa Khad

Valley

△5685

△5960

△6005

Ramabang (6135m)

Base Camp ③

△5820 Camp-1

A.B.C.

△6045

△5845

East △6160

Upper Debsa

△6080

△5560

△5805

△6055

West Upper Debsa ②

△5845

Snelson's Col

Kulu •• Spiti

△6110

△5910

Thwak Debsa

Bauli Khad ④

Col (c.5600m)

△5820

△6410

6507

△6130

△5795

△6222

△6243

△6262

Ratiruni Glacier

△5655

△5741

△5500

Kulu •• Spiti

△5730

△5710

△5620

△5520

△5810

Dibibokri Glacier (Dibi Ka Glacier)

△5680

△5855

Ratiruni Nala

△5601

Dibi Ka Nala Valley

Parvati River Valley

Pulga 19km

N
W — E
S

INDIA

Expedition Area (white dot)

State of Himachal Pradesh

1 Peak 6055, Debsa valley.

2 The Spiti Expedition team at base camp. Back row L to R: Craig Scarlett, Paul Mitchell, Masthi Manjunadha (LO), Darach O'Murchu. Front: Manbahadur (assistant cook), Gerry Galligan, Raj Kumar (cook).

3 Paulie on Peak 6135 (Ramabang) and the East Upper Debsa background. Photo: *Darach O'Murchu*

1 Bridge traffic, Spiti.
2 Three men in a tent. Paulie, Darach and Gerry in the Parvati valley, Kulu, after crossing the divide.
3 The view west up the Parahio valley from the settlement of Kaho Dogri.

1 The vast Dibibokri glacier.
2 Darach, Craig and Paulie at ABC, East Upper Debsa valley.

Col | Bauli Khad Valley | (6,507m)

Kangla Tarbo (6,315m)
First ascent, IMC team
led by Paddy O'Leary, 2000.

Shigri Parbat (6,526m)
First ascended by
Joss Lynam, 1961.

1 Ramabang summit view northward, 22 June 2008.
2 Darach celebrates on Ramabang's summit.
3 Paulie and Gerry celebrate on Ramabang's summit. Photo: *Darach O'Murchu*
4 Gerry on Peak 6135.

1 First exploration. Paulie, Craig and Darach venturing up the West Upper Debsa valley.
2 Paulie, river-crossing the Dibi Ka Nala.
3 Moving towards the col at the head of the Bauli Khad valley, with unclimbed six-thousanders on either side.
Photo: *Darach O'Murchu*

1 Life back in town; the snake wallahs of Old Manali.
2 Craig and Gerry on the Southwest Ridge, Ramabang. Photo: *Darach O'Murchu*
3 Himalayan winters frequently destroy mountain roads. Passing a repair crew at work, Spiti.

1 Gerry on the final steps to the summit, Peak 6135 — Ramabang. Photo: *Darach O'Murchu*
2 Spitians, Sagnam village.
3 Darach and Paulie on the summit snowfield, Southwest Ridge, Ramabang.

ennui associated with all long bus journeys. Conversations came and went. Mothers fed their babies. The engine rattled beneath us and bodies stretched out and slept. The scenery rolled by. We snaked around hills thick with spruce, birch and tall bamboo. The muddy Seti river flowed on our right, with terraces of rice creeping up its banks. Everything was green and the soil was wet. We passed by huts of corrugated iron roofs secured with rocks and truck tyres, and bright advertising hoardings for Castrol oil and Tuborg beer. Farmhouses dotted the route. Their verandahs bedecked with vegetables strung out to dry.

Sam chatted away as I half-listened. My eyes toggled between the bus and the road. It is not unusual to think about calamities when you're inside a bus on a winding, mountainous road in Asia. All the more so when there are sharp drops to the side. Typical news headlines you've encountered at home enter your head: *DISASTER IN ASIA. BUS PLUNGES OFF CLIFF. 60 KILLED.* To our right the road dropped sharply in places and there were few crash barriers. I looked down thinking, what were the chances of us making a wrong move and being tomorrow's headlines? We passed a corroded minibus which lay sideways, 100 metres down a ravine. Its nose was stuck in the dirt and foliage crept up its body, entwined in its rear axle. How many unfortunates were in that? A few miles later we were put to the test. We came out of a bend and bore down on another bus heading the same way. As was his wont, our driver blew the horn to signal our overtaking intention. He pulled out and drew up alongside it. Both vehicles were doing a fair speed. Another bend lay ahead and, around it a 4x4 came hammering towards us. Two big buses on a narrow, two-lane stretch of road. Now I thought, there's hardly any room for three? And the way things looked we didn't have the speed to finish the manoeuvre. Surely our driver must brake? He has to. He's not going to … ? Christ, no! Incredibly, he swung out wider, off the road onto the tight shoulder. There was no barrier. I looked down in horror as the bus teetered over the drop. How the wheels kept purchase I do not know. My heart skipped a beat. The horns of three vehicles blared out and plumes of dust filled the air. Amazingly the 4x4 sailed between us and the other bus. Then our man veered back onto the asphalt and finished the move. The whole thing was over in seconds. Strangely nobody on-board seemed to notice. People daydreamed or slept and Sam kept jabbering away. Oblivion had been a hair's breadth away.

At the next stop the students came down off the roof and filed back inside. They looked paler and were much quieter now. Maybe the roof wasn't so great after all. Surprise, surprise.

It was raining cats and dogs by the time we made Pokhara. Sam had already booked a resthouse for herself. I hadn't, so I tagged along. The next morning I went to see the bikeman. But at his workshop I learned he was in England and not expected to return for a few weeks. I had a problem now. Other Bullet dealers were few and far between. Some were known cowboys and I was reluctant to trust them. This put a new slant on things. Time was important. I had hoped to be on the road in three weeks, four at the most with a bike and all documentation in place. However, getting the paperwork processed isn't easy. Days earlier on an internet forum, I had read of a German punter who had recently done the same trip, Nepal to Europe on a Bullet. It took him five weeks to get all this paperwork done and he claimed this was quick. 'Allow for six', was his advice. Other recent postings concurred with this. Hence if my dealer was out of town for a few weeks, adding up all this time meant a wait of up to two months. This was no good, my time and patience had limits.

All afternoon and evening I mulled over things — ideas and possibilities — before coming up with four options. The first was to get a bike, forget about the carnet and take my chances at border crossings. The second was to wait around Pokhara until bike and carnet were ready and then ride home. The third was to forget about a bike trip altogether but still do an overland journey home on buses and trains. The fourth idea, a new one, was to go on another expedition in the mountains and then head home, overland on buses and trains and any other vehicle that served the same purpose.

I dismissed the first. Without a carnet I knew the chances of making it across borders was slim. The second was a waste of valuable time. The third was very possible. But it was the last idea, the combination of a solo mountaineering expedition followed by the overland trip home that piqued my interest most. This raised a few questions. For the mountain part, where would I go? What would I do? Being rainy season and with no research done, was anything feasible? A first ascent even? Who would I ask to find out? Would I need a permit? How much would it cost? And of course, going solo anything I attempted couldn't be too technical.

My first problem was I was in Nepal during the monsoon. This was the wrong time to be going into the hills. Continual snow and rain would scupper any serious mountaineering. I would have to return to India, to ranges in the Himalaya that aren't affected by monsoon. To places like Spiti or Ladakh.

I knew enough about Spiti but nothing about Ladakh, an area further north. Consultation with an expert was needed, so I phoned Harish Kapadia, a Mumbai-based explorer and scholar on all aspects of Indian mountaineering. I explained my predicament. On both regions he was encouraging; Ladakh especially so.

'Yes there are several valleys in Ladakh that have not been explored, Gerry, and a lot of peaks that are still unclimbed. Lower peaks mainly — five to six thousand metres high. The region is not heavily glaciated, so you can easily do things on your own. Go and talk to Motup. He is the one who knows the most about Ladakh and what can be done there.'

Motup, of course. Why didn't I think of him? Motup Chewang and his wife Yangdu run Rimo Expeditions, the agency we had hired for logistics and catering for the Spiti expedition. They run their business out of Leh, Ladakh's capital. Both are well-regarded and knowledgeable mountaineers. So I phoned them. The word was good. There were plenty of unclimbed peaks in accessible valleys not far from Leh. Few glaciers and no monsoon. There were donkeys available for load carrying and no hassles with permits.

'The best thing to do is come here to Leh, Gerry,' Motup advised. 'We can meet and talk. I will show you maps of different areas and tell you what I know. I can also provide you with any equipment you need. A solo expedition would be no problem.'

This all sounded good.

Meanwhile Sam and I hung around together. Sam didn't have any fixed itinerary about where she was going and what she wanted to do. She was happy enough being a rolling stone.

Compared with Kathmandu, Pokhara is small, quieter and less congested. It is situated beside Phewa Lake, a tranquil spot with wooded hills on one bank and rice paddies on the other. The city is largely flat, spread out and has wide streets. But the city's main attraction are the mountains to its northeast. The immense cirque of the Annapurnas and the shapely, fish-tailed Machapuchare. It was unfortunate that while I was here it was impossible to see them, even though they were only a few miles away. Thick, seasonal cloud persistently obscured them. Other attractions, natural and man-made, had to take precedence. However, just like some Delhi sights I visited, for grandeur and importance, none could compare with the mountains.

We rowed across the lake and walked up a hill to see a white construction that looked like a lighthouse. It was a pagoda, dedicated to world peace. No doubt it was a well-intended monument, chosen by city officials. But to me it seemed pointless. Its only saving grace was the view it gives of the lake, the city and the surrounding countryside. A visit to the International Mountaineering Museum wasn't much better. This place has some scientific and cultural merit, with information on the geology of Nepal and references to mountain communities world-wide. But it concentrates exclusively on 8,000 metre peaks, with reference to the first ascents. All of this information is well documented elsewhere and I could find nothing new to learn here. Of peaks below 8,000 metres, there is almost nothing. Annapurna I, the local giant, Maurice Herzog's epic is well represented, but shamefully I could find nothing on Bonington's South Face expedition of 1970 — possibly the finest Himalayan climb of the 20th century.

A trip to a bat cave on the edge of town was nearly as disappointing. Like most caves, it was dark, cold and damp. And there was no sign of the bats. Given the dreary environment I couldn't blame them if they had decided to move out.

Staying on a somber note, movement of a different kind came home to me as I scanned through new emails in an internet shop one evening. Annalisa, a girl I had broken up with several months earlier, wrote saying she had met someone else and was in love. The news came as a shock. Just two lines said it all. At home we had been together for over a year, until she got a job in her native Italy and returned there. We had always got on well and we kept in touch regularly but it was impossible to maintain a relationship given the distance. Our separation was amicable, yet part of me had regrets. She was the one person I felt most comfortable with. But I had not given her enough attention. My mountain projects came first and she suffered because of it.

'You love your mountains more than you love me', was a comment I occasionally heard. There was a grain of truth in that which I couldn't refute. But my focus on the Spiti expedition and the preparations that went with it hadn't helped. I was hoping our separation was only temporary and I anticipated spending time with her on my journey home to see if we had a long-term future together. But now that was impossible. A long phone conversation confirmed this. I felt sad knowing I had lost someone special. But at the same time, part of me was glad she had found happiness.

The following days were a blur. To Sam I must have appeared distant and strange. I found normal conversation difficult, mostly irrelevant. There was too much personal stuff going on in my head. Nevertheless, a decision had been made. I scrapped the idea of a bike trip home. Waiting weeks in the monsoon for a carnet was just too much and the logic of heading off without one was unsound. Motup's words were too enticing. Ladakh was a new place to explore; to attempt another first ascent and feel a sense of accomplishment. And also to experience another culture. My mind was made up — I was going there. Afterwards I would make my way home, slowly from country to country, using local transport and any other means except aeroplanes. This could be a great adventure, something quite different and unanticipated. Perhaps Annalisa's news had a bearing on fresh thinking? And that little voice of direction that had been at me since the end of the Spiti expedition insisted on having its way. I wanted and needed to get away ... back to the mountains.

❄ ❄ ❄ ❄

Thursday 24 July. It was time to head back to Kathmandu. Sam was heading back also. Her plan was to do a course in meditation and Buddhism at an ashram before returning to India for more lecherous torment.

But getting back to the city wasn't easy. Students, demanding a 45 percent discount on their transport costs, blockaded the road. Also, word spread of a cyclist in some village who had been knocked down accidentally and killed. The villagers were making their own demands for government compensation and they also blocked the only road. After waiting a day, a trickle of buses got through and we were fortunate to be on one of them.

Strikes and stoppages seemed to be the norm in Nepal. The country was also suffering a chronic petrol shortage. In Pokhara, I'd seen a petrol station with a queue a mile long. Its owner was only allowed to sell a few litres to each customer. Earlier I learned all petrol was imported from India. The price was high and making the interest payments was always a struggle, so the government had to subsidise it in an effort to keep the economy going. Hence the high price at the pumps, the shortages and rationing.

The bus journey was uneventful. We kept a healthy distance from cliffs. Farmers and their families worked the fields, harvesting corn and rice. Spells of sunlight broke through the cloud and combs of silver shone from the bending grass. A young lad got on for a stretch. It transpired he belonged to the Gandharvas; a caste of musicians who play their repertoire of songs from village to village. The songs reflect their lives and pay homage to known heroes lost in battle. He sang and played a sarangi, a guitar-like instrument which he worked with a bow, much like a violin. It was raw Nepalese blues.

❄ ❄ ❄ ❄

Back to the bustle of Thamel. I was looking forward to moving on and getting the second mountaineering project underway. As I hadn't foreseen things, all my expedition gear was on its way home. I had what I needed for a bike trip: boots, gloves, base layers and so forth, which I would still use. But I now had to get the essentials needed for the hills. Things like a down jacket, a reliable stove and a half-decent tent. Second-hand stuff would do. Being Kathmandu, there was no shortage of outdoor shops, so off I went.

In one shop I met three young Tibetan girls who were very keen to sell. None of them had ever been to Tibet, their families having left nine years after the Chinese invasion. However despite having been born and raised in Nepal, they felt passionate about their homeland and were angry at the ongoing injustice there. They cited the example of the hundreds of monks who had been killed or had disappeared from Lhasa several months earlier during Olympic protests highlighting the Tibetan cause. The girls were now planning their own protest, marching on the Chinese embassy on the 8th August — the date of the Olympic opening ceremony. They got excited when they saw I had a video camera.

'Come, you join us. Film us protesting. You tell the whole world.'

'I wish I could,' I said with some guilt. 'But I'm sorry I won't be here.'

In consolation I felt obliged to give them some business. So after some jovial haggling I bought a down jacket. Before leaving I asked them their names and what each one meant. Their answers were a far cry from the experiences of Tibet: Pema, *Lotus*; Kyilhamo, *Happy Fairy*; and Sonam, *Good Fortune*.

The girls weren't the only ones with a reason to protest. That same morning in Thamel I heard some commotion down an alleyway. The noise grew louder, then a mob of a hundred or so men appeared. They marched up and down the street, shouting slogans and waving their fists in the air. At the front they carried aloft a crude effigy made from bits of wood, cardboard, twine and torn plastic. It represented the country's recently elected vice-president. His crime? Swearing into office the previous day in Hindi — not the national language, Nepali. It didn't take much to stoke some people's ire.

The next afternoon I was in another gear shop looking at tents when I noticed all the other shops in the street were closing abruptly. Their steel shutters came clattering down almost simultaneously.

That's strange, I thought. 'Another protest?'

'Yes,' Tent-man said.

'What's it this time?'

'Hotel strike. Now I must close too,' he added, motioning me towards the door.

Onto the street I went. Another large mob had assembled at the junction outside the Kathmandu Guest House. The story this time was of a hotel manager who absconded owing his staff a month's wages. They were out to get him. He didn't get far, being holed up in a second-floor apartment across the street from the hotel. The mob, mostly young fellas, were bawling, demanding he come out. There followed much fist-waving and animated chanting. The antics attracted onlookers and more young fellas keen to join in. Then a paddy-wagon rolled up and a riot squad spilled out, batons and shields at the ready.

Some heaving and half-charges followed. The tension mounted. Not surprisingly, the culprit wasn't coming out. This stand-off continued for half an hour. Eventually the leaders grew restless. Something had to be done. If they weren't getting their man then they had to have a go at something or someone. In an amusing twist, yesterday's villain, the vice-presidential effigy re-appeared. It got bundled to the front of the crowd as vexatious individuals took turns swiping at it. Shoulder high it was hoisted again. The mob, by now tired with the lack of progress on the fugitive and with pent-up energy to vent, took off on a parade up and down the streets. The manhunt had morphed into a political protest. Bemused spectators such as myself stood by, watching the rabble shuffle one way and then the other, with the noise ebbing and flowing and the now bedraggled vice-presidential proxy bobbing about. Although noisy and uncontrolled, the whole thing went on without incident. It all ended promptly though. The monsoon rain took care of it. Everyone scattered for cover. The effigy disappeared. The riot police made a bee-line for their van, while the protest leaders legged it back to the hotel. The rest of us on-lookers remained huddled in doorways.

So much for dedication to the cause, I thought. Nature had exposed everyone's true colours.

And that seems to be the way it is in Nepal. Be it student blockades one day, political protests the next, the people of Nepal just seem to enjoy a good demonstration. Materially they may not have much, and politically their powers may be limited. But a good solid protest creates a bit of chaos and helps to blow off a bit of steam. It is a random act by a community expressing solidarity, regardless of the cause. Also, it might not achieve a great deal but it is an entertaining opportunity to show your adversaries that you're thinking of them, and it sends a message to your government that you exist.

This is the new Nepal — a lively democracy, after all.

Monday 28 July. Sam and I parted. I would miss her like I missed the company of the boys. I suspect she felt the same way also. My stay in Nepal was short but I sensed I would miss the place also. It was clear the country was in a state of flux: externally threatened by China and India, and internally, with no current government, the presence of dubious Maoism, a recent violent past and a shift from a monarchy to a republic. Economically it lies in poor state. The one positive aspect I could see is the quality of its people. Everyone I had met I had respect for, and I could see their integrity shining through all the privations and problems.

The plane left for India. It arced around the city, penetrated the cloud and settled on a course west. I was halfway back, starboard in a window seat. As Kathmandu receded I gazed down on hundreds of miles of snow-clad peaks. They were clustered tightly together like eggs in a basket. I judged most were in or around 6,000 metres in height, but dwarfing all were a few behemoths looming through the thick monsoon cloud. Their flanks shone like upturned diamonds, while their summits boldly snagged the jetstream winds. Here were the towers of magnificence I had read about in books, and now I was actually seeing them. The pinnacles of the earth, unveiled for my leaving. Could that be Himal Chuli, I wondered, a mountain just shy of 8,000 metres? And beyond that to the north, is that Manaslu? And over there to the west, at last, was the unmistakable form of the Annapurnas. I couldn't stop looking at them. I had never seen anything so big. What an experience it must be for any man to climb them, I thought. My neck strained by the window as we gradually drifted by them. Awe struck, I told myself I had to return to explore Nepal again some time.

Two

To Leh

Delhi was hot. I took an evening bus to Manali in an air-conditioned Volvo. It was comfortable and the ticket price reflected it, but the bus suffered from that great malignant indulgence of modern life — television. I swore never to take another bus that force-fed you loud, inane rubbish. Give me a clattering Tata with wooden seats crammed with people, which I can handle any day.

The trip wasn't all pain. Along the way we passed hordes of men: barefoot, skinny young types, all wearing bright orange t-shirts and shorts, travelling in the one direction. They carried pairs of pots, flamboyantly decorated with tinsel, tied at either end of a wooden pole, balanced across their shoulders. They looked like crowds of Dutch football supporters gone native at the Rio carnival. Every few miles a mess-tent by the roadside served as a feeding station and, next to each, curiously, were racks for the orange-men to hang their loads. Later in Manali I asked Rajan for an explanation. He told me they were Kanwarias — devout Hindu men who make a pilgrimage to holy sites along the Ganges each year. They fill their pots with Ganges water and carry them back to their villages by foot, some barefoot. The distances travelled are long — up to 250 kilometres — and take days. As the water is considered sacred, it cannot touch the ground, hence the use of racks. Villagers and townsfolk along the way provide the feeding stations and this is considered good karma. Once home, the Kanwarias offer the water to Lord Shiva the river's creator, at the local temple.

I spent two days in Manali. Thick rain clouds built up throughout the mornings, depositing monsoon lakes both afternoons. I bought a jeep ticket for Leh and visited Paul the Tailor to get a suit made; something warm and woolly for winters at home.

Nights were spent in Old Manali, reading and writing. The evenings were best, as the light dimmed and business activity slowed down. Young Israelis drifted into cafés for a drink and a toke. Music spilled out. Dylan from one place,

Santana from another. The sounds inter-mingled and travelled up the street, passing the hippy shops full of beads, leather goods and tie-dyed clothing. Their owners sat outside beckoning you in. Spliffs got rolled and passed around. Lights flickered from the internet cafés, and barbers casually trimmed the hair of their last customers. Near the bridge, the aroma of curry drifted out of the Blue Elephant restaurant. Amid all this I sat on a veranda, nursing a coffee, with my thoughts for company. Every so often an Enfield thumping by would wake me up. The music and laughter carried on.

Through this mix a local man led his yak uphill in the middle of the road. The animal, a piebald, plodded along obediently. It seemed oblivious to the noise and activity; its ruminations probably rested on a night's pasture. Its long coat was clean, well groomed and shone softly under the electric lights. The animal's large size and its rarity in this urban place made it seem strange. It filed by like a presence from another world. A ghost calmly passing in the night.

❄ ❄ ❄ ❄

Thursday 31 July. Manali was very familiar to me now. It almost felt like home. But I was keen to move on. The new adventure awaited, one I had done no preparation for — another step into the unknown.

The jeep left town at 2 a.m., part of a flotilla of buses and jeeps that make the nineteen-hour journey to Leh each day. Eleven of us were wedged into it: myself, three Indians, three French, two Canadians and two Koreans.

We crossed the Rohtang La in the dead of night, then followed the Chandra and Bhaga nalas through Lahaul, over the main Himalayan range and into Southern Ladakh. The landscape varied, from large snow-clad mountains with valleys of scrub in Lahaul, to high desert plateaus and the dry, barren peaks of Ladakh. A few small villages and settlements were passed. Dangerous hairpin bends were negotiated, bridges and high passes crossed. On more than one ascent the tone of the engine changed, struggling under lower levels of oxygen.

It was a long, hard day: cramped, bumpy and full of dust. An expression I came across somewhere summed it up: *Travel to Leh and eat clay.*

But the dust wasn't the worst. Traffic was. Not cars, trucks. There is no railway here, the road is the only modern link between Leh and the south. As a result, all goods are transported on it. I lost count of the number of smelly brown Tatas we passed or got stuck behind as we made our way over the hills. Overtaking them was no pleasure, especially around cliffs and bends. The mind played tricks on me, recalling that wayward bus in Nepal.

However the journey wasn't all bad. Scores of black and yellow road-signs along the way offered prosaic distraction. Each advocated slower speed and caution with captions like: *Don't be a gama in the land of the lama* … and … *Safety on the road is safe tea at home* … and … *If you are married then please divorce yourself from speed*. To perhaps the most memorable: *Are you going for a party? Then why drive so dirty?*

These signs are all over the place. To think there's a team of civil servants in some office somewhere paid to come up with them.

The day wore on. Towards evening we reached the Indus. It channels its way through steep red gorges crowned with aiguilles and gendarmes. To me the Indus seemed surprisingly small, especially given its status as one of the great waterways of the sub-continent. But it still had a long way to go on its journey. That journey begins near Mount Kailash in Western Tibet and continues west through Ladakh and into Pakistan, passing Gilgit before turning south to absorb five other rivers that both name and serve the Punjab before emptying into the Arabian Sea at Karachi. A voyage of over 3,000 kilometres.

At Gya village I was reminded of Spiti, seeing adobe houses of flat roofs with tufts of juniper and scrub on top. The Tibetan influence. Outside the village stand crumbling chortens. Their bulbous shapes grew darker by the minute, in keeping with the silhouettes of the encircling hills. Then with the first sight of prayer flags we knew we were in a Buddhist land. This was Ladakh. Night fell and a vast canopy of stars came out.

Around ten we made Leh. I got a room in the Chospa Guesthouse, where I left my bag before moseying downtown to stretch my legs. I met Olivier, one of the French people from the jeep, outside a café. He was doing the same as me, recovering. We went in for a drink.

Olivier was travelling alone. He was around my age; a debonair type with gentleman looks and a polite, middle-class demeanour. Like me, he held a job in corporate-land, working as a business consultant in Paris. We talked about the jeep trip, the dust and discomfort, and our reasons for coming to Ladakh. For him, he was on two weeks' holidays and planned to spend the whole time on a meditation course.

'But won't you get bored?' I asked.

'No, I don't think so. I am focused and I am interested in meditation. They say there's a strong link between the mind and the body. I know there is — I just want to explore it more. If it means living like a hermit for two weeks, then so be it.'

We discussed women. Of this subject Olivier seemed to know a great deal and he was more than generous in sharing his thoughts with me. He asked me about my personal life. I told him of my break-up with Annalisa and how the future had changed in my head, with me not knowing what would happen next.

'Meditation is necessary for me too, Olivier. So right now I'm disappearing into the mountains for a while.'

He smiled knowingly. 'Everyone must do their own thing.'

❅ ❅ ❅ ❅

Friday 1 August, 9 a.m. Being the busy tourist season, Chospa guesthouse had no beds available for subsequent nights. Its manager, a dapper, agreeable gent by the name of Konchok, urged me to stay with his cousin Stanzin who ran another guesthouse, Druk, across town. We chatted in reception as we waited for Stanzin to show up. I was curious to learn a few words of Ladakhi and the meaning of some names. I learned 'Chospa' meant 'holy man who recites scriptures.' Konchok also informed me that many Ladakhis, like Tibetans, traditionally had only one name. But this was changing. Indian school rules mandated each child to have two names. I asked Konchok what his name meant.

'Konchok means Lucky,' he said. Then as if to pre-empt my next question, he shook his head and wryly said, 'But I am not so lucky.'

Nearby his two assistants chortled.

Minutes later Stanzin walked in. Being an accommodating host, Konchok insisted I let Stanzin take my bag on the back of his scooter over to Druk. Stanzin agreed and one of the assistants was given instructions. As the bag was being lifted, Konchok pointed to my golf umbrella, the one I had with me since Shimla, and laughed.

'This is Ladakh. You won't need that here.'

'Why? I asked. When was the last time it rained here?'

He thought for a moment.

'2007.'

❅ ❅ ❅ ❅

Stanzin looked about thirty. He was unusually tall, lean, and wore an American baseball cap. Like Konchok, he was genuinely friendly and helpful. The pair of them made a good first impression on me. I wondered if all Ladakhis were like them. He brought me to Druk, organised a room and insisted on taking me on a spin around Leh on the back of the scooter to help me get familiar with the place. The vibe I was picking up was good.

Yes, I think I'll make Druk my urban base camp, I thought.

That afternoon I found the Rimo office and met Motup and Yangdu. Mountaineers in their own right, Motup had done many first ascents in Ladakh and East Karakoram, and had the best knowledge of anyone of both areas. I reminded him of what I was hoping to do, namely more exploration and another first ascent of a peak. I broached the names of some the valleys I had lately read about in one of Harish's books, but he dismissed them.

'No. You will need permits for those areas.'

Tackling 6,000-metre peaks would also be tricky, as the chances were accessible ones would have been climbed and remote ones would be in glaciated areas. This meant greater risk for a party of one. I wanted to keep things simple. We both felt the best objectives lay in lower peaks in the 5,000- to 6,000-metre range, many of which were unclimbed, accessible and free of bureaucracy. After some discussion Motup leaned over the map and pointed to an area west of Leh in the Zanskar range — the Kanji valley.

'I would advise going here, Gerry. It is a nice place on a trekking route but few people go there. I think you may find things to do there and you won't need a permit. Also, we can equip you with anything you need.'

The map was small scale and of the kind I knew to be very inaccurate. None better were available. But that was OK. It made going to this valley all the more appealing. What's more, Motup's view was assuring and 'Kanji' had a good ring to it. Already I could feel an expedition beginning.

Two weeks, I thought. That would be enough in the mountains, with a month spent overall in the area.

'OK Motup, that'll do. I'll head there. I'll be back in a few days to pick up some gear.'

And with that I thanked him and left.

Buoyed by this meeting, I hung around town for a few days, to learn what I could about Ladakh.

❋ ❋ ❋ ❋

That evening I ventured up to Leh Palace, a 17th century edifice on a hilltop overlooking town. It is far from its glory days now, being a warren of empty chambers and dusty corridors. But the place affords a great view of the city and beyond. Leh is an oasis in a desert. Tall poplar and willow trees grow in abundance. Small green vegetable gardens are plentiful, bordered by mud-stone walls and narrow winding streets that weave through the old town. Over ubiquitous flat roofs, streams of prayer flags hang limply, then dance like shamans when the wind pipes up. Beyond, a brown desert wasteland stretches for miles up to the snow-capped peaks of the Zanskar range. Zans meaning copper, kar meaning white. Queen of these peaks, is the 6,121-metre Stok Kangri.

The sun was hot and the sky untainted. I padded down the hill to the cool of Namgyal Tsemo gompa. Outside, an elderly monk with a shaved head and claret robe collected an entrance fee. Inside stood a huge red statue of Maitreya — buddha of the future. Nearby, a Romanian conservationist scratched at a wall, restoring a large fresco of buddhas in various meditative poses.

On the way back to Druk I reflected on what I had seen during the day. One thing stood out. Although this was India, Ladakh didn't seem part of it. Politically it is but, like Spiti, in other aspects it is not. Take the Ladakhis themselves, for example. In appearance they are different, having Aryan and Mongoloid features — round faces, flat noses and sallow skin. Most Indians are darker, with thicker hair and angled faces. Language is distinctly different. Many Ladakhis speak a flavour of Hindi, but foremost they speak Ladakhi, a language of Tibetan origin. Spiritually, Buddhism is the main religion, not Hinduism. And geographically Ladakh is higher, drier, with less vegetation than much of India and is more remote from the sub-continent's main cities. With such physical and cultural differences, Ladakh has much deeper ties with its close neighbour, Tibet. So much so it is sometimes referred to as Little Tibet.

❄ ❄ ❄ ❄

There seemed to be a lot of Europeans around Leh. All tourists, travellers or active types, drawn to Ladakh by its culture and outdoor activities, trekking and rafting, without interruption of the monsoon. It was easy to meet people. I hooked up with Juliet, who hung around the French bakery off the Fort road. 'I quit my job in Manchester a while back,' she said. 'I was in Marketing. Planned on coming here with a friend of mine for a while, just to chill out and do some trekking.'

But Juliet wasn't long in Ladakh when she suffered altitude sickness in the mountains, forcing her to return to Leh to recuperate. But she got bored after a few days and decided to put her marketing skills to good use, designing websites for businesses around town.

'I've been doing it for ten weeks now. It pays all right. I quite like it here. I might be tempted to stay, indefinitely.'

It was good to meet her. She was a natural socialite and networker who seemed to know everyone and everything about town. When asked, she rattled off the safe eating houses and places worth visiting in seconds. Through her, I met two local lads, Namgyal and Wangial. Both were genial types, working as organisers and guides in the trekking trade. They dressed in hip, Western casuals and wore dark glasses. I asked them about the trekking game and about life in Ladakh.

'Business is good. We are busy all summer long, from June to September,' said Namgyal. 'After that it gets quiet here. It starts to get cold and the tourists don't come.'

'That sounds ideal,' I said. They both nodded.

'But maybe some day they will not come at all.' said Wangial apprehensively.

'What do you mean by that?' I asked, thinking the situation in Kashmir or new laws might be the reasons. But the answer he gave me was equally if not more unsettling.

'This global warming. Ladakh summers are hotter now than they used to be. The snow doesn't stay on the mountains as long. The sun melts it quickly.'

'Yeah,' added Namgyal. 'I met an old man yesterday and we talked about this. He said the glaciers are retreating at a fast rate. 'Turning black,' he said. This is a big danger. If it continues, our water supply will be threatened. Our crops will not grow and people will have to move.'

'Then Leh and Ladakh will turn into a desert,' I added. 'A wasteland.'

'Yes,' they both said.

❄ ❄ ❄ ❄

The urban exploration continued. I was walking up Main Bazaar road one midday when I noticed a lot of noise and activity around Leh Jokhang, the main Buddhist gompa in town. A high-ranking US-based Tibetan lama was on a tour of the monasteries around Leh. Today he was leading prayers and creating a stir. I followed the crowd.

Several hundred people had flocked into the temple and its grounds. The temple itself was packed with monks, nuns and other devotees. Bells rang out and loudspeakers fed the droning mantras to the crowd outside. Multi-coloured prayer flags streamed from trees and children ran about. In the yard the faithful faced the temple, spinning prayer wheels, fingering beads and mumbling prayers. The ground was hot. There were old folks, men and women with leather-brown skin and wrinkled faces. They wore the traditional dress the people of this region have always worn: brown gonchas — a form of overcoat; *Thickme pabus* — curled-toe straw shoes; Stovepipe hats known as *tibbis*. Many of the women wore their hair in long, plaited ponytails. The whole sight made me feel I was transported to another era.

Clearly the lama's presence had invigorated a deep sense of worship. The faithful meditated, their thin lips moving, their eyes closed. Others hobbled clockwise around the temple, spinning the sequence of prayer wheels fixed on the walls, uttering supplications. I followed them for one circuit.

Arriving back at the entrance gate, I looked down at the ground to find two wooden bows beside quivers full of arrows. More thoughts followed of a distant past. The prayers went on.

Some hours later I was in a bookshop across the street when I heard what I thought was the sound of alpine horns. Sure enough, when I looked out I saw four monks with long horns sounding a fanfare outside the temple gates in a low, earthy tone. Inching out of the gate was a Toyota 4x4. It stopped between the four monks. Moments later, the lama emerged, smiling through the crowd. He was a short, portly bloke of around fifty. His cohorts, other monks of similar size and age, surrounded him and around the lot was the fervent crowd who wanted to see their leader off and, if they could, touch him. The odd thing was this seemed like less of a spiritual departure and more of a Hollywood exit. Along with the robes and shaved heads, the lama and his entourage wore ray-bans, shiny gold watches and smart, Western-style shoes. They made it to the 4x4, got inside and then, like royalty, lowered the tinted windows for a final farewell. Moments later they were out on the street disappearing around a bend. The crowd died down. The horns became silent and the atmosphere settled.

It's an odd faith this Buddhism, I casually thought. Here we have exiled Tibetan monks with flash jewellery and fancy cars, leading prayers for humble folk in old clothes with bows and arrows. No doubt the lama was a pious man. But had he grown too fond of life in the West?

❄ ❄ ❄ ❄

I meandered around town with the video camera. To my surprise few people noticed or were bothered with me filming, which was fine. It was easy to get absorbed into the place.

Its hinterland might be desolate, but Leh is anything but. For centuries it has been an important trading post for various peoples and caravans crossing the continent. From the west, Kashmiri and Balti tribesmen brought saffron, grain and wool to trade. From the east, Tibetans brought tea, wool, carpets and charas. The Yarkandis of Central Asia proffered silver, tobacco, tea and leather goods. Kulu merchants from the south traded salt, wheat, pashminas, spices, cotton and opium. And Ladakhi traders added borax, sulphur and apricots to the mix. All these goods were exchanged and hauled great distances across Asia, on the backs of yaks, donkeys, horses and sheep. Leh is still a prominent trading post and market days remain busy. Only these days currency has replaced bartering and the type of goods has changed.

There's no sign of much borax or opium now, but plenty of electronic goods, penknives, batteries and cheap Chinese clothing.

The town still maintains a cosmopolitan air, indications of which are every-where. From Indian barbers and tailors with premises bearing names like Sharma and Kumar, to Kashmiri merchants selling trinkets and rugs. The latter being sharp-nosed men in skull caps and pathani suits, hustling outside shop doorways. It is no surprise there are a lot of Tibetans also; generations of unfortunates forced from their homeland by a vicious Chinese authority. In tented markets they peddle their wares: Buddha statuettes and thankas, prayer wheels and bowls, assortments of beads, incense and bells.

The old town is a gem. Each lane has its own spell, like the bakers lane, near Jokhang gompa. Here in a terrace of a half dozen chambers, dark industrious men knead bread. They shape them into small rolls and place them, one by one, inside the walls of pit ovens. A mound of baked rolls sit on a cart outside, enticing customers. Halfway along the lane was a gnarled, communal, tree trunk — part of a system of continual fuel supply. Every so often a baker would leave his station, walk over and chop off an armful of wood for his oven.

Behind Main Bazaar road are more alleys of interest. There are fabric shops and goldsmiths and elderly Ladakhi folk in their timeless gonchas, chatting in two's and three's. Children play at their feet. There are tiny Tibetan restaurants smelling of incense and cooking oil, and monks and nuns, chopsticks in hand, nibbling steaming momos.

I came upon a hardware shop. A veritable treasure trove, like the ones we used to have at home before chain stores took over. Its wooden shelves bore an impressive array of tools, all old-fashioned in looks but wonderfully durable. Among them, hammers and hoes, shovel heads, forks, sickles and coiled hemp rope. Crude mallet heads lined the floor like a company of soldiers. In the middle of all this, an old herdsman hunkered on the floor, picking at a box of horse-shoes. He was grading them by size, stacking them on the floor in piles. Again I was reminded of the past — of reliable times. Old and dusty this place was, but looking around I was convinced if a man wanted to make or build anything of quality in Ladakh or anywhere, he would find just what he needed here.

Staying with tools, another afternoon in the same alley, I walked into a barber shop for a haircut and beard trim. The young Punjabi either didn't understand me or had fixed ideas of his own. He reached for the electric razor and was about to go to work when I noticed the thing set to zero, meaning a bald head and face. I pointed to the scissors.

'Here, use that. I don't want you turning me into a monk.'

I mentioned earlier that much of life in India is unpredictable and sometimes eye-opening. In this regard Leh is no different. Perhaps more so. It is one of India's most northern cities. It has a rich trading history and a varied ethnic mix. It is surrounded by barren land in a remote, politically sensitive place, with Kashmir and Pakistan on one side, Tibet and China on the other. The atmosphere on its streets elicits a frontier sense. But these days it is a peaceful town and one I felt safe in. In many ways it is quite ordinary. It has roads and cars, businesses, many buildings, a water supply and intermittent electricity. Fortunately it still has some way to go before it apes the look and character of many cities of the West. Perhaps Leh will always be a frontier town, where a bit of excitement is never far away. One example. I was waiting for breakfast outside the Lamayuru restaurant one morning. The sun was well up but a wind was blowing and it was chilly. Suddenly two kiangs — wild Tibetan asses — ran down the hill chasing one another. They galloped by me, turned the corner sharply and high-tailed it up the Fort road in a carefree manner. There was no handler to control or stop them, only a dust cloud when they had gone. They probably ran right through Leh. But the odd thing was, this seemed quite normal. There were plenty of people around. Others had seen and heard them, but no one gave it a second thought.

At night the town is pitch dark and quiet. Well ... quiet except for the bands of stray dogs marauding the streets, barking and howling. They stick at this for several hours until they feel hoarse. One by one they fall silent, like the rest of us, yielding to sleep. Then at some ungodly hour in the morning a muezzin leads prayers from Jama Masjid mosque. The wailing supplications are enough to waken the dead, and then the canine din begins all over again.

THREE

Politics and Protest

Politically, Ladakh sits in the Indian state of Jammu & Kashmir. Kashmir as a region has been a bone of contention between India and Pakistan since partition. Most of Kashmir is Muslim and this is also the case on the Indian side. I had thought, looking around Leh, there didn't appear to be any tension between townsfolk, be they native, immigrant, or belonging to different religions, but my perception was slightly misplaced. It is one thing to travel through a place and experience it, quite another to live in it and know it. I was reminded of this by Stanzin as we shared a chai one afternoon at the French bakery.

'Stanzin, I notice a good number of Kashmiri men running businesses here in Leh. Tell me, what do you think of this?'

He stiffened before answering. 'I do not think much. It is not easy with them here.'

'How so?'

'Kashmiri people are not Buddhist like us. They speak a different language to us. The ones that come here and set up businesses can be greedy.' He sipped before continuing. 'In their shops they sell Tibetan things, pashmina, shawls and other things. Don't buy from them, Gerry. They always put a lot of pressure on foreigners to buy. All they want is money. We Ladakhis are different; we do not believe in living like that, we are not greedy. That is bad karma. We do fair business and we want everyone to be happy ... to be looked after.'

He was firm in his view and went on to tell me of tensions between shop-keepers and of occasional trouble.

'What about other Ladakhis, Stanzin? Do you think they feel the same way?'

'Yes, I think many others do.' He continued, saying he considered Ladakh to be the poor relation in the regional government of Jammu & Kashmir, that state representatives in parliament were biased towards Kashmir, and dispro-portionately lower levels of funding were too often allocated to projects and public services in Ladakh.

'We don't have power in Ladakh,' he claimed. 'We're controlled by Kashmir.' Emphasising the point, he raised a fist. 'We need our own independence. A Union Territory.'

'You mean a separate Ladakh state, though still within India?'

'Yes.'

'And again, do you think many Ladakhis think the same way?'

'Yes, many do, but more and more Kashmiris are moving into Ladakh, taking business away from us, and that is not good.'

Another chai, another day and another unrelated conversation at the same place. Only this time it was with Juliet and a German friend of hers, Suzanne, who was working as a conservationist for an NGO, spending the summer restoring frescoes in a gompa outside Leh. The job was no holiday. It involved squatting on a scaffold in the dark with a head-torch, scraping seven centuries of mud and bird-shit off fragile paintings. It was a tough, mentally draining activity requiring a high level of concentration and care. Moreover, Suzanne didn't get to see much daylight; only early in the morning, late in the evening, and a spell at midday for lunch. Miners probably had it easier. Some days she would scratch half a square metre off the wall, other days just a few centimetres. It depended on the toughness of the dirt or its position on the painting. When scratching around faces or body parts, she had to be particularly careful; a slip of the hand could decapitate a figure or chop off a leg.

'It's hard work, I know,' she said, 'and very tiring, but I enjoy it. Some days I could be scraping for hours, not knowing what's underneath, but by the end of the day a baby Buddha appears — one that has not been seen in five hundred years. This makes it satisfying.'

Suzanne and I had one thing in common. In the same way I get my kicks from the mountains, by first ascents and exploration, she delights herself uncovering treasures whose existence no one has been aware of. Suzanne is an explorer too.

❄ ❄ ❄ ❄

An educational afternoon was spent with a visit to The International Society for Ecology and Culture. This organisation was started in the 1980s by a Swedish linguist, Helena Norberg-Hodge, when she witnessed the changes taking place in Ladakh after it was opened to the outside world in 1974. Prior to that Ladakh was largely unknown.

In the '60s and early '70s, the Indian government decided to strengthen its borders with Pakistan and Chinese-controlled Tibet through an increased military presence. It also set out to show the world that regardless of border disputes, Jammu and Kashmir was firmly Indian territory. Consequently, a road was built linking Manali to Leh, and industry and tourism was encouraged. Norberg-Hodge was one of the first Europeans to enter Ladakh. Her interest in the Ladakhi language and folk tales brought her close to the people, helping her understand the culture and environment. As an outsider, she could see a traditional way of life being eroded by the imposition of a Western-style ideology brought about by government policy.

Ladakhis have long lived a peaceful existence in close-knit villages and in harmony with their environment. Their survival has been one of interdependence and self-reliance. Historically, they have grown their own crops and built homes from available resources — mud, straw and wood. Their animals help them on the land. Yak, cattle, dzo, sheep and goats have provided meat and milk and wool and leather for clothing, and dung for fuel. Wild herbs have been the source of their medicines, administered by amchis — local doctors with knowledge handed down to them through generations. Polygandry has kept population levels stable and all work is done on a shared, communal basis. Theirs has been a frugal, sustainable existence, where nothing is wasted and anything in short supply is obtained by bartering. This way of life, based on agreed customs and rules and free of outside interference, has proven itself over centuries. As well as that, their Buddhist faith, which emphasises the impermanence and interdependence of all things, teaches them to value each other, their communities, their animals and surroundings. Since '74 Norberg-Hodge has fought hard to preserve this traditional way of life and protect the natural environment. She told me of the many changes she witnessed over the years, few of them positive. After '74, locals saw outsiders, Western tourists especially, going around seemingly with lots of time and money. They smoked cigarettes, wore fancy clothes, sunglasses and jewellery. They came in bright cars, motorbikes and trucks, and they brought a new culture of music, films, odd gadgets and strange food. It all seemed sophisticated, enticing and bamboozling. They also brought a money economy with them. Suddenly bartering no longer worked. Heavily subsidised imported foodstuffs and building materials made it unviable for Ladakhis to trade their own goods. The money system, jobs and subsidised housing drew many off the land and into Leh. Leh was transformed from a quiet backwater with no traffic, clean water and air, into a noisy, polluted sprawl. Then came further roads, more settlements, government buildings and an increased army presence.

This new culture was one of alienation. No longer were Ladakhis part of an interdependent community, supporting one another, sharing resources and balancing work. Many now lived isolated in small urban boxes, competing for jobs and money. The support they once relied on from networks of family and neighbours were diminishing and the traditional skills which enabled them to live self-sufficiently were lost. They became servile to the money economy. Psychologically, this new environment changed them. It taught them to view their own culture as backward and made them feel inferior. A vicious circle ensued. The money system brought inflation. Inflation drove prices higher, forcing people to work harder to make ends meet. Money changed the way people valued each other. Co-operation and sharing was no longer important. There were new rules — competition and money transactions were king. Everything had its price, and a new culture of self-centredness to the point of greed was instilled.

Norberg-Hodge had her work cut out. 'As a Westerner in the early days I could clearly see the destructive effects the Western-style culture would bring,' she told me. 'Something had to be done. I've seen the damage on the environment, on a healthy, sustainable way of life and, saddest of all, on the happiness of the Ladakhi people. We have been campaigning against government policies and vested business interest for thirty years. We have been educating as many people as we can about this — here and around the world. It's a constant fight but we have had some success. And that's worth it. If anything, the lessons of Ladakh apply to the whole world.'

It was hard to disagree with her. From what I could see, Ladakh is at a crossroads. A continual one. In the past it may have been a great crossroads of Asian trade. Today it is a junction facing external threats and internal challenges. One is global warming and its impact on water supply and food production. The other is security, border conflict and international politics, with a sabre-rattling Pakistan on one side, an ambitious China on the other. However its internal challenges are different. In my view the Ladakhis have the ability to manage them; be it squabbles between locals and Kashmiris, gaining a degree of independence from Delhi, or dealing with a culture that values individualism, competition and money above self-reliance and co-operation. Certainly, thinking about the Ladakhis I got to know, all of them have a deep appreciation of their people and culture. They see the changes happening around them and worry about Ladakh's future. So despite all the challenges I feel people such as these have the brains, pragmatism and tolerance to overcome them.

They also have the strength of their Buddhist faith, and this is not something to be underestimated. As I was to see in the coming weeks, Buddhism is the corner-stone of all Ladakhi life. It is a teaching that professes the sanctity of all living things, including a respect for the environment. A person should only take what they need to survive. Desires and all forms of attachment are disapproved. Furthermore, a person should transcend the influences brought to them by their senses of seeing, hearing, smelling, touching, tasting and thinking, in order to liberate themselves from an earth-bound, ignorant state. This unenlightened state is known as samsara. Karma — spiritual credit — is earned by practising compassion and tolerance for others by kind words, thoughts and deeds. Rewards are obtained when a soul reaches a state of spiritual perfection, buddhahood, otherwise known as nirvana. This is hard to reach and usually requires a soul to live out many lives through re-incarnation. The cyclical nature of re-incarnation reminds the faithful that everything in this life — thoughts, actions, physical matter and presence — is connected to the next life and all previous lives. Thus, Buddhists believe everything is transient and everything is interdependent, hence everything is infinite. It is by this paradigm that Ladakhis value their traditional ways. Buddhism helps them evaluate and manage any physical, social or political challenges they may face. It can also help them build perspective and come to terms with the shortcomings and changes brought on by the imposition of another culture.

❄ ❄ ❄ ❄

Tuesday 5 August. My focus returned to the mountains and preparations. I went back to Rimo and got everything I needed: a rope, mountain axe, crampons, climbing hardware and seven canisters of gas. Next came a trip to a grocery shop for two weeks' supply of food, covering the duration I expected to be out. The lot was hauled back to Druk on the back of Stanzin's scooter. The plan was to leave Leh by a shared jeep early the next day and head west to the village of Hiniskut. There I hoped to get donkeys to carry the loads south, through a valley to Kanji village. Motup assured me that I would also find animals in Kanji for the same purpose, allowing me to explore the area.

Things were looking fine. This would be an easy expedition to mount, I thought.

There was only myself, no paperwork, no detailed kit-lists, no complicated logistics. I was looking forward to leaving Leh and excited by the unknown possibilities ahead. I was raring to go.

But as they say, God smiles whenever you make a plan, and if that is so then he was laughing at me this evening. During my stay in Leh I had only eaten in safe, Tibetan restaurants where vegetarian food only is served. Up until now, in India and Nepal, I had been careful, abstaining from meat of any kind, other than the tinned stuff Raj had given us at Thwak Debsa. Only this night I strayed and wound up eating contaminated chicken and lamb in a dubious place. I should have known better. Vomiting kept me awake all night and leaving the following morning was impossible. I was only fit to stay in bed and that's where I remained for the day and following night. I lay there shivering, sweating, and cursing everything. Now I knew how Paulie felt.

Thursday was much the same. Flat coke and a handful of pills helped clean out the system. Still weak, I managed to shuffle back to the offending restaurant for my money back. I was angry. Livid, I let the manager have it; how the food poisoned me and what it had done to my trip. Fortunately for him he paid up. If he hadn't, Plan B was to return with the axe.

Later that evening I met Juliet and told her what happened. She wasn't surprised.

'Yeah a lot of people have been coming down sick lately. Do you know what it is?'

'No. What?'

'The chicken. I could have told you. Word going around is that a truck bringing refridgerated chickens from Kargil got delayed. It was meant to supply the restaurants around here. Some bridge out west collapsed and it couldn't get through, so the fridge was switched off. It took a week to get the bridge fixed and when they did, there was still a load of chickens to deliver. You know what happened next.'

❄ ❄ ❄ ❄

Friday 8 August. I was feeling better and was confident about leaving the following day so I walked into town to arrange transport.

This was no ordinary day. The opening ceremony of the Beijing Olympics was on and demonstrations against the Chinese occupation of Tibet were taking place in cities worldwide. Leh was no exception. All Tibetan businesses and shops were closed for the day and a protest march was being held in the morning. I joined it. Two thousand turned out; Tibetans and Ladakhis mostly, young and old, monks and nuns. It was like a religious festival. Claret and saffron robes everywhere. People wore their finest, traditional clothes. Women wore their best jewellery; many carried bouquets of flowers. Faces were painted in the colours of the outlawed Tibetan flag — a sunburst of yellow, red and blue. Scores of banners and flags were held aloft and the mood was passionate. Interestingly, this mood was driven by young women, with one of them near me leading the cries:

'WHAT WE WANT? WE WANT FREEDOM, IN TIBET … STOP GENOCIDE IN TIBET … RELEASE RELEASE PANCHEN LAMA … LONG LIVE DALAI LAMA.'

Baton-wielding police stood by. I filmed the crowd passing through the bazaar. Then I joined the back and got swept along as we made our way across town, past the market and uphill to the polo ground. Speeches were made denouncing Chinese policy and a litany of the atrocities committed against the Tibetans called out.

To say the Tibetans have been victims of crimes over the past sixty years is to do them an injustice. They have suffered a holocaust. In 1949 after forty years of civil war between Nationalists and Communists, Mao Tse-tung's Communist force declared China a People's Republic. This new Beijing-based regime was centralised, tightly controlled, aggressive and ruthless. Very quickly Mao set about expanding his power and territory. In October 1950 he sent in 30,000 troops of his People's Liberation Army (PLA) to 'liberate Tibet from feudal oppressors and Western imperialists.' The Tibetans, with no standing army, weapons or means to defend themselves, were no match for the PLA. In the months and years ahead Mao's forces went on a genocidal spree. The Buddhist culture was to be destroyed. By 1980 1.2 million Tibetans, roughly one-fifth of the population, had been killed or had died of starvation. One hundred thousand had been imprisoned in labour camps. Countless thousands had been tortured and mutilated. Stoning, lynching, crucifixion, disembowelment, starvation, electric-shock treatment, forced sterilisation, infanticide and rape were commonplace. Tibet had become the world's largest laboratory on human torture techniques. 6,254 monasteries, nunneries and temples had been destroyed, their precious metal artifacts and statues melted down or sold off. The Tibetan language and education system was outlawed and 60 percent of the country's literary heritage had been burnt. What's more, the destruction wrought on the environment was massive. Entire forests had been felled to serve Chinese needs. Farmland had been exhausted to dust. Wildlife, once plentiful, had been largely eradicated and swathes of the country had been given over as nuclear dumping grounds. In total a 2,000-year-old civilisation was being systematically wiped out. That was 1980. Shamefully, the same horror continues today.

But where was the help and why were these things allowed happen? In 1950, as their world caved in, the Tibetans inaugurated a fifteen-year-old boy, Tenzin Gyatso, as their Head of State and spiritual leader: their fourteenth Dalai Lama. Understandably he was too young and politically inexperienced to effect change.

His pleas and those of his cabinet for international support fell on deaf ears. Cravenly, members of the UN and the governments of Britain, the US and India in particular, heard these cries but chose to ignore them. In 1950 China was the big new player in global politics and it was considered unwise to antagonise it. Moreover, for each of these three powers there was a more important matter to deal with, namely a growing Russian threat, so conveniently and disgracefully, Tibet, incapable of defending itself, was left to face the jaws of evil. Ignominiously, in the sixty or so years since, the situation has barely changed.

As the Leh protest continued, I thought about the three Tibetan girls I met in the gear shop in Kathmandu and how they pleaded with me to film them marching on the Chinese embassy. Later I was to learn four hundred demonstrators had been arrested there. Were the girls among them?

But here the protest passed without incident. The speeches lasted a couple of hours and the crowd drifted home, satisfied with their work. But one image of the day stuck in my head. As we entered the polo ground I spotted a lone Tibetan monk, a frail man advancing in years, who was easily overtaken by the crowd. On seeing my camera he stopped momentarily to allow me film him. With the rugged Zanskars in the background, he held an anti-Chinese declaration in one hand and a Tibetan flag in the other. It was a defiance beyond words. If he was caught carrying either object in his homeland, the punishment he would face would be severe. Click. I got him on film. If language was a barrier between us, I hope the sentiment I felt as I looked through the lens got through. 'More power to you, mate.'

Back to the Mountains

Saturday 9 August, 7 a.m. I finally got moving, sharing a Kargil-bound jeep with several others. The plan was to hop off at Hiniskut, 138 kilometres west of Leh, then travel by foot, 10 kilometres south to Kanji. Using Kanji as a base, the intention was to explore valleys further south, hopefully find and climb a suitable peak, then cross a known high pass — the Kanji-La — and descend the far side to the village of Ringdom. This would make for a traverse of the Zanskars. It was roughly 30 kilometres between Kanji and Ringdom, with a height gain of at least 1,200 metres, not counting any peak attempt. A metalled road passes through Ringdom. Once there, I would hitch back to Leh via Kargil.

With our bags on the roof, the 4x4 snaked its way west, through the barren desert, past numerous army compounds. Military presence aside, it felt great to be out of town and into open countryside.

The Indus flowed on our left. To the right, we passed high banks, sweeping hills and walls of conglomerate. Up ahead, as we climbed through the mountains, thick clouds gathered. The temperature dropped, the mood changed and our world became grey. Half an hour later it began to rain. We laboured uphill to Lamayuru village; a place well-known for its erstwhile monastery. The oversized gompa stood out like a crumbling fortress above the village which looked as if it had seen better days in a previous century. Perhaps it was just the rain, or the effects of the harsh mountain environment, or both. I promised I would stop on the return journey and do the village and gompa some descriptive justice. Slowly, we chugged on.

At Fatu-La, a high pass, the road was a morass of mud and gompa-sized potholes filled with rainwater. Out beyond, the mountains resembled a lunar landscape, much like Spiti. There wasn't a twig in sight. The gloomy enveloping clouds didn't help and for a moment I felt I was being driven up the Wicklow Gap on a miserable wet Sunday in winter, wishing I had stayed in bed.

The rain eased off by the time we made Hiniskut, early afternoon. I was expecting to find a settlement. Instead I found an empty dirt road above the Indus, with two locked sheds and not a soul in sight.

What had I let myself in for? I wondered. This was the middle of nowhere. What were the chances of meeting another human, let alone donkeys or horses to take my gear into the hills? It looked like the kind of nowhere I would be marooned in for years … where my skeleton might be uncovered by a road repair crew in 2056. The folks in the 4x4 looked similarly concerned. As my bags got untied from the roof, one of them in broken English, asked what my plans were. I had to bluff.

'I may stay a day or two here,' I shrugged, laconically. 'Maybe three. I shall see.'

'Are you sure?'

'Absolutely.'

They left me, waving forlornly and mouthing empty 'Jules'. I watched them go, the 4x4 getting smaller and smaller until it rounded a bend and disappeared. Wonderful, I thought.

I looked around and kicked a few stones. Then came the recoil of doubt.

'Right Galligan, what's the story? What have you let yourself in for and where are your great ideas now?' But frankly I didn't have any ideas. I never thought I would need any and now all I could do was look around and be thankful the rain had stopped.

I had four bags with me. Three of them heavy. I had to stash them somewhere and go and look for someone. Anyone. So I dragged them off the road behind a pile of rocks. As I was doing this I spotted two shifty-looking characters up the road. They were looking at me.

Bollocks, I thought. This is dodgy. They're eyeing up the gear, and probably eyeing me up also. It was anyone's guess what was going on in their heads. There was only one thing for it. Confront them.

As I drew close to them my impression changed. They weren't the dodgy types I suspected, merely marooned punters like me with all the time in the world at their disposal. One of them had reasonable English.

'Kanji?' I asked.

He pointed to a trail that led to a valley, the other side of the river. I asked him if there were any horses for hire. He shook his head.

'Any donkeys?'

'Em … yes. Maybe donkeys.'

With that, his mate whistled then shouted up the hill. Moments later, another fella appeared. Galstan the donkeyman. Obviously.

It's funny, I had noticed several times in India, whenever I thought I was alone in a rural or empty place, I invariably wasn't. India's huge population isn't confined to big cities. People lurk everywhere. You have to go well off road, into unknown valleys and places to get away from them, and even then it's hard to be alone. I was reminded of our stay in the Debsa. At base camp we thought we had the place to ourselves, until the gaddis and four-hundred animals showed up. But no matter. That's India and part of its charm.

Now I was happy to have met these lads. Quickly we cut a deal. For 300 rupees Galstan's donkeys would haul my belongings to Kanji. We would leave immediately, it was quite a turnaround.

Like the water wallahs and taximen of Delhi, everyone chipped in to the activity in hand — loading the donkeys. The two lads were curious to know what I had in the sacks. I slipped them a few rupees for their help, then off we went.

Galstan's donkeys were unlike their Spitian cousins, being less dedicated, preferring to skive off in any direction to eat plants. He continually had to work a stalk on their backsides to drive them along. The trick was to stay close behind them so they couldn't see you. Walking in front or leading from the side led to certain disobedience.

We headed south, tracking up a nala unnamed on the map, which cut through Kanji gorge. Also not marked on the map was a gravel road. By my reckoning it rarely saw vehicles. Nevertheless it made easy going. On the flat the animals raced along. They forged ahead while I slowed down to study the gorge and surrounding valleys.

Here the peaks weren't as tame as I had hoped for. They were all steep, big-walled structures with long serrated ridges and difficult pinnacles; much like the Dolomites and of the same rock type — limestone. As climbing objectives they were all technical and very appetising, but impractical for me going solo. There was far too much risk involved. Interestingly, there wasn't a glacier or snowflake in sight.

We made the village around six. A campsite lies below it next to the nala. Galstan had unloaded my gear by the time I arrived. He was keen to get back to Hiniskut before dark. There was little time for me either as rain returned as he set out. Sharply I erected the tent and threw everything inside. The rain got heavy and it grew dark. Night fell. I managed to fix up a brew in the porch, eat some food and then crawl into bed. My thoughts were on the tent. Would it withstand a torrent? It was a cheap Chinese thing I picked up in Kathmandu. Outside, the patter was loud. I looked around. So far so good. I thought about the journey here; the rain-soaked jeep ride through Lamayuru.

Then I recalled the conversation I had with Chospa Konchok on arrival in Leh and the declaration he made when he spotted my golf umbrella.

'This is Ladakh. You won't need an umbrella here.'

Yeah right.

❄ ❄ ❄ ❄

Sunday 10 August. The rain continued all morning, finally clearing up at noon. I wasn't alone in the campsite. Four Germans had moved in for the summer. They, like Suzanne, were conservationists, restoring murals in Kanji's 700-year -old temple, the Tsuglag-Khang. They had a cook, in the form of the campsite manager, another lad by the name Konchok. He spent his summers here, looking after the camp and operating a small shop for passing trekkers. We got talking. Konchok asked me how long I intended to stay and I told him my plans. I asked him if any climbers came to the area.

'No. No climbers. We only get some trekkers that stop here.'

That's OK then, I thought, encouraged.

Konchok also told me the meaning of the word Kanji: 'Junction of four valleys.' Looking around this made perfect sense. The village lies at the junction of four valleys going north, south, southeast and west. The main nala runs south–north and is fed by another river, the Chomo nala, from the southeast. Kanji sits on the West bank of this nala and is split in two by a dry riverbed from the west.

I wandered around. There were many similarities to the villages of Spiti. The same square, two-storey, adobe houses with flat roofs and wooden windows. Prayer flags, battered by the elements, flew from the rooftops. White, domed chortens stood in common places and hundreds of intricately-carved mani stones were piled up in walls, here and there. I got lost in the warren of lanes. Nearby were green fields of barley planted in stages and carefully irrigated by a network of water channels.

There were women and children about. Some were washing clothes and carrying baskets to and from houses and fields. Two teenage girls giggled and posed when they saw my camera, and a dog cowered in a doorway. I heard hammering across the dry riverbed. Three men were building a new school. Large wooden window frames were being erected. The roof had yet to go on, many stone blocks lay to one side awaiting use. Curiously I couldn't see any other men about, although I later learned many were away working as herders and guides in the trekking trade. I did see oxen though. Eighteen or twenty of them crammed into a stone pen. Big, black brutes with sharp, coathanger horns. They weren't a happy looking lot; jostling and head-butting one another while throwing me dirty looks.

In the afternoon the sky remained grey. It was time for a little exploration. I walked south, up the side of the nala for two kilometres and came to a feeder nala flowing from the west. The Kanji valley widened to half a kilometre at this section. I turned right and made my way up this feeder nala for a look. Here the geography changed. There were no steep, technical peaks, just valley walls of easy-angled earth. It didn't get any better the further I went. Ridge-tops were flat, making insignificant hills as opposed to defined peaks. I followed a track until it ran out by a stone hut and tilled fields. More ragged prayer flags shivered on poles. The view ahead remained uninspiring, more bland hills and no peaks. By now I had mentally scratched this valley off my list. I was more interested to know what lay to the south. Were there better mountains there? Besides, the intention was still to traverse the range in that direction to Ringdom.

I turned and made my way back to Kanji. Past the confluence I met a group of children and their father driving a herd of donkeys toward the village. The eldest child looked about ten and spoke the most English. We had a good chat, with him informing me about all the crops they grow in the village: potatoes, barley, cauliflower, cabbage, peas and beans. When I pointed to a weed which was widespread in the valley, with an oily, pungent smell, he knew its name and purpose.

'Hotong.'

Once dried it made winter animal feed and was also used as broom material.

As we walked, some donkeys ventured into the barley fields and his siblings ran to shoo them out. I asked him why the oxen in the village were penned up.

'They don't look happy,' I said.

'They misbehaved,' he said. 'They eat crops they shouldn't have. We give them punishment for a few days.'

'Ah, that explains it.'

Light rain fell as I got back to camp. It was cold. I introduced myself to the Germans, cooked a pot of noodles and tinned vegetables, had a coffee and went to bed.

❄ ❄ ❄ ❄

Monday 11 August. I woke up feeling rotten. My head ached, my eyes felt like lead, my stomach churned and my whole frame shivered. I remained in the sleeping bag for hours, no part of me wanting to move. My energy level had dropped and I could only put this down to the poisoned food I had in Leh. The body still hadn't recovered and now it was exacting its vengeance. All I was good for was wasting the day in a heap in the tent. Late afternoon I managed to surface, for toilet needs only and staggered across the field to the loo. A few words exchanged with the Germans made me feel vaguely human. On return I swallowed a handful of pills left over from the Spiti trip, not knowing or caring what they were. Food and drink was out of the question.

The hours stretched by and the evening brought rain. I had noticed heavy cloud building up all day. I listened to the muffled voices of the Germans and the staccato drops on the tent. Night fell, the voices grew silent and then a storm came. The rain became a downpour and once more I worried if the tent had the strength to prevail. Thunder boomed and lightening flashed, creating murky shadows in the tent and monstrous thoughts in my head. I felt wretched and was unable to sleep. Doubts and anxieties ganged up on me like a bad hallucinogenic trip.

What am I doing here? Alone, sick, in a flimsy tent in the middle of nowhere, in the eye of a storm.

I swore at myself. I should never have eaten in that restaurant. I knew meat was risky. I broke the first rule of self-preservation and now I was paying the price. Talk about stupidity? And as for coming here? There are no mountains for me here … only steep, technical stuff, or easy bloody hills. Maybe it was a waste of time. I might have been better off staying in Manali, getting stoned.

The rant expanded. As for Annalisa? Yeah, you messed up royally there, didn't you? Letting her go. That email said it all. You didn't deserve her.

Then came the voice of the Frenchman, followed by more anger: You and I are getting on, you know?

Yes I know. So what? You mean I'll never replace her and I'll grow old on my own, full of anger and regret. Is that it?

Religion wasn't spared criticism either: My head filled with images of contemplative Buddhas, Hindu gods, idols, serpents and temples. Then pictures of Catholic priests and bishops in spotless robes, performing absurd rituals with hosts, chalices and incense. Is there a God at all? I asked. What's the purpose of life? Are we all eejits scratching around this earth? Is religion just an elaborate joke?

The anger turned on politicians, large business interests, cronyism, corruption, globalisation, greed and the human condition. Chospa Konchok got it too. The blasted umbrella.

Meanwhile the storm raged on and I felt no better. The tent remained intact. There was some seepage but no leaks. Inside was a bomb site, with clothes and gear everywhere. There were enough metal objects about to attract lightening, plus seven canisters of gas to make an inferno.

Will I bother doing anything about this? Nah. Stuff it all.

❄ ❄ ❄ ❄

Tuesday 12 August. The rain stopped. I woke up marginally better and was able to shuffle about. Campsite Konchok offered me food. But I had to refuse: anything edible was still off-limits.

I made my way up the village for a look at the old temple. It is seven centuries old, a tiny windowless chamber having the look and feel of a tomb. Red frescoes in various state of decay and rejuvenation cover the walls and three life-sized Buddha statues face you as you walk in. All sit in the customary lotus position and each displays the inkling of a grin. In my beleaguered state I found this particularly difficult to take. Imagine spending hundreds of years locked in a dark box in all kinds of weather and still come out smiling as the day you went in. More luck to them, I thought. I had enough problems just with one night in the tent.

The Germans were there, busy with their head-torches on. It was painstaking work; pasting filler into tiny holes in the walls with small penknives; laboriously mixing powders to match original paint colours, and delicately injecting glue behind bits of flaking paint. They had a local artist, another Konchok, working with them. I left them at it and returned to the tent, still being in no mood for much else. Further valley reconnaissance was out of the question. I just had to tough it out and rest. I lay half-dozing in the sleeping bag. The hours passed. Heavy clouds gathered up the valley again, the drizzle began and evening slipped into night.

Brooding thoughts on Annalisa re-surfaced and these brought on the same black dogs of the previous night. I tried reading as a distraction and picked up the only book I had, *The Four Noble Truths*, by the Dalai Lama. But concentration was impossible. Chapter One's title said it all … 'The Truth of Suffering.' It was too much to take. I tossed it aside, sank deeper into the bag, blocked out all light and contact with the outside world, then prayed for another storm.

❄ ❄ ❄ ❄

Wednesday 13 August. I felt a bit better. Much of the morning was spent lying on the grass, allowing the sun to heat me up. The rain had stopped. Campsite Konchok remarked he hadn't seen such prolonged rain in the valley before.

A large contingent of French trekkers rolled in. They took over the camp with their animals, boxes, tents, supporting cooks, guides, and themselves. I was in no mood for socialising and retreated to the tent. They came from the southeast and were planning to head out to Hiniskut the next day.

What was southeast? I wondered. From the door of the tent I had noticed a mountain down the valley, several kilometres away. It was an unusual shape;

brown and flat-topped, with a ridge down the side facing me and a feature that looked like a rhino horn appearing to project from its north. To its south lay the hint of a glacier. It looked ugly and unappealing but uniquely, this character made it interesting.

If I was to give it a name, what would I call it? Probably 'Druk,' after Stanzin's guesthouse. 'Druk' being Ladakhi for Dragon. I thought there was no harm in getting a closer look. It might even prove a worthwhile objective. So I decided next day, if I felt OK, I would do a recce.

I managed some food that night: biscuits and pasta. After dark, with the French army in bed, I ventured out for a breath of air. I wandered the river bank to the junction and looked at the village. The night was calm, the moon was out and this all made for a pleasant change. The village was dark, except for the dim lights of a few solar lamps. Great silhouettes of rock towered beyond. For the first time I heard the sound of a motor, a lorry, making its way around the bend, past the campsite and into the dry riverbed that bisects the village. Up it went, slowly bouncing on rocks. A good way up it stopped. The lights switched off and the night's tranquility returned. Two men with glowing lanterns got out. They paced their way back downhill, keeping together, treading carefully over uneven ground. Through the darkness it was hard to make them out. But their lanterns looked like a pair of eyes. The eyes of a snow leopard creeping down the nala.

FIVE

Hassle in Herderland

Thursday 14 August. I woke up late. I was still weak but felt a lot better, and it was getting easier to eat. The weather looked encouraging, cloudy but without rain. Thankfully the French pulled out hours earlier and camp reverted to quiet normality.

I packed a light bag and set out. Up over the Kanji bridge, past barley fields, then straight southeast, following a track on the southern bank of the Chomo nala. An hour out, the valley walls obscured Druk. But to its north, another finer peak came into view. Classic triangular in shape, it stood at the head of the valley, adjoining a pass to its north. This pass was the one the French had crossed on their way to Kanji. It was marked Yogma-La on the map with a height of 4,700 metres. If that figure was accurate I judged the summit of this new mountain to be roughly 5,200 metres. Again, it was worth a closer look.

Campsite Konchok told me that in order to progress along this valley I needed to cross a stone bridge over the nala, about an hour and a half out of camp. I had forgotten this and missed the bridge. But for the day's purpose it didn't matter. I continued up the southern bank until passage was cut off by the nala flowing around a bend. Here easy ground gave way to a vertical bank, and other than back-tracking and crossing the nala, I couldn't continue. Instead, I ascended a ramp up the valley wall and looked out from on top of the bend. The view was great. Beyond the nala was the small settlement of Dumbur, consisting of a few stone shelters, prayer flags and grazing fields. There were few signs of life or movement of any kind. Beyond that, Yogma-La, the new peak and Druk. Druk looked less of a dragon now and less interesting. The rhino horn wasn't part of it but a feature on a connecting ridge. However the other newer peak was more attractive. It had good shape and wasn't technical or committing, unlike others. My eyes meandered over it, scouting a route. Its North Ridge from Yogma-La was long and had numerous steps, some large, possibly tricky.

The shorter ridge on the south seemed easier but its broad west side looked fine. I could visualise some zigzagging over loose ground and a few obstacles, but nothing onerous, except possibly close to the top, where firm, steeper stuff led to the summit. Overall though, it appeared possible, which was encouraging. Already I was thinking ahead. Cross the nala and bypass Dumbur. Then head up towards the Yogma-La. I knew this was feasible as the French had come that way. But then I could stop short of it and cut right, south, to traverse the lower slopes of the peak to an appropriate attack point at its southwest. Yes, this all looked OK from where I stood. The only drawback might be a river somewhere. But from my vantage point I couldn't see traces of a river, nor was there anything marked on the map — not that this was any guarantee.

Returning to Kanji I felt upbeat. Here was a surprising new peak, one that would probably make an interesting, feasible objective.

❄ ❄ ❄ ❄

Friday 15 August. There was more rain during the night. As the morning cleared, snow was visible on high ground. Druk wore a thin, white coat.

I had a good rest and I felt my appetite coming back. Today's agenda was to return to the original plan — an exploration of the valley south. Off I went.

According to the map the Kanji nala is fed by glacial melt off the Zanskar watershed to the south. Four rivers spawn from four glaciers and converge at a point midway between the village and the watershed, forming the nala. Beyond this nexus a trail leads up the Western-most glacier to the watershed and a pass, the Kanji-La. I reckoned, not counting any peak attempt, it would be a two-day trek from the village to this pass, with another day needed for descent to Ringdom. This was assuming the main obstacle — river crossing — was possible. Mindful of this, the day's aim was to advance as far south as possible, ideally to the confluence, to assess the feasibility of passage and to hopefully find a possible climbing objective en route.

It was a relief to be active again, to be in pleasant daylight, breathing cool mountain air and to have purpose. I could feel my health and spirits returning. I had to admit the recent days and nights had been miserable. There's little comfort in being imprisoned in a tent, sick and alone, with violent weather outside and nightmarish thoughts in your head. I retraced my steps from the first recce, got to the wide junction and crossed a stone bridge to the eastern bank of the Kanji nala. The nala meanders north, cutting a series of S-bends. I followed it south, keeping on a distinct track — the product of villagers herding their animals to and from high ground. According to the map, the valley was fairly straight, bending only gradually from the southwest to south and straightening well in advance of the converging tributaries. However I knew the map was inaccurate, so I wasn't surprised to find the direction of the valley altering sharply, ninety degrees to the southeast. I continued, admiring the many pillars and towers looming on either side. Three hours out I came to another significant bend, right-trending this time, after which the valley reverted to a southerly direction. A minor tributary joined the bend's apex. This area formed a flat pasture and standing in the middle of it were six square gaddi shelters and a circular animal pen. Later I was to learn this place was called Mendhi. I had to stop and admire both the location of the shelter and the craftsmanship of its builders. The place was deserted and, with grass growing in abundance, looked as if it hadn't seen man or beast all summer. The shelters were beautiful; each one an L-shape to keep out the winds. None were high, their walls built with stones carefully chosen and placed on top of one another without the use of mud. Inside, they were cleverly laid out. Raised slabs served as sleeping berths. Other long flagstones provided seating and shelves. Some shelves were built into walls, others were freestanding. A fireplace stood in the middle and next to it, an alcove to store fuel. One tiny window was strategically placed to allow the shepherds to keep an eye on the pen. All requirements seemed to be catered for. However the most impressive part of these huts were their roofs. In Spiti I noticed few gaddi shelters had them. But here was different. Each had a thick load-bearing beam with rows of willow branches on top, then straw, followed by stone slabs, and all of it sealed with mud. Chimneys weren't built and all fireplace and roof areas were burnished by tar and soot. I had to commend the builders on sourcing the wood, as there are hardly any trees of note in this part of the world. In one regard the huts, with their grey limestone, reminded me of old sheds and cottages in Connemara. Half a world away but no different. I sat inside one, ate lunch and considered them fine, comfortable places to shelter from any kind of storm. Certainly they out-classed the tent.

Moving outside I spotted a beautiful, fawn weasel on the walls of the pen. He was small, with a cream chest and he peered at me as if to say, 'who let you in here?' This is my place. I gave chase, playing a game of hide and seek with him, with the idea of getting him on film. But he was too cute and quick, and just teased me by spying behind different rocks, urging me on. Whenever I thought I might get close, he scurried behind another rock, denying me a clear view through the lens. I conceded defeat and pressed on, upriver into the gorge. The view was impressive all round: fine red, stratified walls, with spires and pinnacles on top. Again, these were lovely structures to climb, but not solo.

Up ahead, past the gorge, on the left-hand side, I could make out the edge of a glacier. And as I neared the head of the valley, I thought, the confluence mustn't be far now.

However the passage along the bank ran out, forcing me into the nala. Other than technical climbing there was no way of breaching the sides of the gorge. I waded up a shallow stretch and then stopped. Water covered the entire width of the gorge. The only way of advancing was to venture deeper into the nala, and try to navigate a line across islands until the gorge widened. If getting through this valley is tricky under normal conditions, then the heavy rains had made it a lot worse. I spent half an hour looking for an easy way through, but there wasn't any. Progression alone was stupid. I thought about another possible attempt later, with animals carrying loads and the support of a herder. But even with a drop in water level it still appeared risky. What about further on? There it might be worse, with possibly more river crossings to take on. The more I thought about it, the more hazardous it seemed, and the more pessimistic I became. This was an attractive and dramatic valley right enough, but a remote spot. People seldom ventured here. Any mistake in a crossing — an innocuous slip — with or without others could prove very costly. Rescue or help would be highly improbable. It made little sense to go on.

Forget the Zanskar traverse, I thought. There's only one objective left — the southeast valley with that dark, pyramid peak.

Still in the water, I circled around taking footage of the valley. I had a final look at the glacier and wondered what the junction of tributaries might look like. Then I turned and retraced my steps back to Mendhi. I wasn't disappointed. How could I be? I had no power over the fickleness of nature and the limits of self and geography. But I was satisfied with a good day's exploration, seeing a fine valley and unexpectedly stumbling upon a unique habitation.

Marching back to Kanji I was conscious of time passing. Clouds were gathering again. Nearing the village, it rained. I sheltered under a couple of nylon sacks I had and waited for the shower to pass. It didn't last long. When it cleared a rainbow came out and the sun shone brilliantly across Kanji, painting the swaying fields of barley in a fresh, golden light. I felt good. The body was gaining strength and the mind was much clearer. I sensed the spell of bad luck and bad weather was over. A new mood of optimism caught me. I had enough knowledge of the area now and was looking forward to the next step. By a process of elimination I now had one focus, with several outlying thoughts: The southeast valley … the pyramid … an approach … an attempt … a trek … an exit.

Two days earlier, I asked Campsite Konchok what he knew of this valley, or more pertinently, what he knew about the pyramid peak. He knew it, as he knew the Yogma-La, but he wasn't aware of anyone having climbed it, or having attempted it. He corroborated what Motup told me earlier.

'Trekkers in these parts climb mountains as guided parties only, and the only mountains they do are 6,000-metre ones and there are not many of those around, so I don't think anyone has climbed that mountain.'

Again, this was encouraging. Also he was of the view no locals had climbed or attempted to climb the mountain, as they had no reason to. Certainly he had not heard of anyone having tried. Mountain passes were more important to them. This made sense, so I happily deduced the pyramid was a virgin peak.

Next I explained my thoughts on the mountain, about an approach, cutting south from Yogma-La and attacking it from its western side. He listened and nodded patiently as I spoke and drew in the air with my finger.

'Yes it should be possible to climb the mountain from that side,' he said, before adding, 'Around that side of the mountain there is another pass — an old one used by the locals.'

My ears pricked up. Here was interesting news. Questioning him more I learned that in order to get to a high pasture in the valley further beyond, known as Shilakang, some of the locals use an adjoining ridge, south of the peak by much the same approach I had been thinking about. I had noticed this ridge was much higher than Yogma-La. However judging by the map it appeared to be a more direct way to Shilakang. There had to be an advantage, otherwise the locals wouldn't use it, I thought. Given the height difference it may have been harder going than Yogma-La, but it was probably quicker. I repeated the key question: 'No one you've heard of has ever climbed that mountain, Konchok. Is that correct?'

'That is correct.'

Right, that settles it, I thought. Well, almost. Climbing the peak was one thing. What to do afterwards was another. The Ringdom traverse was off-limits and a direct return to Hiniskut didn't appeal. Once more I studied the map. There was one other possible option. Instead of returning to Kanji I could continue in a general eastward direction, passing through valleys beyond the peak to arrive on the Leh-Kargil road at Lamayuru. There were two ways of doing this: following one track leading northeast, or another, semi-circular route via the southeast. The former would be shorter and more direct, but involved multiple river crossings. The latter was longer, had higher passes, but fewer river crossings. I put it to Campsite Konchok, who knew both routes.

'What do you think, Konchok?'

'The longer way. With all this rain and the stronger rivers, no donkeyman would want to take his donkeys the first way. It is too dangerous.'

This made sense. Having seen the gorge the previous day I knew exactly what he meant. Local knowledge should never be ignored. Already my mind was shaping a plan. I would attempt the peak by the western side, come off it the same way and cross the local's pass and head down to Shilakang. Then I would take the long route through the valleys until I reached Lamayuru. Overall I estimated the trip to take five days. It's funny, sometimes you go into the mountains expecting to do one thing, such as my first plan of a Zanskar traverse, but you wind up doing something different and entirely unexpected. That's the way it is in the hills — flexibility is the name of the game.

I was enthusiastic now I had a clear objective, and I was determined to salvage something from a venture which had, up to now, been a bundle of setbacks. But a vital matter had to be dealt with first. I wasn't going anywhere without donkeys.

❋ ❋ ❋ ❋

Saturday 16 August. The Donkeyman was difficult. He had visited me days earlier while I was sick, offering his services. His price was 300 rupees per animal per day, 100 rupees more than what Motup and Yangdu told me was the going rate. Yangdu's words stuck in my brain. 'Don't pay any more than 200.'

When I offered him this he scoffed and walked away.

Now I'm not mean, but the notion of paying over the odds for anything, especially when the vendor knows it, bothers me. But the thing was, in Kanji this lad held a monopoly. All other animal handlers were either away or not in business.

On this morning I sought him out to see if he had changed his mind. He was in the main temple, lighting butterlamps with a monk and two others. Although he spoke no English, he knew the value of money, especially when counted on fingers. My pitch was plain:

'Two donkeys, five days to Lamayuru — two thousand rupees.'

He shook his head. 'No.' Again he scoffed. 'Donkey, 300 rupee.'

No reduction, he wasn't budging. His cohorts, aware of the stalemate, closed rank. My subsequent attempts at negotiation were met with snorts and derision. It was pointless. I had to leave.

Back in the tent I heated a soup and thought about this. To an independent mind, the situation was clear. I was the outsider, the European, and most Europeans such as me have plenty of money. At least in the eyes of Ladakhis. I needed the donkeys more than the donkeyman needed my business. He knew this and he also knew he was the only supplier. There was no competition. What's more, his season was short. If he chose to work at all he may as well work for good money, so why not overcharge me? But something in this rankled with me. He is a Buddhist, I thought. Buddhists are meant to be above greed and the accumulation of wealth. No, cop yourself on; this is naïve thinking. If he is anything like me he is shaky with his faith and he'll bend the odd rule to suit himself. After all, he isn't a lama or a monk. And besides, Ladakh is changing. Bartering is gone. The money system with all its short-comings, has embedded itself as the mechanism of trade. He knows this and is just playing the game, why are you bothered by it? Just cough up and be done. More fundamentally, the difference between what he is asking and what you're prepared to pay is 1,000 rupees. That's just around 15 euro. Bloody peanuts, man. You want to get moving tomorrow, don't you? Well don't be a gobshite for nothing. Pay up now and be done with it.

It was a compelling argument. But I still couldn't do it. Then came the counter argument. If I pay what he wants then I'm only condoning greed, I thought. I'm a man of principal, I think, and the one local price is the price after all. Motup and Yangdu who know the score here can confirm this. Besides, if I let him fleece me then he knows it is OK. He will do it again and the next punter who comes along will be fleeced even more. How would I feel about this? Wonderful.

I was getting nowhere. Thankfully a distraction in the form of Artist Konchok emerged in the afternoon. He was painting with the Germans in the old temple but broke away from his work to take me to his house to show me some thankas he painted during the winter. In his large, sun-filled drawing room he unhooked four paintings from the walls and lined them up for view. Three were complete and each remained stretched on their wooden frames like looms. All were religiously symbolic, with Buddha the main figure depicted in various yogic poses. Each was as good as the next. The colours were all strong, the compositions well balanced and the level of detail minute and exact. One piece in particular caught my eye. Its central motif was a Yamaraja — a fearsome winged beast, with four heads, twelve eyes and eight arms. Striking a malevolent pose surrounded by fire, its job is to determine which souls go to nirvana, which go to hell and which are compelled to live out another life. Various weapons and body parts were gripped in its hands. A slew of heads were pinned to its dress and a tiara of skulls encircled its heads. Its feet stomped on two naked repentants, a man and a woman, who looked beyond redemption. It was a creature of nightmares and I was glad I hadn't come across it days earlier.

Below it were a couple of serene Buddhas and more body parts, while above it a third Buddha, meditating atop a lotus flower floating in the sky. Mountains, sky and clouds made up the background and a small bird with a snake in its beak — a Garuda — flew by. Konchok explained the whole message. The Yamaraja was the judge. The body parts — eyes, ears, noses, tongues, hearts and nerves — were the sensory influencers of thought and action. These are associated with the ignorant, samsaric state, of which it is necessary for all individuals to overcome. The skulls were a warning, as were the naked couple … live a good life or else. The floating Buddha represented the heavenly state, and if the Yamaraja deemed you worthy, then the garuda would take you there. Overall it was a powerful work and I was taken by it, not just for its artistic merit, but for the lesson it gave — a lesson fit to unsettle any heathen.

'You want to buy it?' Konchok asked.

'I'd love to, Konchok, but I don't have the cash. And if I did, it would only get damaged going over the mountains.'

As I made to leave an idea came to me. Konchok spoke well. He was bright, a man of ideas and obvious talent.

'Konchok?'

'Yes?'

'Tell me, do you know anything about donkeymen?'

❄ ❄ ❄ ❄

Sunday 17 August. The day was warm and sunny and I was back in Artist Konchok's kitchen, having tea with him and Tsewang the donkeyman. I had explained my predicament to Konchok who agreed to help as negotiator and translator. However on a price reduction, his influence was of little use.

'He will not drop his price,' he said.

'Will he see me halfway then, 250 rupees a donkey?' I asked.

Konchok translated.

Tsewang shook his head. I could see by his body language he wasn't keen enough in getting the business. He had his rate and that was it. 300 rupees an animal — take it or leave it. So much for my ethics and ideals, reluctantly I had to concede.

'All right then. I presume he will bring his own shelter and take his own food, Konchok? And he understands we're not going by Yogma-La, but taking the old, local route?'

More translation followed, with Tsewang nodding.

'Yes, he understands,' said Konchok.

'Right, lets confirm then. Two donkeys, five days to Lamayuru, going by Shilakang. 3,000 rupees. OK?'

'OK,' said Konchok.

I needed assurance Tsewang understood. 'Is that OK with him?'

Further words were exchanged. Then Konchok turned to me and said, 'He agrees. But he wants you to know it will take him one day more to return to Kanji with the donkeys. This will be another 600 rupees.'

I rolled my eyes in exasperation. 'All right, all right, I'll pay it. But that's it.'

I packed up and paid Campsite Konchok. The donkeys were loaded and we were away mid-morning. Finally I was moving again, exploring, only this time committed to a known objective. Our small caravan, two men and two animals, crept up the Chomo nala. Hopefully the poor weather and privations of base camp are behind me, I thought. The day was bright and all was well with the world.

We saw the bridge this time, crossed it and plodded up to Dumbur where we stopped for a rest. Again, no one was about. Munching cattle and dzo looked up, inspecting us from a distance. On a drystone wall another playful weasel appeared.

I'm not chasing you, mate. You lads are too quick for me.

We looked up at the pyramid peak. Although it wasn't the tallest mountain around, there are higher, steeper ones to its north, it had the strongest presence in the valley. Its classic shape, darkness and location emphasised this. The Yogma-La was visible now. It was substantially lower than the opposite pass on the Southern Ridge. Drawing on the ground, I explained again the day's plan to Tsewang: head towards Yogma-La, cut south well before it, cross the west side of the pyramid, then move up until I found a high camp spot below the South Ridge. He appeared to understand.

We continued, ascending a trail towards Yogma-La. On the way, I heard a squealing whistle. Looking up, a fat marmot scurried out of a bush and up a hill. In seconds it was outside its hole, next to its mate. The mate having raised the alarm. We were still quite near them. Their tails were long and their black and tan coats thick. Tough creatures, I thought. They have to be to survive winters up here. Then like all other fauna, they eyed us curiously as we walked by.

A while later I stepped to the right, off the trail. 'Come on, Tsewang, this way.'

But Tsewang had other ideas, with the Yogma-La fixed in his head. The two donkeys were in front of him with the same objective. Raising my voice I motioned with my arms and walking pole.

'Tsewang — Not Yogma-La. This way.'

I continued uphill over scrub and broken ground. Looking over I could see Tsewang still had his doubts. I found myself shouting at him now, not out of communication but of frustration, as I pointed the intended way with the pole.

'No Yogma-La!'

This went on for a bit. So much for the clarity of earlier. I had lost patience with him, what with the hassle over the price and now this. Struggling, he eventually marshalled the donkeys and reluctantly left the trail. I could see he still didn't understand. Once on the hill, the animals veered off different ways. Fifteen minutes later, with each of us chasing to retrieve a donkey, we regrouped and resumed our direction.

The terrain was awkward over bushes and rough, dessicated earth. The gradient was fine. The higher we got, the sparser the vegetation. In several places I was surprised to find clumps of wild rhubarb. This at over 4,000 metres.

For over an hour we paced up this western apron. The ground opened out the more we ascended to reveal fine views of summits to the west and the south. I pressed ahead and, some 300 metres short of the summit ridge, found a good camp spot on a hump of scree. There I waited for Tsewang and the animals.

It took him an age to come up. Clearly this route was making him work. That's not a bad thing, I thought. If I'm paying over the odds he can earn his money. So long as the donkeys aren't suffering.

They eventually arrived. I thought it unusual Tsewang didn't use a stick to goad the animals. Like Galstan's charges, they had the habit of wandering off looking for food. As a result Tsewang had to persistently chase both. This meant zigzagging his way up the hill between them. A stick would have given some measure of control, but that wasn't his style. Nonetheless they reached me in one piece, although tired. We unloaded and talked, or tried to. The plan was obvious enough. I would spend the night here and make a summit attempt in the morning. Tsewang would bring the donkeys back halfway down the hill to pasture. They would camp and return by noon the next day. Then we would all cross the ridge and descend towards Shilakang. We checked our watches. I pointed towards twelve on Tsewang's and gestured the rest.

'Twelve o' clock here tomorrow, Tsewang. Then Shilakang. OK?'

'OK.'

Off they went. Quickly I erected the tent with the idea of getting a recce in before sundown. I was curious to see over the ridge and look for a line up the peak. Camp established, I pressed up the slope, with my feet sliding in the grit. I made the ridge and looked over. More equivalent peaks lay to the east, but to the south, were several snow-clad, glacially connected summits which made up a section of the Zanskar watershed.

That must be Chomotang, I thought, looking at the highest. I remembered

Motup mentioning it. It is estimated to be around 6,000 metres, making it one of the most prominent in the range. Then I looked up at the pyramid. The crest of the South Ridge was crennellated, with some short, steep sections. That might take a bit of work and time, I thought. Probably best to leave it.

The near side stretched from the south to the west, where it met a broken, scrappy ridge. Roughly speaking, half was loose, the other half firm. All of it made an easy 40-degree angle. There was no direct line up but several possibilities, all similar and worth exploring. None of this worried me. But it was the summit crest that drew my attention, as it had from the recce. A wide arch, it comprised fingers, grooves and blocks. As a ridge crest it wasn't particularly high but its side was steep and I couldn't spot any immediate weakness. Certainly it didn't seem the place where mistakes would be easily forgiven.

That'll be the fun part, I thought. The best saved for last.

I stood for a time examining everything, but after a while I accepted I was no wiser. Like all mountains I knew its secrets would be revealed as I ascended it. And rightly so. After all, this was exploration, and most likely a first ascent attempt.

A chill wind swept across the ridge. I pulled up my hood. There was no point in hanging around any longer, and besides, I was hungry. The mountain could wait until the morning.

Monday 18 August. I hadn't slept much. Not from anticipation, but from the glare of a full moon penetrating the tent. Everything was calm. The temperature had dropped, and at first light I could see a frost coat everywhere. The sky remained clear. I heated some porridge and tea and was out of the tent, staring at the hill at 6.30. The body felt OK and well-enough rested.

I started in a direct line from the tent up the southwest side. The scree was a series of shelves with coarse rock of broadly consistent size. My feet slipped frequently on the rime. I would have fallen a few times were it not for the poles. The toes soon became numb.

I came to a wide gully, the first section of solid rock. Stopping for a look, I chose to veer to the inside right, supporting myself by its side like banisters. Thoughts of Ramabang came back to me; the hard work, the possibilities, the thousands of small decisions.

I continued up, zigzagging over sections. The toes remained cold and the thigh muscles strained with each step. I looked up at the summit crest. It was short but vertical and overhanging in places, and I still couldn't identify any weakness. Anxious thoughts crept in. Be useful to have a belay partner, I mused.

The scrambling continued. I stopped twice to film the route, the summit ridge and surrounding peaks. All was silent. The air was perfectly still. A rising sun cast a shadow of the mountain over me and a full moon lingered, refusing to disappear. At one point I thought I heard one of the donkeys cry out below, and I grinned knowing he hadn't anticipated spending a cold night high on a mountain.

Rocks clattered beneath me. I was making a trail. Up the last shelf and then the scree ran out. I was approaching the base of the ridge. Was there a line up? I still couldn't tell. Up I went, over small buttresses, gripping loose flakes and small holds. And then another gully. I bridged upwards on ledges. My feet felt clumsy in the boots. More stones clattered down. I was right under the ridge now and, looking around, I still couldn't see anything obvious. To my left was a slab, five metres high, with a crack running down its centre. Why not? Go for it, I thought. I knew I was close now. But first, a leftward traverse. Delicate steps were needed on small ledges. The rock was poor. Chunks came off in my hands, and I was conscious of balance. It's funny the things that go through your head at times when you're climbing. In this instance a descent three of us made on Mount Assiniboine, Canada. Myself, Rob MacCallum and Jim Osborne. We had finished the climb and were coming down a head wall, abseiling sections. The abseil points were a series of fixed, stainless steel, ringed pegs, driven into the limestone. On the second-last pitch, Rob went first, followed by Jim. While clipping-on for my turn, I thought I saw something moving. It can't be the peg, I thought. Fortunately I checked it. It slid effortlessly out of the rock like a knife through butter. I held it aloft.

'Hey, look what you two just abb'd off.'

To say there was surprise in their eyes would be an understatement. But I digress. Now wasn't a good time for such reflection. My hands went into the crack and jammed. My feet got purchase on side ledges. I looked up. I still wasn't certain but I had to commit. Carefully now. Two steps over a sloping foothold got me a better position. Then a mantelshelf move onto a wide enough ledge brought on a bomber hand-hold. That was the crux. I did it. Another pull up and I was on the summit. At last the sun shone on my face. There was no denying, it felt wonderful.

I looked around. Ah, this is sweet, I thought. A clear day, peaks all around and not a breath of wind. Just silence. Looking down, the tent was a mere orange speck while further back, retracing the approach route, the grey nala and green pastures were tiny. Now no longer cloistered by valley walls, my range of view was extraordinary. Brown graceful mountains stood to the west. The white lucid Chomotang cluster dominated the south, while to the north I could make out the iced summits of the Ladakh range and on up to the edge of the Karakoram. It was a superlative sight.

I sat on a flake, allowing myself to warm comfortably in the sun and just gazed and thought. I knew I had reached the pinnacle of this small expedition and this was no small thing. The view before me and the fact that I had made this summit, a likely first ascent, was, I felt, sweet reward for the tribulations endured earlier: the sickness and doubt, the anguish over Annalisa, the bout of depression. Moreover, just sitting here was a mark of tenacity in exploration. I had come to a little-known area. I had worked around the challenges of poor weather and natural obstacles. I had been flexible and practical enough in sizing up alternatives and modifying my plans, and I had the determination to go for new objectives. There lies the rub of any type of exploration. You can aim for one thing, but you never know what might happen along the way. You can find yourself doing something different and unexpected. Ultimately, pragmatism, persistence and a belief in oneself pays off.

I loitered at the top for half an hour. There was a fair run-out down the east side, with a gentler slide down the north towards Yogma-La. I piled up some stones to make a small cairn. And then a final job: I wondered what name I would call it. Pyramid Peak was hardly original. But I didn't have to think hard. There was really only one name to propose. A name I had come across a lot recently and one which seemed appropriate: Konchok. Konchok meant lucky, after all. I considered myself lucky to have ascended this mountain, in that I had the health, freedom and resources to do so. But I was also lucky in the help I got along the way from Stanzin, Motup, Yangdu, Harish, Galstan, Tsewang, and particularly from the three Konchoks for their contributions. The suave Chospa who helped me with good accommodation in Leh. Campsite Konchok for the local knowledge and for offering me help when I was sick. And Artist Konchok, who stimulated me with his work and who brokered the donkey deal. 'Konchok,' the lucky peak. It couldn't be anything else.

Six

Campcraft, Donkeys and Mandalas

I down-climbed a different section of the ridge, which turned out to be easier than the ascent, before traversing back onto the route I had come up. I wasn't long descending the scree when I caught a shadow passing over me. I looked up. A lone griffon wheeled overhead. He made for the west, riding the thermals, turned and swept down towards Dumbur before disappearing behind a ridge. It all looked so easy up there, to be able to glide from one summit to the next in less than a minute. Seeing him reminded me of my last view of the Debsa and Ramabang.

The scree slope was a doddle going down. In no time I was back at the tent. I brewed a coffee, ate some chocolate and nuts, packed up the gear and stretched out on the thermarest dozing, waiting for Tsewang to show up. Yeah, not a bad morning's work, I thought.

They arrived on time. We loaded the bags and continued on, plodding up over the ridge and down towards Shilakang. Two cairns marked the old way. Further on, we crossed the vegetation line. Meanwhile, grey clouds had been gathering. Then it started to hail. It came down heavily at one point, forcing us to seek partial shelter behind a rock. As we waited, the bleached skull of a sheep stared up at us.

We crossed the Shilakang nala, then ascended the opposite bank, taking us to the Shilakang settlement. This was nothing more than a couple of ram-shackle stone huts, with neither animals or gaddis about. We pressed on, following a trail around a ridge that led to open scrub to the southeast. More small cairns were passed, then a mani wall and a boulder with prayer flags flapping in the breeze. From this spot I looked back at Konchok; at its East Ridge, at the col we crossed and the green flora lower down. It was a fine sight.

Soon the sun re-appeared. It wasn't the only thing to come out. We came upon a stray donkey braying at us from across the scrub. He was a small animal who was either forgotten, lost or had wandered away from a trekking party. With his dirty matted coat he looked like he had been in the wilderness for weeks. Not surprisingly, he was glad to see us and happy to tag along.

The lucky thing, I thought. He now had company and a new owner to look after him.

'Tsewang?' I called. 'Konchok donkey.'

Tsewang laughed. He and the animals were doing well by this new arrival, with fresh legs and company. We were all on a winner today.

But I was curious. I wondered what price a donkey such as this would make on the market. By mono-syllabic exchanges and counting on fingers I put it to Tsewang.

'Well Tsewang, 600 ... 700 ... 800 rupees?'

He looked at the animal, tilted his head and held up three fingers.

'Three hundred rupees?' I exclaimed. You've got to be joking? That was the price I was paying for hiring one of these animals a day, never mind buying one. What's more, I was paying fifty percent over the odds. You cute hoor, Tsewang, I thought. Had I known that I might have bought my own animals and avoided hiring them. They wouldn't have cost me anything. I would have made free use of them for as long as I liked and could have sold them in Lamayuru at the end of the expedition. Perhaps made a profit. This made me think. Until now I had considered myself a bright-enough man. I have been around. I have a business degree and hold down a white-collar job in corporate-land. I am capable at most things I put my mind to. I am assertive and can drive a hard bargain with anyone when I want to. But now I was flummoxed. It seemed no matter how well I considered myself, I obviously wasn't good enough to take on a Himalayan donkeyman.

❄ ❄ ❄ ❄

Soon we made camp in a sheltered hollow next to a small nala. The sun was still out but the wind had dropped and it was a pleasant evening. We were all tired. Unburdened, the animals grazed assiduously on thorn bushes.

I was intrigued by Tsewang. Typifying what I had learned about rural Ladakhis, he was frugal and resourceful. He didn't carry much in the way of a load, only a rolled-up canvas tarpaulin containing a pot and his food. This was hitched to my stuff on the back of a donkey. The canvas had a double use as a tent and as a back protector for the donkey under awkward loads.

A woollen blanket on the back of the other animal did the same job and also served as Tsewang's bed. The ropes used to secure the loads on the beasts were made from yak hair. Meanwhile, I frequently saw Tsewang with a ball of raw yak wool and wooden needles, spinning a thread while we walked. Also at camp he made the most of nature by allowing the donkeys to feed off bushes and by collecting scrub for fire. My approach to camp may have been more sophisticated, though not necessarily superior. I had everything I needed, all of it manufactured, such as a nylon tent, a foam mattress, a sleeping bag, canisters of gas and a steel stove. At one stage I thought Tsewang's traditional methods and few belongings might make me look foolish. But this wasn't so. On the contrary, I was surprised at some of his shortcomings. As mentioned, he didn't carry a stick, but he started to use one at Shilakang, probably after all the donkey hassle. And now at camp he tried to use it to erect his tent. It made a comical sight. The stick kept falling, with the canvas sheet collapsing on top of him. Moments later after much poking, a head would appear, followed by the rest of him crawling out to begin the process again. After several failed attempts I couldn't bear seeing him struggle any longer. Intervention was needed. I went over, planted my two walking poles firmly in the ground and balanced the canvas over them. The shelter wasn't exactly storm-proof, being riddled with holes the size of your hand. He also lacked other necessities, such as a knife or sharp object to cut food and a warm hat for the cold nights. I had to lend him both. This wasn't a problem. In fact it was very worthwhile. We each had our own ways of doing things and by helping each other the Buddhist principle of interdependence and sharing for the common good was being exercised. I helped Tsewang and he helped me by supplying donkeys and his knowledge. Other than the old pass we crossed south of Konchok, he knew the route well. The map I had was poor. It was easy to make a mistake and find yourself in the wrong valley, or in the wrong place in the right valley. Alone, I might have spent a lot of time and effort finding the proper way, but here Tsewang came into his own. Also, communication between us wasn't as difficult as I thought it would be. The lack of a common language was no barrier. We both knew our objective and what we needed to do. We knew when to camp, where to camp and how to deal with the donkeys. Little things like rest stops or water sources, or thoughts about the weather or the terrain were expressed by simple mimicry. The company of one another and the long silences were accepted, indeed welcome. Travelling with few interruptions and a steadiness of pace, we slipped into our own reveries. The sun beat down. The valleys absorbed us. The winds brushed our faces and dream-like clouds sailed over our heads.

I reflected on yesterday's events and in particular how I had lost patience with him over the Yogma-La. In all my annoyance the one thing I noticed about Tsewang was that he never got irritated. At first I found this perplexing. I know if someone is angry with me I often find myself reacting in a similar manner. But not Tsewang. I half expected a robust argument, but instead he remained silent and calm and even seemed bemused by my outbursts. This led me to question the way I had behaved. Had I been right to get angry with him? Was it merely self-serving? Was what I wanted all that important? Perhaps. I tried to think of other incidents of annoyance in Ladakh but other than the restaurant episode there were none. Moreover, everyone I had encountered up to now had been gracious and even-tempered, just like Tsewang. I put this down to religious teaching. In Buddhism anger is considered a characteristic of the ignorant, unenlightened state. It is disrespectful and bad karma. Thus it was no wonder everyone I met seemed polite and even-tempered. It dawned on me how refreshing this was; to live in a society where anger and self-regard is frowned upon. I thought, what if other cultures — countries and societies — felt and behaved the same way? How powerful could that be?

If there is one thing Tsewang taught me, it's that it's hard to get a Buddhist angry, even if you want to.

❄ ❄ ❄ ❄

Tuesday 19 August. It was a mild night and we all slept well. Having slept on mountains, inhospitable glaciers and moraines, I was reminded of the basic comforts that make up a good rest. Like camping in a sheltered place, or being able to pitch a tent on soft grass, or being close to a water source. These things, often taken for granted, now had a greater value.

We had a long day ahead, about 20 kilometres, still going southeast and over a high pass, the Shinguche-La. We washed, had breakfast and fed the leftover porridge and tsampa to the animals. It was another mild morning. The light was soft, there was little wind, and man and beast were in good form.

A word here about the donkeys. Other than the latest arrival, we had got to know each other. This morning for instance, they plodded over to my tent and stood outside, not expecting anything, merely to say hello. The kind of greeting you might expect from a pet dog, not a working animal. Naturally I had to return the gesture, patting them on the heads. They each had their own personality. The smaller of the pair, a male, was quiet. Mentally and physically he wasn't as sharp as the other, and being smaller and weaker, was given the lighter load. I nicknamed him Dozy. The other, a female, was bigger, stronger and bore the heavier load.

She was very assertive and had no qualms growling at the others as Tsewang distributed the leftovers. Clearly she was the boss. She was clever too. I noticed that whenever we moved on easy ground, be it downhill or on the open flat, she would gallop ahead in order to generate enough time for grazing before we caught up with her. The other two never twigged this and so never got a decent nibble as Tsewang and I were always on their heels, harassing them along. It was because of this and her feisty nature that I named her Trigger. Konchok was well named. He was the smallest and, because of this, wasn't given any load. He wasn't as vocal now compared to when we met him yesterday. He now assumed a placid, subservient air, much like Dozy. Actually, a lot like Dozy. Without fuss, he did what he was told.

By half-nine we were off, crossing the nala and descending further along the valley. Our first aim was to make a pass, the Shinguche-La. We travelled northeast for a stretch, then took a right into an adjacent valley, continuing southeast towards its head. The soil and rock type changed from a brown to a dull grey. The animals moved steadily and nipped at available scrub. I lagged at the back, stopping occasionally to film but also because I felt no need to rush. What's more, I found I was still tired.

We crossed a river, stepping over stones and started up a muddy bank with a series of long zigzags to the pass. I remained at the back, plodding along, panting hard. The crew were waiting for me at the top. On arrival I noticed tiredness got the better of us all. Tsewang sat on the ground and the animals stood motionless with their heads down. A cold wind whipped over the col. We couldn't rest long. Several small cairns had been placed along the pass by others, along with the customary streams of prayer flags, all of them weathered and torn. Poor Dozy had a look of dejection on his face. Being high up the ground was bare, not a shred of flora to nibble on. Not that I had much sympathy for him. I reached into my pocket, pulled out a Snickers and started chewing it.

'Sorry Dozy, this ain't donkey food.'

I looked back at where we had come from. It was a fine view down the valley and out over the rugged brown Zanskars. I could see Konchok, with its dark, familiar shape, its cols and its bigger neighbour to the north with a long, serrated South Ridge. Similar to the Debsa exit, I knew I would feel sad turning my back and losing sight of it as soon as we moved from the pass. Irrational I know, but that's the captivating power of mountains; they grow on you. Often when you're drawn to a place you allow it become part of your sub-conscious. Then when you have to walk away, you feel like you're abandoning an old friend. But all is never lost. Usually you are left with good memories and thoughts to draw upon for a long time afterwards. That is why I find myself going back to the mountains again and again. They replenish the soul.

On the subject of soul, it runs deep in Ladakh in the form of Buddhism. No traveller can fail to notice its influence. Buddhist symbols, chortens, mani walls and prayer flags, are found everywhere there are people. In towns, villages, roadsides, fields and mountain passes. Monasteries are numerous, as are the monks and nuns who inhabit them, and who dedicate their lives to learning, teaching and practicing the faith. And it's not just clerics who noticeably practice. The ordinary person does, a lot. Throughout my stay in Leh and Kanji I saw many people, elderly folks particularly, spending their time spinning prayer wheels and reciting mantras. Even Tsewang, while walking with the animals and spinning his yarn, spent hours mumbling prayers in his own mildly detached way. Once, while waiting for me by a stream, I found him etching the syllable *Hum* in Tibetan script on a boulder. *Hum* is the last part of the all-powerful mantra *Om Ma-Ni Pa-dme Hum*, where each syllable represents one realm of existence in the Wheel of Life. Reciting *Hum* sends a compassionate thought to all beings suffering from aggression and hatred and bad karma in the world of hell. Was he trying to tell me something? I wondered.

The literal interpretation of the chant is 'Jewel in the Lotus' — referring to the desired state of divine purity, or Buddhahood. Other interpretations by syllable aim to overcome the temptations and sins associated with earthly life. *Om* deals with ego and pride. *Ma* defeats jealousy and lust. *Ni* quells passions and desires. *Pad* does away with ignorance and prejudice. *Me* renounces possessiveness and poverty.

The mantra is inscribed on temples, prayer wheels and thousands of mani walls all over Ladakh. It is on everyone's lips, not just at these holy sites, but in everyday existence. What struck me most about a great number of the people in India, Nepal and later in Pakistan and Iran is that they live their religion every day. Regardless of whether they're Buddhist, Hindu, Sikh, Muslim, Christian or Jain, they practice their faith everywhere — alone in private spaces, in their workplaces, at temples, markets, bus stations and so forth. With such dedication, it is fair to say most really believe and try to abide by the rules of their faith. This is a marked contrast to the developed West where religion is practiced by some, not all. We tend to question it much more, we often ignore it, sometimes ridicule it and frequently consider it of limited importance in everyday life. It seems the wealthier a society gets, the more secular it becomes. Occasionally I found myself wondering who is better off? Are Asians too humble? Too deferential? Or are we in the West too arrogant, superficial and sure of ourselves?

We moved on. Down the other side of the pass, southeast and into another bare valley. Flora may have been scarce but the impressive formation of peaks and rocks all round made up for it. All were of limestone of various hue: green, grey, burnt sienna, yellow ochre, purple and brown. Pinnacles and needles stuck out from the tops of buttresses and ramps that resembled ancient fortresses. I was reminded again of the geological history of the Himalayas — a one-time sea floor, crushed and uplifted into giant stacks and left to the mercy of weathering and erosion to form a mass of distorted shapes. Here Gaudi-esque, they were at their surreal, colourful best.

The further we descended, the wider the smorgasbord of colours and shapes became. Daubs of red lichen and black moss peppered the stones at our feet. The ground flattened somewhat and Trigger, sniffing imminent vegetation, however sparse, raced ahead.

Way off to the south stood two conspicuous mountains. Both looked like six-thousanders. One, slender with defined ridges and faces and a pointed summit, reminded me of the Matterhorn. A huge scoop of a hanging glacier sat threateningly high on its North Face. The lower section had sheared off, littering a terrace below. Nearby was a dissimilar mountain; a broad black and white dome which, if scaled down, might resemble a Christmas pudding. I could imagine icing being poured over it, to spread and run liberally down its sides, to remain in that state for thousands of years.

We walked and walked, tracking an energetic nala by our left. The sun beat down and the valley broadened out. Around two o'clock we spotted a couple of figures ahead. Gaddis. But no sign of the herd. Tsewang seemed to know them. We met and they led us to their shelter, inviting us in for tea. I politely declined. Tsewang went in and I lay on the ground dozing in the sun. Tiredness was creeping up again.

We continued northeast, over a rocky moraine bank with shallow ravines and patches of scrub. Steadily we lost height, still surrounded by dry, jagged peaks. There was some traffic now. A caravan of forty horses and mules and their handlers came up the valley towards us. I stepped aside, watching them go by. They were heading south to Lingshed, having come from Wanla. It was strange to hear the sound of so many hooves.

We made Honupatta before dark. It wasn't so much a village as a campsite among irrigated fields, in a V-shaped valley accommodating the Spong nala. A few other trekking parties were here; some Europeans with their pony men and cooks. I was too tired and disinclined to talk to them, or to anyone. I pitched the tent, heated some dinner and slept.

❆ ❆ ❆ ❆

Wednesday 20 August. This was another fine day with a full moon floating high over a wall of peaks. We continued down the valley. It narrowed, with a well-worn single track sandwiched between steep cliffs on our left and the roaring nala on our right. We hooked up with another donkeyman for part of the way. His charges carried odd loads. One had a child's pink tricycle on its back. Another a black sports bag with the word *Speed* emblazoned on it. There was nothing rapid about them or us. All animals trotted along with Trigger out front assuming a leadership role.

Donkeys are unusual creatures, I mused. Their big heads and long ears seem out of proportion to their small bodies and thin legs. I imagined if their heads were any bigger they would cause them to topple over. Not that they seemed to know this.

We aimed to reach the next village, Wanla, by evening. On the way we passed people heading up to Honupatta. Various nationalities. And mani walls. Dozens of them. In keeping with Buddhist convention, Tsewang walked clockwise around them. To pass anti-clockwise would unsettle the spirits. Bad karma.

The track widened after an hour and the valley tightened to a gorge. A while later we passed some ragged tarpaulin tents. Encampments. Who are they for? I wondered. Why would anyone choose to live here?

Further along I found out, having gained a clue by the caterpillar tracks on the ground. Then I heard the engine. A mechanical digger was taking chunks out of the valley wall—rocks, dirt and trees—after having carved a wide passage behind, ostensibly for vehicle use. They were road builders. Further down we passed more tents and people. Two blokes were drilling into rock with pneumatic equipment.

'For dynamite?' I shouted at one of them.

'Yeah dynamite,' he answered.

It was a depressing sight. And an equally depressing thought. Nature was being tamed. Man blasting a passage up the valley to bring more people and settlement into it. This would create traffic, noise, litter, ugliness and pollution. There didn't seem to be any reason for it; there were only a couple of tiny farms up the valley and the farmers seemed to manage well enough by themselves. Beyond that, there were just the mountains. A natural wonderland. Unless of course, officialdom wanted to destroy all this with a road to Lingshed in order to stamp the word 'progress' on it. It made little sense. Why don't they put the money and effort into their existing main roads? I thought. God knows, that would be better. All they would be doing here is creating a mess.

Leaving the upheaval we carried on, following the bends of the gorge. We crossed the nala by a shaky wooden bridge. On the far side, in the shadow of the gorge wall was a character coming towards us: a ponyman leading four sandy horses. Nothing unusual there, I thought, except for his appearance. As we drew closer I noticed everything about him was old world. A Ladakhi of around thirty, he had strong mongol features and a striking black moustache. His attire from head to toe was all traditional: goncha, tebi, and thikmey pabus — straw hooked-toe shoes. The horses also displayed an antiquated charm, with coarse leathers and wooden chests on their backs. They all looked as if they had stepped out of the 15th century. I was reminded of those ancient caravans of merchants, plodding the length and breadth of Asia. There was only one flaw. A dirty red sports bag hung on the man's back, with the words 'Fortis Bank' stamped in pale white letters. I wished I hadn't seen it. The nostalgic delusion was instantly dashed.

It remained dashed. We passed more workers drilling. Another party swinging picks into the earth and shovelling the loads away. Then a gang of women squatting in a line, breaking rocks with lump hammers. Scarves covered their faces to keep the dust out.

This is slavery, only without the chains, I thought.

Bit by bit, the gorge was being chipped away. The scene was gloomy and unsettling. It certainly shattered the idea of a peaceful hike through an earthly paradise, far from civilisation and the cares of the world. Once more my reaction was to consider turning around and marching back up the mountains for comfort.

We came out of the gorge, passed hills of brown conglomerate, crossed a concrete bridge and stepped onto a smooth metalled road. No more upheaval. It felt odd walking on a hard, flat surface again. Lizards danced over the asphalt and Trigger raced ahead. Several kilometres later we stopped at Fanjila village and had a drink. Parties of English and French trekkers went by. Slowly I was returning to people and settlements. I was so used to my own company in calm surroundings that I didn't want to return. The same feeling I had after the Spiti expedition. Give me wings and I'll fly into the hills, I thought. Only this time I'll stay there.

But a return to society offered one consolation — different food. I had been living on the same diet of tinned vegetables, noodles and pasta for two weeks, so I was looking forward to a change. Nothing special. A plate of fried egg and chips would be nice. Well, more than nice. Frankly, divine.

Back on the Wanla road we were the only traffic. It was harvest time. Ripened barley swayed in the fields. Women reaped with sickles, gathering the crop and bundling it into small stacks which chequered the fields, awaiting collection. There was no machinery, everything worked by hand. In the village and on surrounding homesteads people were busy threshing and winnowing. Threshing involves spreading the barley around a wide flat circle. In the middle stands a pole, and roped onto this a half dozen cattle or dzo. The animals are driven clockwise around the pole and their hooves break the grain from the straw. Winnowing is more artful. Here two people stand facing each other around a smaller circle, with the crop in the middle. By the use of forks they scoop up the sheaves, flick them into the air and let the wind blow away the chaff. The grain falls to the ground and is collected. This is a very simple, elegant process.

We passed a woman at one stage on the road. She was bent over, carrying a large bale of straw over her shoulder and moving slowly. For Trigger the temptation was too much. No sooner had the woman walked by when Trigger turned, bit a mouthful of straw and proceeded to sneak along behind her for more. You had to admire her, she wasn't one for wasting opportunities.

Barley wasn't the only crop in abundance. As we entered Wanla we passed orchards rich in apricot and walled gardens of marigold, alfalfa and sunflower. The village was quiet. We settled into a campsite on its outskirts. It had been a long, hot tiring day and the donkeys were glad to be rid of the loads. I was happy to be rid of my boots. My feet were sore and I put it down to the hard road. Relief of a sort was found bathing them in the cold nala.

Before eating I padded back into the village. Earlier I had noticed all houses in the village had large wooden windows. This was nothing unusual, as it is the architectural style of Ladakh. However what struck me was their craftsmanship. Every one of them was decoratively made. It was little wonder; I passed the carpentry shop moments later. Inside was a teenage lad, hacksaw in hand, bent over a vice. With the aid of a template, he was delicately sawing a complicated lotus flower out of a plank. Wood shavings littered the floor and stacks of beautiful, ornate chests stood in a corner behind him. The familiar smell of varnish and shavings stirred childhood memories. Days at home in my father's workshop. The pair of us making bookshelves and go-karts. Projects that went on for weeks, involving all manner of activities: drawing, measuring, cutting, drilling, chiseling, hammering, sanding, assembling and varnishing. The master and apprentice. It was so long ago. I didn't realise it then but the practical skills I learned from him have stood to me all my life. The projects were great lessons on resourcefulness and problem solving. Not only that but they built up my confidence on being able to create and achieve things. It had been ages since I had worked with wood, but here, seeing this workshop, breathing its air and feeling its atmosphere made me long to turn the clock back — for the old man and the past.

❄ ❄ ❄ ❄

Thursday 21 August. Our last day. I woke up, had my usual porridge and tea and packed up. It was another fine day. Tsewang came around with the donkeys. But there was only two of them. No Konchok. It transpired another herder in the village had recognised him as his and Tsewang had to hand him over. Tsewang was out of luck. I couldn't make out if he got any reward for Konchok. Probably not. So we were back to four again.

It would be a short day; no more than 8 kilometres northwest with a 600 metre height gain over a pass, the Prikit-La. This would bring us to Lamayuru and the Kargil-Leh road. We loaded up and left the campsite. Everything was quiet. But on the way out of the village we heard the sound of a tractor starting up somewhere. I had to sigh. More bloody progress.

A track led the whole way, through fields then scrub, then up a dry river-bed, forming a narrow channel through the hills. We hooked up with two other donkey teams, of which Tsewang knew, to form one long caravan. Naturally, the assertive Trigger led out front. Several parties came the opposite way, mostly French tourists staying in Lamayuru and out for the day.

'Bonjour Madame. Ça va, Monsieur. Wanla? Oui, c'est pas loin.' It felt odd hearing myself say these things. Actually it felt odd talking at all.

We padded up the track to the pass, zigzagging up a pile of choss. A mani wall and a brace of prayer flags marked the top. I knew once we stepped down the far side the expedition would be over and thoughts would turn slowly towards home. The time had been well spent. Considering the initial setbacks of sickness, poor weather and low spirits, this little trip had been very rewarding. Another mountain had been climbed, another valley system explored and a mountain community experienced. But there was a lot more. In fact my sojourn in Ladakh had been one educational expedition. I now had a great sense of its culture, its main religion and above all, the nature of its people. Tsewang, Stanzin, the Konchoks and others had taught me a lot about living peacefully and co-operatively, with care. I had also seen that it was possible for society — any society — to live without greed, self-interest, competition and aggression.

Down we went, towards the Sangeluma nala and Lamayuru. With the sun out, the gompa looked impressive and the village appeared more inviting than last sighting. Poplar trees dotted the way. However not far away, the tranquil mountain atmosphere we thought we had reclaimed, was undermined again.

A dirty Tata truck clamoured along the road while a digger noisily excavated a hill. Black smoke billowed from its exhaust. Welcome back to civilisation.

We walked alongside the nala and padded the final metres uphill to the road and the village. I would miss Tsewang and his easy-going ways, and I would miss the donkeys for their characters and hard work. We had been a good team. The three of them, still with the caravan, would walk back to Kanji, taking the road by Hiniskut. It would take them a day and a half.

We unloaded, I paid up and we exchanged pleasantries of which neither of us understood. It didn't matter though, the sentiment was mutually agreeable. Then we shook hands. But with cash fresh in his hand, Tsewang the businessman wasn't one to miss a final chance. He looked down at my boots and intimated he would like them. They would be much better than the sandals. I had to smile. He already had my cash and my spare hat. But full marks for trying.

'Are you joking? Not my boots, Tsewang. You'll take the shirt off my back next.'

With my belongings stashed at the back of a dhaba I crossed the road to a guesthouse for lunch. Nothing would do other than a plate of fried egg and chips. Then a second plate, with the lot washed down with a tall bottle of Kashmiri apple juice. Rarely had simple food tasted so good.

Sated, I was able to visit the gompa. A winding, hilly lane took me there. Dozens of monks, many of them young boys, were present. They behaved no differently to any other boys of their age, running about, horse-playing. Despite the size of the complex, there wasn't a great deal to see. Much of it was closed to outsiders. A good view of the valley could be found and on the roof terrace of the oldest temple, elderly villagers shuffled around a cluster of chortens and prayer wheels. Their faces were sun-beaten and wizened. Their clothing was old and layered. Silver bangles hung on their wrists and well-worn sheepskin bags sagged on their backs.

An afternoon breeze whipped up clouds of dust. I roved into the main temple. In the dim venerable calm, amidst hanging thankas, trumpets, drums and glass cases full of brass statues of Buddha, four monks busied themselves creating a mandala. It was being copied from a photograph. Mandalas are multi-coloured pictures with geometric patterns containing arcs, circles, rectangles and squares. They are abstract designs having no obvious connection to anything of this life. Thus it was impossible for me to guess what it represented. Clearly its significance was profound, so I asked one of the monks what it meant. But he gave me such a weighted look as if it would take him years to explain.

'Don't worry about it,' I said.

I learned they were making it for an up-coming festival. I watched them work.

It was a long, laborious exercise mainly because the material used appeared to be dry powder paint. The mandala's outline had been drawn on a flat wooden board, one metre square. A monk sat on each side. The powder paint was scooped into steel funnels by each, held in the fingers and brought over a given shape. By scratching the funnel with the stem of a spoon, the powder was evenly sprinkled onto the shape. As there were many shapes, there was an awful lot of scratching.

'How long does it take to make?' I asked another monk.

'Four days.'

They were about halfway there. They scratched away feverishly. Judging by some of the pained expressions, they were behind schedule. Other monks came and went, passing comments. This couldn't have helped the pressure. But no doubt once finished it would be a beautiful work. It would form the centre-piece of the festival. They would do puja with it and destroy it afterwards; in Buddhism nothing is permanent. That said I couldn't help thinking that on a practical level there was no guarantee it would make the festival. After all, it was only a pile of fine powder on a board and it had many monks hovering around it all day. What if someone sneezed?

In the late afternoon I hitched back to Leh. I was lucky. One lift got me there. It was a 4x4 with two men coming from the monastery. One of them was a monk. We snaked along the Indus. I was mindful of its long voyage west through Kashmir, Pakistan and out into the Arabian sea. The sun set behind us. It grew dark and a raft of shimmering stars appeared. I asked the monk if he had seen the mandala. He had. I was still curious to know what it meant, so I asked him. But like the earlier monk, he sighed heavily at my question. Again the thought of unravelling years of wisdom and teaching it to a foreigner of a different culture and religion was too much. It would take all night and he still wouldn't get to the bottom of it. Did he really have to explain? He wavered, searching for an excuse not to. But I was keen to know something, anything, about it. It couldn't all just be an arrangement of colours on something vague and indescribable.

'Look,' I said, offering a way out, 'I know Buddhism is deep and complicated, but just give me an idea, a general idea, of what the mandala is all about. In just one sentence, please.'

He thought for a moment. 'In one sentence?'

'Yes.'

'OK. It is a map to help you reach nirvana.'

SEVEN

The Wisdom of Monks

Friday 22 August. I woke up in my old room in Druk. It was luxury to be sleeping indoors again, not having to think about storms and leaks or having the sun baking you inside or outside the tent. Sometimes it's good to be back from the mountains, sometimes not. Now there were other luxuries, like Stanzin cooking me breakfast. Why would anyone look for hardship? I wondered. A man could get used to this.

The afternoon was spent in a leisurely way, returning the Rimo gear, writing postcards and emails and having chai with Namgyal, Wangial and Juliet.

❄ ❄ ❄ ❄

Saturday 23 August. For all the time I was in Ladakh I was interested in talking to some monks or nuns. There were always a few around Leh at any time but it wasn't easy approaching them or anyone as a complete stranger. I was interested in getting a view of Buddhism and life in general from their perspective. So I asked Juliet, the network.

'I'll speak to Wangial,' she said. 'Some of his friends are monks. Let's see what he can do.'

One thing led to another and an appointment was made to meet two monks, Samten and Angdu from Tserkarmo monastery, in the garden of The Penguin Café that afternoon.

Both men were young. Samten about twenty-eight, Angdu around thirty-five. Both were quite different in character and had taken different paths to their vocation. Samten was just six when he decided to join a monastery, of his own accord. I was immediately struck by his sharpness and intensity. Angdu on the other hand, was a late-comer, having entered the monastic life at twenty-seven, after renouncing bad behaviour and trouble. He was the quieter of the two and seemed calmer. On Samten, I thought it strange that a boy as young as six would choose to become a monk. After all, with such little life experience how could he know what was best for him? I put this to him. His response was forthright.

'I just knew it was the right thing for me. I felt it in my heart. And I still do today. It is difficult to explain, I just knew. Other people join the monastery at different times in their lives. Look at Angdu here who joined later in life. He will tell you he joined when he knew it was right for him.'

Angdu agreed. Nevertheless I still thought it odd.

'But it must have been hard, Samten, leaving your family at such a young age? And life in the monastery must have been hard. Is it?'

'Yes, it is not easy leaving your family, but you gain a new family instead. Although as a young boy, you are not so special. You get less attention. And yes, life in the monastery is hard. Meditation is hard. But as you get older you experience more and you get more wisdom.'

Neither man had any regrets. Both were firmly of the view the monastic life was for them.

'And what of this wisdom, men? I am aware Buddhism is a religion that is both simple and complex. But tell me, really, what is it all about?'

Samten was direct. 'Buddha means clarity; clarity like when we were born. As we grow up we become conditioned by life and by others. We get clouded in our thoughts and in our understanding. The aim of Buddhism is to strip away all that cloudiness and seek the truth in everything. In other words, to be able to see clearly like a new-born child again.'

'I see,' I said. 'But isn't Buddhism also about forgetting yourself? About losing your vanity and desires and putting the well-being of others first? And by doing so, you earn good karma?'

'Yes it is,' answered Angdu. 'We call this nangpa.'

'Nangpa?'

'Nangpa means the one who follows the inner heart. The one who seeks truth.'

'We all try to live by nangpa,' added Samten. 'But not all monks do.' He held up his robe. 'You see these robes? They are red to remind us of fire. If we don't overcome our egos we will be burned by fire.'

'OK, that's the ego,' I said. 'But what of meditation? What do you get from it?'

Samten again: 'Meditation is a reflection; a reflection on your thoughts and actions; and on the choices you have made, which can be good or bad. Your intellect controls your heart. If you have good thoughts this will strengthen your heart and will be reflected in your choices and actions. Mediation will train and improve your intellect and heart. You see, your mind is your workshop. But your heart is your real home.'

'You mean the intellect is the tool of the heart?'

'Exactly.'

'I see.' I was enjoying this now. The conversation was going well and I had many more questions. One thing I wasn't sure about was Buddha himself. I had thought there was only one Buddha. But in my travels so far I had seen many Buddhas on thankas and murals in monasteries and temples. They were often grouped side by side, each Buddha varying slightly from the next by size, colour, clothing and pose. Also, they serve different purposes. One being the Medicine Buddha. Another being the Future Buddha. Another, Compassionate Buddha, another, Energy Buddha and so on. 'What is behind this?' I asked. 'Can either of you tell me?'

'You are right,' Angdu replied, 'there is only one Buddha and he was the original teacher. All the other buddhas you say are manifestations of him. Consider for example, a full moon shining on a lake. If the wind blows and there are ripples on the lake, how many reflections of the moon do you see in it?'

'Many,' I said.

'Correct. Each reflection is a different manifestation. But there is only one moon. And so it is with Buddha.'

Point made.

However there was another, bigger aspect of Buddhism that was unclear to me. One I had been struggling with for a long time. A conversation I had with Nima back in Tabo came to mind. The notion of re-incarnation. I have always thought the prospect of having to live many lives over, depressing. There is enough anxiety and suffering in most people's lives, so surely one spell on earth is enough for anyone. Seventy years or so is a good stretch; long enough to make a contribution to the world and to fulfil any objectives, assuming you have any. I was interested to know if either man had ever thought the same way and, if so, did they reject it.

They hadn't and didn't. Samten was first to explain. 'We see death as the end of one life and the beginning of another journey. In other words, your soul leaves your body and you go someplace else. Would you agree?'

'Eh ... yes, I would,' I said.

He continued. 'You were born a Christian, right?'

I nodded.

'So, you don't know when you die whether your soul goes to heaven or hell or some other place, do you?'

'True, I don't know,' I said.

'Well neither do we,' he added succinctly. 'We don't know whether we go to a heaven or a hell, or carry on as another being. None of us do.'

My brow furrowed. 'So what are you saying, Samten?'

'I am saying the soul continues in another form after death — whatever form that is. We have no control of where it goes. It can go anywhere. That is re-incarnation. This means that you, me, Angdu and all of us here will go on another journey when we die. We will all be re-incarnated.'

His words were simple and yet so disarming. It didn't matter what religion you were. If you believe in an afterlife, you accept the concept of re-incarnation. In one sense I could accept this. But in another, the misgivings I felt towards re-incarnation had increased. Now it seemed the chances of returning to earth to live out many lives had grown. Moreover, Buddhists alone don't hold any monopoly on it.

Changing subject, I brought up the changes that have taken place in Ladakh since the 1970s; namely industrialisation, the rise of the money economy and its effects on people and culture. I asked the monks for their views. Both were well aware of the negative changes and the loss of the old ways. Also, like Wangial, they acknowledged most Ladakhi's weren't fully aware of the consequences. Nor had they any regrets, as yet. Samten noted people were busier and more money-oriented today.

'In the past you didn't need much to survive. Money wasn't important and you could get food and shelter anywhere for free. People just gave you this. But now I have seen how modern life and modern culture creates insecurity — paranoia — and it is built on lying to people.'

'Lying? What do you mean by that?'

'Modern culture is a system built on getting money and giving money in order to get by. It forces you to lie to someone else. For example, this cup of chai costs twenty rupees. But in reality it only costs five rupees to produce. By selling for a higher price — higher than necessary — you are telling people a lie. In this way money and its value becomes more important than people. It takes over your thoughts. It complicates them. Then it influences your actions, and this is a bad thing. This is bad karma.'

Angdu agreed. 'Earning and striving for money and material things is like drinking salt water. You feel you must have more and more in order to satisfy your thirst. This is an empty way to live.'

Samten again: 'Yes. As I say, it changes you and makes you insecure. For example, if you have ten rupees in your bag, you don't care if you lose it. But if you've got a hundred thousand rupees, you are obsessed at not losing it. So you become insecure and paranoid. And again, this influences your intellect, your heart and your actions, but never in a good way.'

These were firm views on money and the effects it has on people, irrespective of who they are or what society they come from. I had to acknowledge there was truth in their words.

My pre-conceived notions of monks and nuns had been of pious, ascetic people living quiet, hermetic lives in isolated monasteries. I hadn't considered them mixing freely in society so much, let alone formulating such strong, salient opinions. Neither had I associated them with marriage. But again, the lads presented an unexpected view here. They told me there were no hard and fast rules in Buddhism. Occasionally monks and nuns get married and have children, if they feel strongly inclined. Their abbots don't prevent them. Also many monks spend a lot of time outside the monastery, working on community and educational programmes. They work on agricultural projects, for the benefit of society and the monastery. Indeed many travel widely, not just to other monasteries, but to other countries. This was news to me. I was surprised to discover Samten had travelled extensively in Europe, America and Canada. I asked him what he thought of life in the West and how it compared to Ladakh. Again his response was illuminating.

'Life is much easier in Europe in many ways — practical ways. Europe is heaven. You can have an accident and get looked after quickly. You have running water, clean streets and heat in your homes. You have a lot and you are not even aware of it. But in the West many people are self-orientated. They are individually focused, above all else. And because of this, everyone suffers.' He gave examples. 'Young people leave home at eighteen. They move away from their families. Old people, when they can no longer work are left in nursing homes. People get separated and lonely. Everybody thinks they alone are important and they each want to do their own thing, like going after big jobs, chasing status, getting more education and more money. They don't think how their desires and actions affect others, and so, many around them suffer.'

'They live like a horse with blinkers,' said Angdu.

Samten continued. 'When I was in Germany I was there for three months. I did not meet my neighbour once. In my village here you would know everyone in a short time and they would know you.'

I asked both men which place they preferred to live, Ladakh or the West. Their answer was an emphatic 'Ladakh.'

'We feel lucky living here,' said Samten, 'where everyone knows and cares for one another. Being in the West has taught me a lot about the good things of Ladakh; of the value of our close society, our Buddhism, culture and simplicity.

I also think Ladakh can offer a lot to the West as many Westerners are disillusioned and they come here seeking lessons and answers to their problems. Ladakh can teach the West.'

This last comment was a view shared by Helena Norberg-Hodge. So I openly asked, 'How can Ladakh help the West?'

Both monks thought for a moment before replying. Samten first: 'Live for the present. Don't be striving for things that may or may not come tomorrow. Now is important.'

'Yes,' said Angdu. 'You in the West have so much. You have enough. You are lucky. But you also want more and more. Just be thankful for what you have.'

Two hours passed. It had been an absorbing conversation. The lads had plenty to say, with much wisdom and common sense thrown in. Although most of it wasn't new to me, it was still good to be reminded of it. Their views on Western society were especially poignant. Not surprisingly, what struck me most about them was their strong Buddhist belief; a belief which lies at the heart of their societal values and general outlook on life. I had seen and experienced this a lot in Ladakh, by the considerate people I had come to know and like, and symbolically, by the many flags, chortens and mani walls I had seen everywhere. The more I thought about Buddhism, or more accurately, the principles of Buddhism, the less difference I could see between it and the teachings of Western-held Christianity. Yet somehow I think we in the West have strayed. Unlike Buddhists, we don't seem to live and practice our beliefs and traditions and have them reflected in our behaviour and in society to anywhere near the same extent. Perhaps these monks, Helena Norberg-Hodge and the other Ladakhis I met, have an important point: the West could learn a great deal from Ladakh.

❄ ❄ ❄ ❄

My last few days in Leh were spent doing odds and ends: making phone calls, emailing, buying *Free Tibet* T-shirts and sending them home, having chai and coffee with friends.

Stanzin coaxed me into a raft trip on the Zanskar for a day. This was an odd experience, with several Israelis, a tall Ladakhi and a Mick, all in an inflatable dinghy pirouetting down a cold, silty, river with steep mountain walls on either side. Shades of *Deliverance*. Strangely at one point, I thought about life back at the office; of meetings and suits, deadlines, troubled projects and flaky contracts. This lasted all of five minutes and then I quickly forgot about that life again.

Druk guesthouse was changing. In a week Bollywood would descend on Leh. According to Stanzin, half the film world would be staying in Druk. He would hand over the keys and go back to his village for a month. After that all would be quiet until spring.

With my mountaineering and exploration objectives achieved, my thoughts turned to the road. The plan was still to go home by any means other than plane, in the spirit of latter-day hippies and Silk Road traders. There would be no rush. For the most part I was happy the original idea of a bike trip home hadn't worked out. If it had, I would never have returned to the mountains, done new things in them and experienced a remarkable Himalayan culture. Ladakh had been an education. It had also been an adventure. I learned a lot about what it means to live and get by on simple needs; to thrive in small communities and to challenge Western thought. Ladakh had changed me and I would miss it. I would miss its people and the friends I had made here; people with much to give and who expected little in return. It was all good karma.

Stanzin arranged a ticket for me on a night jeep back to Manali. My last night was spent in Leh Chen bar with the gang. Summer was drawing to a close and I could sense people doing new things. Stanzin would be returning to his village. Chospa Konchok would be starting his own guesthouse in the New Year. Suzanne would be returning to Germany. Juliet and Wangial were planning to drive south to Goa for the winter. They saw me off, to much celebration and handshaking. My last abiding memory was of them all plus Namgyal in the back of Wangial's pick-up, heading down the Fort Road in the early hours. Stanzin in the back, with a bellyful of chang, hollering up at the stars:

'Independence! Union Territory!'

And all the dogs in Leh woke up and barked.

PART 3

The Open Road

One

McLeod Ganj

It was a long jarring night in the jeep, on a twisting road — cold and impossible to sleep. To his credit, driver was alert and skillful, facing down many trucks and negotiating flooded rivers and bends. It was a pity I had to listen to a ceaseless amount of tinny Hindi music which he played to keep himself awake. But at least it was better than television.

A cold wind blew down from the mountains. The Zanskars gave way to the Himalayan range and a rose-tinged dawn heralded a fresh day. There were numerous police and dhaba stops.

Into Lahaul early afternoon. Around the villages of Darcha and Keylong we passed many lovely, snow-capped, mountains. Some were six-thousanders. Normally such as view would whet my appetite to climb, but not today. I had played long enough in the mountains for now and the thought of organising another expedition, no matter how small, was too great. There was so much mental and physical effort involved. I knew I needed to be away from the mountains for a while in order for my hunger to grow. Essentially I needed to miss them again.

We rolled along the Chandra and chugged up hairpin bends to the Rohtang Pass. I spotted an ibex on the road bank. As soon as we approached, he scarpered. By now the landscape had changed. The barren earth had given way to green scrub — indications of a trail to the monsoon. The road was a mess, broken at the edges and potholed in the middle from flooding and landsides. Repair gangs were out in force. The Rohtang is a high gap between ranges. It is a cloud-breaker and rain-maker, hence the top of the Pass was misty and forlorn. People and horses shuffled around in the cold and mud. We slid down the far side on rutted tracks, nervously skating around hairpins and jousting with on-coming lorries under the clamour of horns. Appropriately, the road-signs warned of danger, although of a lascivious nature.

Horn is to honk. Please do it on my curves.

Those civil servants again.

New terrain now; the Kulu valley, with much pasture and greenery. Water streamed down rocky hillsides. Tall pine and sycamore trees were being fed by energetic nalas and huge granite boulders teetered on cliff tops. We passed nomadic gaddis by the roadside tending their flocks. Two stood out. Both were middle-aged, slim, bearded and shawled, holding long wooden staffs and standing bolt upright. They looked like prophets from the Old Testament and had they said as much, I would have believed them. This their promised land. Weary, we made our way down the valley and picked up the faint smell of weed as we neared a muggy, overcast Manali. It had been nineteen hours since Leh and everyone needed a rest.

I stayed two days doing odds and ends. To lighten my load I posted some mountain gear and several books I had collected, home. I picked up the finished suit from Paul the Tailor and tried it on before leaving his shop. As usual in the mountains I had lost weight so it came as no surprise to find the trousers too loose at the waist. Paul was surprised and concerned.

'I can take that in Gerry, if you wish?'

'No Paul, leave it be. It's grand. Expansion will be needed for the years ahead.'

Although my motorbike trip home was a non-starter, I felt I couldn't leave India without having spent some time on an Enfield Bullet. So I hired one for a day. I was looking forward to it and was in upbeat mood that morning. But that soon changed.

Like all abused rental machines, the bike was hard work. Being single cylinder, it cut out at low revs. There were no indicators. The clutch was stiff. Changing gear was rough and kick-starting it required the leg power of a horse. All of this was bearable to a degree, but the ride wasn't. It was a traumatic experience.

I took the road north, up the Kulu valley, which was a bad choice. Half the Indian army had the same idea. The Bullet and I got swallowed in a convoy of stinking military trucks. The noise was intimidating, the dust and fumes suffocating. Escaping those clutches I turned to head south. It was no better there. I found myself playing chicken with on-coming maniacs. Moreover I was bullied into the ditch by kamakazies attacking me from the rear. Horns blared everywhere. Jamming on for tardy rickshaws and pedestrians was one thing, being at the mercy of flying death-traps springing out of nowhere was another. My heart was in my mouth most of the time. At one stage on my way down a hill, I took a bend to find a bus stalled in the middle of the road. I narrowly missed it. Added to this was the state of the roads — rutted tracks full of potholes and floods.

By lunchtime I could take no more. Up until this point I had accepted motor-cycling as a dangerous and sometimes stressful activity in most countries. But now I realised here in India it is a lethal undertaking at all times. I was just glad I had decided not to travel home this way. In Ireland we often complain about high speed, poor driving standards and deficient roads. But none of this compares to what you get on the Indian sub-continent's roads, which is another world.

In between sorties I stopped for a chai at a roof-terrace café in Vashisht. I was taking in the view of the Beas when I overheard an Irish accent at a nearby table. A Dublin fella with a guitar and trilby hat was proselytising the achievements of our nation to an Israeli. How Ireland is a wonderful little country with a fine literary and musical heritage, and how unique it was to be the first country to rise against the British empire and bring about its downfall. Hearing this guff was nothing new to me and it made me cringe. Would this lad be rabbiting on like this at home? Hardly. It made me think there must be some flaw in the Irish psyche that compels some of us to boast about our country whenever we go away. Like spoiled children craving attention and praise. Doubtless other nationalities suffer to varying degrees of the same ailment. Don't get me wrong. I think it is good to have a quiet pride in where you come from. So long as that pride doesn't get overblown. Otherwise it becomes self-deluding and the culprit, be they an individual, nation or group, loses the will to question itself objectively and form a healthy criticism. Insularity creeps in and worryingly, the offending party loses the capacity to think.

This fella kept at it like a broken record and I found myself thinking, there are only two things worse than having to listen to a vain Mick abroad on his holidays: loud Brits and loud Americans. Oddly I was glad to get on the bike and face the mayhem again.

The Bullet was changed for a bus ticket to Dharamsala and McLeod Ganj. The latter being home to the Dalai Lama and the Tibetan government in exile. In an email Darach had advised me to take the night bus as there wasn't much to see during the day. Like me, he was going home overland by way of Pakistan, Iran and Turkey. He had finished his work in the Karakoram, was two weeks ahead of me and presently somewhere in Iran. We stayed in contact by the odd email, which for me, was useful. As we were both taking roughly the same route, he was able to offer tips on logistics, money changing and places to stay.

If the day bus was dull, the night bus was anything but. Me, some Indians, some French and a clatter of Israelis were crammed in. Bodies and bags littered the aisle. It was pitch black inside and out, making it feel we were travelling blind.

Also, poor suspension mixed with speed and a broken road dispelled any ambition for sleep. I now know what it feels like to be an astronaut blasting into space. You can't see where you're going. You have no control over anything. The G-forces rattle you violently. You're fearful of flying objects and you're never sure if you'll survive the ordeal. The only relief is the calm, weightless feeling you get once you've penetrated the earth's atmosphere. But no relief here. Other than pit-stops for thali and chai, as an exercise in psychological torture, I would rate this journey eight out of ten. All wasn't over when the sun came up and we rolled into McLeod Ganj. In our bleary eyed, dilapidated state we may as well have landed on another planet. The doors swung open and swarms of aliens accosted us with taxi rides and rooms to sell.

❇ ❇ ❇ ❇

As well as being home to the exiled Dalai Lama, McLeod Ganj has for decades been a refuge for thousands of Tibetans forced from their homeland by an oppressive Chinese regime. The town, set high among wooded hills, has a distinctly Buddhist air. Prayer flags abound. Shops sell Tibetan-inspired, Indian-made goods, and many monks and nuns can be seen ambling about.

The Tsuglagkhang complex near the town centre is an important multi-functional place. It is the town's main temple, the residence of the Dalai Lama and the administrative offices of the government in exile. It also houses a museum. On the day I visited, hundreds of monks and nuns had gathered in the temple to fast and pray for an end to Chinese tyranny. I was free to move among them. Hundreds sat on the floor, filling the nave and cloisters; a tide of shaved heads, sallow skin and maroon robes. Incense filled the air and an abbot led chants through a tannoy. Some read prayer scripts, others looked about, more retreated down paths of quiet contemplation.

Following on, I paid a visit to the museum, where a photographic exhibition on Tibet illustrated the suffering inflicted on its people since the 1950 Chinese invasion. Tibet was no idyllic place prior to then but a chronicle of images taken before that year show a peaceful civilisation and reasonably contented people. Pictures taken later show a haunted people. Mao-Tse-tung and his nascent People's Liberation Army went on the rampage. They destroyed monasteries and villages with the aim of eliminating all sense of Buddhist-Tibetan identity. Lamas, monks and nuns were rounded-up, tortured and killed, and citizens of all types were sent to gulags to be tortured, experimented on, worked to death, or simply disappear. The regime bribed, threatened and tortured thousands into becoming spies and informants, ensuring all defiance to their rule was brutally met.

I left the museum sickened and angry, knowing the injustice and oppression continues today.

In 1959 the young Dalai Lama, fearing for his life, went into exile, crossing the Himalayas by foot for asylum in India. Since his escape it is claimed 250,000 others have followed, most by the same desperate means. Many have settled in Nepal and India, among other parts of the world. I met two such refugees separately while wandering around town.

Tashi was 35. She left Tibet as a 17 year old, conscious of opportunities for a better life to be had in India. She crossed the mountains disguised among a party of monks and nuns. She never told her parents of her plan, and understandably they were angry later when they found out. Since then she had been alone in India and she told me she would like to return home some day, although she didn't have a passport. Nor was she likely to get one. Her family are farmers in the Chamba region of Tibet. They live in a village with no phone or electricity. Contact with them is rare, usually by an arranged phone call through relatives in Lhasa. Tashi's story reminded me of the plight of many East Germans, having escaped the Iron Curtain to new lives in the West. Many experienced loneliness after being cut off from family, friends, and loved ones left behind. They often suffered intimidation or job loss as a result of defection. By the same token, exiles couldn't return for fear of imprisonment, torture and other reprisals. But here in McLeod Ganj at least she had the support of a large expatriate community.

Sonam, a pleasant 27 year-old working in a co-op, had a similar story. He journeyed with others over the mountains to a transit camp in Nepal. He spoke of harsh conditions en route, of cases of severe frostbite, with many badly maimed or dead. I could only imagine the suffering. Yet Sonam was remarkably positive about it all.

'I was lucky, I made it OK. I have a job and can now help other Tibetan refugees.'

Here help is at hand. In this Tibetan enclave of India, the Buddhist ethos of unconditional support is palpable. There are educational programmes and business enterprises, such as carpet-making, which give arrivals and settlers some opportunity for establishing new lives. I was to witness one small but telling example of this spirit of co-operation, not in humans but unusually, transposed to the animal world. A well-worn circular path set among trees, hugs the outside perimeter of the Tsuglagkhang complex. To the faithful it is a prayer circuit. Each day hundreds walk clockwise around it, reciting mantras and stopping to spin the many prayer wheels. Not being one of them I still enjoyed the walk, the fresh air and the views. At one point I stopped to admire the work of a carver chiseling mani stones when I noticed a herd of cattle ambling by. They were Friesians; clean, well kept and without a herder. To Buddhists all animals are to be respected, as each one is a soul charting its own course to nirvana in the same way as humans. These cows gave the impression they seemed to know this. Given their pace and movement as a group, it looked as if they had organised their own religious procession. I noticed one straggler was lame in the hindquarters. It hobbled along at the back, obviously in discomfort and having to stop frequently. But what fascinated me was the cow behind it. It kept pressing its muzzle into the animal's side to support it whenever it stopped. Here was a nurse, a physical and moral crutch who had probably dedicated its life to this purpose. Never had I seen animals behave in such an altruistic way before, leading me to think how shameful it is that the Chinese government and its servants — all humans — are incapable of behaving in a remotely similar way to the people of Tibet.

Monday 1 September. McLeod Ganj may be a haven for many but as I was to observe, for some it is no land of plenty. Keen to exercise after the bus trip, I took a hike out of town and up the hills to a peak known as Triund. A winding stone track leads there from the village of Bhagsu, up through thick forests of pine and fern. The air was fresh and griffons hovered about. Few others were out. Halfway up I came to a small chai café. Its concrete terrace afforded a good view of the valley, prompting me to stop. The owner was a man named Govinda, a local Hindu who spoke good English. We got chatting and I asked him what he thought about the Tibetans. His opinion was less than favourable.

'There are too many of them here,' my friend. 'And too much building because of them. This has put a strain on our water supply and our forests. Too many trees have been cut down for building and for the Tibetans to make and sell furniture. The government supports them by giving them money and America and other governments give them more money. This is bad for McLeod Ganj. They own all the restaurants and guest houses. Local Hindi people suffer. We have been pushed out of McLeod Ganj to make way for them and we have had to come up here. We don't get much business up here and we don't get any government help.'

He went on, broadening the grievance to other ailments such as police and government corruption, third world hunger, international relations and the nuclear arms race. It was all dismal stuff. I was beginning to regret I'd asked him anything.

'There are too many problems here, my friend,' he reiterated. 'Hopefully in the next life things will be better.'

He got up to leave, picking up a crowbar, lump hammer and chisel.

'Hold on. Do you think all Hindus believe in re-incarnation?' I asked.

He shrugged. 'Many do. Some don't.'

I pointed to his tools. 'What are you doing with those?'

'I'm going to repair the track.'

'Do you get paid for that?'

He chortled. 'No, I don't get paid.'

'Then why do you do it?'

'For good karma. Maybe it will help me in the next life, my friend.'

TWO

An Afternoon with Lhasang

Tuesday 2 September. I've always had a healthy disrespect for power. Or more specifically, for those who crave and wield it, irrespective of political ideology. This is because many that get it, frequently abuse it for their own self-interests, and usually with destructive consequences. The usual culprits are despots, megalomaniacs, business tycoons and military generals. Ministers and rank and file parliamentary members, be they democratically elected or not, tend to be blind and compliant. As are high-ranking civil servants, lobby groups, media moguls, spin-doctors and powerful business interests. As a result I find it next to impossible to believe anything I read or hear from them. I don't know why but I've always had a soft spot for the powerless and disadvantaged, the underdog in any walk of life; be it low wage non-union workers, disadvantaged school children, three legged greyhounds or hopeless football teams. This must be down to a sense of social conscience, an uneasy awareness of inequality in the world and of wrongs that should be put right. It's hardly a surprise but I've always noticed that the wealthy, the brightest, the well-connected and the powerful always do well in life. Such people are more than capable of looking after themselves and their kind. But what was niggling me now was the plight of the Tibetans, especially after having been in Ladakh and of having witnessed the Olympic protest and knowing their struggle. On the bus here I had been thinking about this and about their spiritual and political leader, the Dalai Lama. I couldn't understand how with all the suffering inflicted upon his people, he could adopt a pacifist stance against the Chinese and maintain it for decades. History and human nature has shown that aggression is rarely overcome by passive resistance. The unfortunate reality is aggression is usually only beaten or diminished when opposed by an equivalent or greater force, usually another violent one. Otherwise it continues, so long as the perpetrator knows he can get away with it. Buddhism teaches non-violence and I can accept the Dalai Lama is a deeply

174

spiritual leader who laudably follows this principal of faith. But you have to ask how practical and ethical is this when pacifist resistance hasn't worked with the Chinese now or in the past? Factually, the latter continues to occupy and terrorise, while Tibetans continue to suffer.

As I travelled I thought, if I ever meet the Dalai Lama, I would challenge him on this. But I knew the chances of meeting him were nil. Instead I resolved to seek out a man who knew him well and who, according to the India Times, was McLeod Ganj's resident expert on all things Tibetan. If I could talk with this man I would get his perspective and see if he agreed or disagreed with me.

I found him. Not far from the Tsuglagkhang complex Lhasang Tsering runs a bookshop called Exiles. He is a middle-aged, thin, energetic man with a slim, grey goatee. Lhasang was seven years old when, in 1959, he fled Tibet with his family for asylum in India. They were taken to Manali, where his parents were given work labouring in road repair gangs. The young Lhasang was educated by an American charity in Dharamsala, where he excelled in his studies and was given a scholarship to study medicine at John Hopkins University in the States. But he turned it down, choosing instead to become a freedom fighter in the Mustang province of Nepal in the early 1970s. In '74 Nepal came under pressure from the Chinese to expose guerrillas. The Dalai Lama ordered all freedom fighters there to surrender. Reluctantly they did and most spent time in prison. Bitterly disappointed, Lhasang returned to India, where he became a teacher, then a school principal and then an information officer for the government in exile. In 1988 the Dalai Lama declared his 'Middle Way' policy for Tibet. The idea being to negotiate an arrangement with the Chinese where, given they share the same landmass, the Chinese would control Tibet's foreign policy and security matters, leaving the Tibetans to govern their own internal affairs as an autonomous state. Lhasang was the first to publicly denounce this policy, calling it unworkable. His belief was, why would China negotiate? They had full power and control over everything already. Why would they want to concede anything? There was nothing in it for them. It was a fair point, but as a result he paid a high price for his criticism. He lost his job and all governmental and educational assistance for his family. When I asked him if he still felt the same way about it today, he said yes.

'It has been twenty years now and we are still waiting to get to that negotiating table. Still waiting on a breakthrough,' he said dourly. 'I hope I am wrong but that will not happen.'

'So do I take it you are still against the Dalai Lama and the government's policy?'

'Yes, I am. You consider this — Tibetans in Tibet are protesting and dying for full freedom. Tibetans in exile are proposing autonomy. We as a people are not of the same view in both our aims and how we achieve them. This is our fault. A nation that is not free does not exist.'

He had his own strategy as an alternative to the Middle Way. He called it the 'Three Musts.' The first involved clarity of purpose. 'We have lost this,' he said. The second 'Must' was the need for a belief that freedom could be achieved. And the third was a strong action plan to follow it up.

'But all this takes strong leadership,' I said. 'The skill to inspire and motivate people.'

He nodded. 'Yes, you are right.'

'So are you saying the Dalai Lama and the government in exile are giving ineffective leadership?'

'Yes.'

It was interesting to hear this given that most of the world's leaders and much of the world's press, plus countless millions have such a high regard for the Dalai Lama, although in my view, a blind one.

'I hear your Musts,' I said. 'But do you not also think you need strong international support to oppose China's policy?'

'Yes, of course we do. That is also important. But we are running out of time.'

He went on to explain how the Chinese were purposely serving their interests by placing hundreds of thousands of Chinese into Tibet, giving them jobs and business support, all in an effort to swamp the indigenous population. Thus the more Chinese in Tibet the more powerless the natives would feel and the harder it would be for them to attain freedom.

'They don't care about the interests of Tibet,' he remarked, sourly. He then compared the situation to that of the native American Indian — slaughtered en masse and banished to tiny enclaves of their own land by an avaricious white man.

'What chance has the American Indian of regaining their homeland now, with full power over all of it?'

'None,' I said.

He nodded. 'Well that is what will happen in Tibet soon. The Chinese know this and are playing at this.'

One thing puzzled me though. 'If that is the case, what about the Tibetans still fleeing? Why then do the Chinese stop them? Isn't it in their interest to let them go? To open the floodgates?'

'Ah yes, but they are very clever, you see. They won't open the floodgates to allow them leave. That would bring too much international attention, which would be a bad strategy. Instead they will keep on letting Tibetans trickle out in manageable numbers. That does not cause a stir.'

The conversation returned to leadership, the Dalai Lama and the Middle Way. On the Middle Way we were both in agreement. It wasn't working. On this and the Dalai Lama's leadership, my own view hadn't changed: Tibetans need to have a firm style of leadership, one that does not exclusively adopt a passive stance. Bullies and oppressors don't change unless they are stood up to. Sometimes this necessitates the use of force, which is always undesirable and should always be the last step. However it is not the only step. Building alliances, getting the support and commitment of other states, trade sanctions and embargos, enforcing international regulations all have their place — provided powerful nations can be convinced. And of course, talking to your enemy, finding common ground and working out a settlement is best. Buddhism, with its key message of universal compassion is fine in a peaceful state. But in a state of fear and terror such as Tibet, governed by a barbarous Chinese regime, it is tragically naïve.

'Don't get me wrong, I have the highest respect for his holiness the Dalai Lama,' said Lhasang. 'But what annoys and frustrates me is he is not prepared to admit his policy is wrong. It has failed and he is unwilling to change his view. Time is running out. Soon the chances of Tibet recovering its freedom will be less and less.'

Time was also ticking by in the bookshop. Hours passed. Heavy monsoon rains came and went. A couple of passers-by joined our discussion and Lhasang sold the odd book. I sat on a stool by the window and probed to find a better, more optimistic angle on the struggle. I raised the internal question.

'What if China changes from within, Lhasang? What are the chances of that happening and what opportunities might that offer the cause?'

He remained doubtful. 'It's a long shot. Something I wouldn't bet on. No Chinese government, or any aspiring one even if you had a regime change, would want to concede on Tibet. Internally that would be damaging. That would only show weakness and give their political adversaries ammunition to attack them. So that is unlikely. However if you get a change in the quality of life among the Chinese themselves, in other words the many poor seeing many others getting richer, then you have a case for civil unrest. This would destabilise the government. Also, don't forget, China is made up of 60 percent occupied territory. If you can unite the people of these occupied lands in one freedom movement, the Uighurs, the Mongolians, the Manchurians, along with the Tibetans, you can increase international support and put more pressure on Beijing to consider the possibility of their independence. After all, no colonial power lasts forever.

Just look at the former British empire; where is it now?'

True, both these points were legitimate but I didn't think they were wholly viable. In the first case I felt if a distinct wealth gap became apparent in any region, one that threatened unrest, the government could inject money and jobs into that area and appease any dissent. Moreover, seeing the Chinese economy getting stronger, the ability to do this grows by the day. On the combined freedom movement, I argued that such an alliance was unlikely to be effective. Coalitions rarely are. Each group pushes its own interests. Faction fights and partisan politics take over. Besides, the Chinese would exploit this and set each group against the other, manipulating them and emasculating any collective will.

Again, neither of us could find much ground for optimism. Continuing, Lhasang raised another point:

'I have a plan. It is also part of the three "Musts". It is implementing the action strategy.'

'And what is that?'

'It is called the Strategy of the Mosquito.'

I raised my brow. This sounded intriguing. 'Please explain,' I said.

'What happens if you lock a big, strong, muscled man into a room full of mosquitos?'

'He is overwhelmed and his strength is no good to him,' I said.

'That's right.'

'So?'

'So if we get one person in every Tibetan family to upset the Chinese economy in some way that they would cause havoc, then the Chinese people and government would be affected and would have to take action. Remember, the Chinese economy is growing enormously and the government wants to protect it. But if you stop trains by putting obstacles on the tracks ... or cut power lines ... or cause important factories to shut down, and you do these things on a wide scale, then that will hurt the Chinese into action.'

'Economic sabotage, you mean?'

'Correct.'

I was in two minds on this. A guerrilla campaign would be effective in creating instability. However it was high risk. It could easily get out of control and cause much bloodshed. Innocent civilians would suffer. Equally, the backlash against ethnic Tibetans would be great. The Chinese authorities would vilify such actions and paint all Tibetans as terrorists. They would then spin this view to the world. Given this, such a strategy may be counter-productive to the Tibetan cause. What's more, the Chinese might redouble their efforts to destroy all traces of Tibet as a distinct place, culture and people. Such a strategy would require formidable leadership, exceptional organisation and communication, plus the commitment of a great many people. Were these fundamentals in place, or could they be? I was sceptical.

We moved on, debating the international dimension. We both felt Tibet was low on the list of other nations' priorities, especially wealthy, developed ones. Tibet offered little in the way of business or resources and the human rights situation, though unsavoury, was something that could be conveniently ignored. Countries, or more specifically, corporations, were more concerned with protecting their stakes in China, whether as a low-cost manufacturing base, or as a huge, lucrative new market to exploit. On the subject of low-cost manufacturing, Lhasang had one simple thing to say:

'You know why the Chinese economy is so strong?'

'Largely because labour is cheap,' I said.

'Yes, and you know what? Most of it is slave labour.'

It was hard to dispute this. He had other interesting points to make on China's relations with its near neighbours, Russia, India and Japan. He cited Russia's growth, its need for energy and its unease over an increasing Chinese influence in its oil and gas-rich former Soviet states. Russia would not want to see China 'meddling further.' He mentioned Japan as having old scores to settle with China and he spoke about strained relations between India and China since the 1962 Sino-Indian war which saw the loss of Indian territory. Today both countries share a huge border and both are nuclear states. He was of the belief India wouldn't want to antagonise China, but equally India wouldn't countenance further threats on its territory. Lhasang's view was that all these tensions offered small opportunities for Tibetans to take advantage. I failed to see how, nevertheless he made salient points about geography. Tibet is the source of some of Asia's largest and most vital rivers, which flow through China and India. Global warming and glacial melt will threaten these rivers. China has made noises about constructing large damns on them to meet growing energy needs. The impact of both would severely affect India, denying it adequate water to irrigate the plains, and the loss of power to drive its hydro-electro power stations. 'Again, India would not allow this,' he said. 'Also, China has long being dumping nuclear waste in Tibet. We all know this. But Tibet is a land of seismic weakness. If they continue to do this, they threaten the well-being of not only Asia but the entire world. So it is in foreigners interests to prevent this getting worse.'

Global warming, damns, water control, power supply, nuclear safety — yes these were all important matters for regional security and the interests of Tibet, but hardly catalysts for achieving independence? I put this to him.

'Ah yes, but they all add up. When you put them in a global context, they affect everyone else. So the focus of other, powerful nations then becomes Tibet, and that can influence change.'

As he developed another point, his eyes brightened, his voice grew in excitement and his hands became more expressive; 'Just look at the size of Tibet. It is a huge landmass of 1.2 million square kilometres. Can you imagine a place that size? Just think, a free Tibet would be a buffer between India and China and other states. It would help defuse all political and military tensions. You would have less of an arms race, more peace and more money in China and India which could go into trade and would, of course, help the welfare of their people and the people of Tibet. So you see, it is really in everyone's interest, here in Asia, Europe, Russia, Japan and America to have a free Tibet.'

I nodded. 'And that would be your message to everyone outside of Tibet?'

His answer was an emphatic yes. 'But first we Tibetans must get our act together with a change of policy.'

'Or a change in leadership,' I reiterated.

He shrugged. It came back to this. He didn't see much chance of this happening soon.

'This is one of our great weaknesses,' he said. 'When the Dalai Lama passes away in ten or fifteen years time, another re-incarnation will be appointed. A child. And it will take twenty-five years of training and education before that person is of any political use. That is too long a time for our struggle. We do not have that time.'

'But what about a leadership change sooner than that? Perhaps a newer, more secular one, with a different structure?'

He thought this likely to happen, but not yet. 'In future generations maybe. Thirty, forty or fifty years, but definitely not soon.' Then gloomily he added, 'As I say, Tibet cannot wait that long. We simply have no time.'

It was a long, insightful discussion. I didn't have the answers to the problems of Tibet and I still don't. But it did get me thinking. Lhasang's ideas of industrial unrest and an alliance of ethnic groups had merit and were worth exploring further. The Middle Way and the effectiveness, or ineffectiveness of leadership was another matter. I also think there is a responsibility on all of us non-Tibetans to force a change. There are ways to do this. We can influence our governments, our business and trade organisations, the media, to demand the Chinese get out of Tibet. Quite plainly, they should not be there. And if they won't, then have them radically change their ways. This may appear daunting at first, but it is not as hard as it seems. Those of us who live in democracies have the power to vote. Why not make the Tibetan cause, or more specifically, the Chinese question, a national political issue? Demand to know what politicians think of the Chinese treatment of Tibetans over the past fifty years. Are they happy to let China continue with its Tibetan policy, or do they want to see change? If they say they don't care, or fudge the issue, then vote them out. If they say they care then ask them what they are going to do about it, what specific actions? Then hold them to it. These are not irrelevant questions. Far from it. China's domestic affairs are intrinsically linked with ourselves. China is a rapidly growing country, with increasing political and economic clout on the world stage. Many of the things we buy are made there. Many of our businesses, hence jobs, are dependent on it, and this will only grow in time. Its record on human rights, freedom of speech, internal governance, property rights and regulation is abysmal. Hence increasingly we need to be more aware of who we're dealing with. Making China and Tibet an important debate will raise national and international awareness. Those in power must be forced to listen. We must ask ourselves, are we comfortable putting up with immoral, destructive Chinese behaviour? If opinions are strong enough, citizens, journalists and activists can force these same politicians to enact laws, strategies and policies that compel corporations and the Chinese government to take notice and change. And that's just one tactic. What if we as individuals refuse to buy goods made in China, or at least reduce the amount we do? Assailing the Chinese export market. Wouldn't it be interesting if we did this as part of an international, high profile movement, with a message for China: to trade you've got to be ethical. Hands off Tibet and treat your own citizens better. And if we are to trade, are we prepared to continue where the Chinese government spies on foreign companies and uses strong-arm tactics to manipulate their operations in China? There are other things we can do. Investments, for example. What if we refused our banks, fund managers, speculators and traders to invest our money in the Chinese market, or in any company that condones current Chinese policy on human rights and the occupation of Tibet? And then there's the Chinese people themselves. In our relations with them, through business, sport, tourism or whatever, we can raise the Tibetan question with them. We can give them cause to question their government's policy and the propagandist education that was fed to them. They are best placed to incite change, perhaps not now, given their indominatable, unelected regime. But perhaps in the future, as their country grows, becomes a bigger player in world affairs and grapples internally with socio-economic, ethnic, religious and political demands.

In the days, weeks and months that followed, after some reading and further thought, my opinion of the Dalai Lama softened. In 1950 even if he had wanted to fight the Chinese, he couldn't. Tibet didn't have the means to. And even if he chose vociferous resistance it would have been pointless — the UN and major powers didn't want to know then — as they still don't want to know now. His choice of non-violent opposition and conciliation since then has, for the most part, been the only avenue open to him. And he has pursued this approach with good reason. Because of non-violence, the world has a lot good-will for the Tibetans and their struggle. So what more could anyone expect of him or any other leader? Although I became more understanding of the Dalai Lama, other views I had, hardened. How we, all of us non-Tibetans, act on Tibet tells us an awful lot about ourselves. Do we use our political powers and freedoms to champion the rights of others? Or do we choose to ignore the on-going tragedy of Tibet because we really don't care? Furthermore, are we happy to accept that those we elect as our leaders care even less?

The rain stopped. I felt I had spent long enough in Lhasang's bookshop, taking up enough of his attention and time. As well as being an activist and businessman, Lhasang is a poet. He read me some of his work before I left. It was graceful verse about Tibet, dreams for its future, and thoughts on his adopted land, India. It was good to see him smile once, expressing warm sentiments on the hospitality of the latter. He had a final word before I left.

'Gerry, you know that railway line they just built from Beijing to Lhasa?'

'Yes.'

'Do you know what I call it?'

I shook my head.

'I call it the last nail in the coffin.'

'Well let's hope you're wrong, Lhasang,' I said.

THREE

Down in Lahore

Wednesday 3 September. I hopped on a morning bus to Pathankot, hoping to make Amritsar by evening. After the last leg, night travel had lost its attraction.

We rolled down to Dharamsala, through wooded hills of pine, birdsong and mist and out onto flat roads of poor condition. I had three bags with me. Two were outside up on the roof. One was a sack with all my outdoor gear. There is one useful thing being a travelling mountaineer: you always have equipment to attach your bags securely to any vehicle roof. Without such resources, I reckon travelling by bus on the sub-continent would be an unbearable worry.

It was hot. The road was dusty. Blaring horns and a noisy engine kept us all awake. My journey was entering a new, physical, state. Going through towns and villages the air was thick with exhaust fumes. There was little wind. Litter was commonplace and once more, people seemed to be everywhere. You can keep these plains, I thought. Ironically they made me feel claustrophobic. Leave me the open hills any day.

A quick change at Pathankot got me another bus for Amritsar, following long straight stretches through the Punjab. Gum trees lined the route, with iron-flat fields of rice stretching as far as the eye could see. More serendipitous observations were made. We passed a teenage boy working a field with a large buffalo. It was a classic Indian scene. Both of them wading in waterlogged earth, out on their own under a milky grey sky. A vapid orange sun hung in the west. I immediately thought of John Constable paintings. His scenes of romantic farm life of peasants and animals, haywains and canal locks, and bygone days where noise was less, technology was simple and time was plentiful. But imagination can be a curse. I was slipping towards a realm of old-world utopia only for this lad to crush my rose-tinged speculations. He took a mobile phone out of his back-pocket and began texting his mates. Yeah, India never fails to surprise.

A surprise of ugliness lies in some of the region's architecture. Every so often we would pass the homes of prosperous farmers. These dwellings are often large, much larger than they needed to be, standing like tacky concrete boxes plonked from the sky. Triumphs of vulgarity over taste. Some had tawdry statues of eagles perched on the roofs. I admit, not every house was like this, but those that were reminded me of the grotesque haciendas that have sprung up in the Irish countryside in recent decades. Was there any connection, I wondered?

But mobile phone and architectural matters aside, I encountered another strange technology common to the Punjab. The Jugaad. These are home-made transport vehicles which are neither cars, lorries, tractors or motorbikes, but a conglomeration of them all. Literally meaning 'innovative fix,' they are three-wheeled contraptions built from any available parts and put together in roadside workshops and backyards. Some are powered by diesel engines which had previous incarnations as agricultural pumps. They have gearboxes and steering wheels but no suspension and, as I discovered later, many have no brakes. Gears are used to slow down and a well-timed block of wood thrown in front of the rear wheels by a volunteer hopping off the side, usually helps them to stop. Although not pretty, they are cheap and reliable to run. What's more, they have many uses; as group taxis, hearses, livestock and crop transporters, even serving as grain and sugar cane processors. I passed many of them on the road. Most were stuffed with people, with more hanging off the side. You can hear and smell them before seeing them puttering along. They may be weird but you have to give full credit to the ingenuity and resourcefulness of their creators.

Now where have I seen things like these before? I wondered. Moments later, I recalled. 'Ah yes, that film. *Mad Max*.'

On the subject of resourcefulness, one thing I noticed about India is that nothing of any value is wasted. If something is broken, be it a motorbike, ox-cart, sewing machine or anything else, it gets fixed. If it can't be fixed it gets taken apart and the pieces recycled to create or fix something else. I saw this everywhere. It's a far cry from today's profligate Western society and very refreshing to see.

The plains gave way to the hectic streets of Amritsar, the capital and spiritual core of Punjab. Here I wanted to see the Harmandir Sahib, otherwise known as the Golden Temple which, to Sikhs, is their holiest temple and home of their most sacred book, the Adi Granth. As expected, as soon as I alighted, a mob of rickshaw riders accosted me. I was heading for the old city and in no mood for heavy sales pressure. Such harassment is common at bus stations in India and as a foreigner you're an attractive target. But when you're tired, such unwanted attention can be frustrating. I don't deny any man a right to make a living, but these hustlers brought out the sharp old git in me. This isn't pleasant but sometimes travel fatigue does that to you. It took a forceful effort to abscond into the first passing auto-rickshaw.

❄ ❄ ❄ ❄

Thursday 4 September. Amritsar's old centre is a busy place of hot narrow streets filled with people and traffic, broken pavements, deafening horns and suffocating exhaust fumes. Like most Indian cities it is a curious mixture of order and chaos. A Bruegel townscape. It is a pluralist place, home to many people of different religions. The most noticeable of these are the Sikhs, and Sikh men in particular with their turbans and beards. Unlike Hindus, they come in all shapes and sizes. Many are tall and heavyset, others thin, and a good many rotund, possibly because of a faith that advocates living and eating well.

I visited the Ram Bag gardens and museum dedicated to the one-eyed Sikh leader, Maharaja Ranjit Singh. Singh lived between the 18th and 19th centuries and early in his tenure was successful at uniting the disparate Sikh clans of Northern India. He consolidated one Sikh state — a Punjab corridor stretching from Amritsar to Lahore, in present-day Pakistan. Following this, he spent years fighting off invading Afghan tribes, driving them back northwest and seizing large tracts of Afghan and Pashtun land in the process. During his reign a Sikh empire rapidly expanded, with further campaigns and the conquering of huge territories, south to Multan and to the northeast as far as Ladakh. Ambitious and visionary, he enlisted French officers to organise and train his men. He upgraded his army's weapons from swords to guns and famously captured the iconic brass canon Zam-Zammah from Bhagi tribes; a gun later immortalised in Kipling's novel *Kim*. His enemies, the British among them, respected and feared him. Yet historical records show he was no bloodthirsty tyrant. On the contrary, being of profound faith, he was lenient with enemies and insubordinators alike and, in keeping with Sikh values, was tolerant of all religions, peoples and castes.

The museum was nothing much. Mainly a collection of colourful paintings of Singh and his men on various campaigns. Lines of well-equipped, confident men in the throes of battle, with Zam-Zammah blasting great holes through enemy fortresses. Everything I saw and everything I read tried to impress upon me the glory and righteousness of the Sikh empire at its zenith. Certainly Singh as a leader was impressive. But my thoughts were very different. The whole ethos was wrong, and what Singh did was equally wrong. It is one thing to protect your homeland and fight off invaders, quite another to retaliate, destroy and usurp their territory. This is flagrant imperialism. Suffice to say, I found it impossible to reconcile this with the principles of Sikhism.

Unsurprisingly Ranjit's empire crumbled after his death. Poor governance, infighting and the avaricious moves of another imperialist, the British, saw to this. The usual stuff. But Ranjit left another legacy before parting, namely the gold plating of the Golden Temple.

If the streets of the old city are hot and stifling, an antidote can be found inside the cool confines of this place. It is tranquil and reverential. Thousands flock each day to worship at Sikhism's holy book, the Adi Granth, housed inside the gold-plated temple in the heart of the complex, at the centre of a lake. This man-made square lake is the namesake of the city; the Amrit Sarovar, meaning 'holy nectar'. As expected the temple's dome and walls shone brilliantly, and the Sikh emblem, an orange triangular flag with a *khanda* — double-edged sword — and crossed scimitars around a circle, flew overhead. The surrounding complex is magnificently constructed in smooth, shining white marble. I walked around, barefoot like everyone else and, in keeping with protocol, with an orange bandana on my head.

The complex is well run. The floors are constantly washed. Stewards wearing ceremonial daggers and spears keep watch, and energetic volunteers give out free chai and sweet rice in the cloisters. At the temple's altar, the holy book sits under an immaculate pink shroud. The faithful file by, offering money and prayers, and attendant priests chant mellifluous hymns to the accompaniment of harmonium and drums. The sound is broadcast all day, every day around the temple. It all makes for a calm, spiritual atmosphere — a far cry from the clamour outside. At the lake, fat, privileged goldfish mouth knowingly at the water's edge.

White is the dominant colour of both the structure and the people's loose cotton clothing. On the ghats below the watch-towers, beefy men strip down to their underwear, enter the water and solemnly pray. Happily I let time and thoughts drift. Some places have that effect … peaceful places such as this. I wandered into one of the cloisters for shade, sat next to others and casually struck up a conversation with a middle-aged gent. It was easy to talk. Being an outsider in most places, people were as curious about me as I was of them.

'How come most Sikh men wear white?' I asked. 'Is it to signify spiritual purity?'

'Yes,' he replied sagely. 'You may be white on the outside, but that is no good if your heart is black.'

Wise words, I thought. And then I was off, lost in another conversation about everything.

Sikhism — developed from aspects of Hinduism and Islam in the 16th century — is a great, equitable religion. All men, women and children are treated the same, where caste, tribe and social standing hold little weight. Sikhs believe in one universal god and, like Buddhists, deplore the malign influences of ego, anger, attachment, lust and greed. Sharing is their hallmark; a concern for the less well-off. In every Sikh temple a visitor, whether hungry or not, can get a free meal. Incredibly the Golden Temple feeds upwards of 35,000 people a day. It is a twenty-four hour operation, manned by volunteers and funded by donations. I had to take a look.

In the gardens next to the lake stands a two-storey dining hall. On the ground level an army of kitchen staff prepare food. Another army washes up. All this takes place in mechanised order under the perpetual din of crashing steel trays and cutlery. To eat, you're given a tray and a spoon and herded upstairs to one of the empty dining halls. There, diners are lined up in long, military-like drills. There are no chairs, everyone sits on the floor. Once the hall fills up, and it does so quickly, a team of volunteers with buckets and ladles in hand, go up and down the aisles doling out food. Today it was black dal, chapattis and rice. Impressively, there's a different menu each day and never any shortage of food. Second helpings are practically forced on you. Some people make the most of this. As I ate, the woman next to me had her portion quickly and I noticed her repeatedly asking for more. Initially I thought this was strange as she seemed to be eating a lot for such a small, thin woman. Then I spotted the dal being spooned into a plastic container and a stack of chapattis surreptitiously hidden in her veil. She spoke to the volunteers and I got the impression they were familiar with her. A regular, no doubt. Had she a large family to feed? God only knew. But I had to hand it to her, she knew how to play the system.

Now I'm a fast eater but I was one of the last to leave. We were ushered downstairs — more crashing and banging with the empties — and then we were back out in the garden. Dinner was over and that was it. The whole exercise didn't take more than twenty minutes. But as I considered this, I realised another four hundred mouths were probably being fed.

For all its good points of altruism and rectitude, there is still one aspect of Sikhism that doesn't sit well with me. Strength, both moral and physical, is considered a virtue. This extends to military strength. Throughout the temple walls are many tablets commemorating Sikhs who fought and died under British, Indian and international command in various battles from the Second World War to the present day, including regional conflicts with China and Pakistan.

There are also dedications giving thanks for having survived campaigns. This is all very well. But it is one thing condoning valour and dedication to service in wars having a moral justification, quite another in conflicts of dubious right. Most importantly, is the ability to distinguish between the two and accept or reject either, whatever the case. As far as I can see, Sikhism does not do this, or if it does, it isn't practiced enough. Followers are encouraged to be strong and be willing and to bear arms and fight. The cause and right is of secondary importance. Blind obedience is the apparent norm. Ranjit Singh is a good example. Here was a celebrated leader, revered today, who unjustifiably expanded an empire to obvious human cost of his enemies and his own men. Where is the virtue in that? Sikhism it seems, in common with other religions, has something to answer for.

Friday 5 September. A short trip in an auto-rickshaw brought me to Wagah. Here a few hundred metres of no-man's land makes up the border crossing between India and Pakistan. This place is famous for the pompous flag-lowering ceremonies held each evening by regimental guards on both sides; but I wasn't prepared to hang around all day to see theatre. However drama of one kind or another is never far away. First were the porters. As I entered the zone I was accosted by a line of them, ardently willing to carry my load. By now I was tired of all the badgering everywhere I went. There's only so much of me India can take. In response they got a series of growls. Then the officials. Irritated, I entered Indian immigration control and arrived at a counter, behind which three dour clerks sat doing nothing. They passed me from one to the other. I was given a form. I had no pen to hand, the closest one was buried in one of the bags and I was damned if I was going to trawl through everything to find it.

'Could I borrow a pen, please?' I asked, directing my question towards the clerk on the left.

'I don't have one.'

Gobshite, I thought. However the fella next to him cut in.

'Here, give me the form. I will complete it for you.'

How helpful, I initially thought, and handed it to him. He filled it out, got me to sign it, checked my passport, stamped both and handed back my passport.

'Am I free to go?' I asked.

'Yes. You are.'

As I picked up my stuff and made to go, he looked at me and brazenly said: 'And now a gift please.'

'Huh?'

He opened his palm. 'A gift. I have completed your form for you. May I have a gift? From your country to me?'

He repeated this. Baksheesk. Now the porters had annoyed me enough. I was hot, sweating and my shoulder hurt from an old injury and the weight of the bags. What's more, I detest all forms of corruption, particularly that initiated by servants of the state. Any state. And particularly by the Indian state, which as we all know is one of the most corrupt in the world. I was in no mood for any of this. But what really got me was the impertinence. The brass neck of this git. I glowered at him.

'Right, you'll get a gift, mate. When I'm home I'll send you a postcard.'

Entering Pakistan was easy. No porters, no hassle, no bribes. In the shade of a drinks stall I waited for a bus to Lahore. There wasn't much traffic crossing the border; a couple of Dutch campervans and a bloke on a British-registered Triumph, all entering India. For a while I thought I was the only traveller on foot. It had felt odd walking down that stretch of no-man's land between gates and guards, like a spy coming out of the cold. Yet I wasn't completely alone. Fifteen minutes later, another character emerged from customs control.

Pascal was a young Swiss fella who was also heading to Lahore. We got talking. He had travelled overland from Turkey to India, eighteen months earlier. While journeying around India he met a Japanese girl and decided to settle for a while in Kerala and study IT. Now he was entering Pakistan to renew his Indian visa. I asked him what he thought of Lahore, and Pakistan in general, having been here.

'Very friendly people,' he said.

On the bus I was torn between listening to Pascal's stories and absorbing everything around me. The land remained flat, with plenty of rice-fields like India. Incongruous smokestacks arrayed the landscape, evidence of an active brick-making industry. Hundreds of buffalo cooled themselves in man-made lakes. And on the road, motorbikes sawn in half and connected to a cab, replaced the Indian-style auto-rickshaw. Few women were to be seen and most of the men, of which there were many, wore the baggy shalwar kameez. On first view, Pakistan seemed a lot like India, but I was keenly aware of the one main difference: this is a land of Islam. This a country where religion and state are umbilically linked — the laws of the latter under-scored by the strictures of the former. You could see this inside the bus. It was divided in two by a steel mesh, segregating men and women. Women at the front, men at the back. Tellingly, the back was packed for much of the journey while the front was mainly empty.

Two unkempt fellas got on at one stage and sat behind us. Both were giddy and looked at us with glazed, bloodshot eyes. We were an attraction for them and every couple of minutes they insisted on shaking our hands. They rambled away in their native Urdu, me having no clue what they were on about and Pascal straining to listen. Bit by bit he picked up the odd word and pieced together what they were saying.

'They are asking us would we like to go to their village in the north and smoke hashish. You see what I mean about friendly people?'

'I do.'

The skies blackened as we entered Lahore. A dust storm blew, followed by a downpour. Pascal led us to the Regale Internet Inn in the middle of town. I remembered the name from one of Darach's emails, being a place he had stayed in. Pascal is a student, Darach is an itinerant and both are used to living on a shoe-string, I thought, so this place won't be the Waldorf.

It wasn't.

Our arrival in Pakistan coincided with the start of Ramadan. This meant most places to eat were closed during daylight hours. We were hungry, but Pascal knew of a place close to the Inn where we would find food. Non-existent in India, I was surprised to find such a place here … a supermarket. In we went. It was something of a culture shock seeing lines of familiar packaged food, stacked on shelves among parallel aisles and with the same artificial light, trolleys, baskets and checkout tills. All of it anachronistic. Only for the locals I could have sworn I was in a Tesco at home. We shopped without haggling, paid for our goods, turned away from the fluorescent lights and air-conditioning, and re-entered the sub-continent.

That evening I went for a wander alone. I found myself in the eponymously named Food Street — an avenue of restaurants and eating stalls. Throngs busied themselves ordering takeaways of chapatti for sundown. Restaurant tables were full. Pakistani cuisine is a mix of the many influences from its neighbours and history; from the hot spicy fare of India, to the cooler yoghurt-based dishes derived from the Mughals of Central Asia. Meat — chicken, mutton and beef — is widely eaten, while fish is popular along the Indus and in the South. Mindful of this I considered a bite. Ever since my sickness in Leh I had been very wary about how food was prepared and I had kept strictly with vegetarian fare. Meat was definitely taboo.

If everyone eats meat here then it must be all right, I thought. Leaving the Leh episode aside, I had survived so far. My body felt fine. What's more I felt I had been long enough in Asia now and had become used to most things.

Perhaps my constitution had grown stronger? Convincing myself, I decided to try some meat and went to the busiest restaurant to see what was on offer. I was no sooner at a table when a menu was thrust at me. Much of it was written in Urdu, which made no sense to me. But the tiny English translation below each selection said enough:

> *Beef brains (by the plate) — 180 rupees.*
> *Sheep's kidneys — 200 rupees.*
> *Testicles and kidney combination — 220 rupees.*

And no sign of a vegetable. Needless to say I lost my appetite.

Moving on I was absorbed by the sights and sounds of the street. Spying a group of men gathered around a drinks stall quaffing glasses of what appeared to be coffee-coloured milk-shake, I wandered over. I just wanted a better look, but being the novelty foreigner I was summoned to join them and was quickly assailed by their curiosity. The questions poured out. 'How old are you? What is your job? Why are you travelling alone? Where is your wife? How much money do you earn? How do I get to Ireland? Can you help me get a job? Can you help me get a visa?' And so on. In a convivial way answers were given, many appropriately vague but good enough to keep us all engaged. I threw in a few questions of my own. Interestingly, given the public place, most of the men seemed to know each other and a few were related. They worked at all things, from taxi driving to dentistry. Meanwhile as we talked, one of those drinks was presented to me. It was a milk-shake all right, frothy on top, with crushed almonds and chunks of ice.

I looked at the ice. A reluctance came over me.

Ice? That's dodgy, I thought. Tap water. Bacteria. And what if the milk isn't pasteurised? Most likely it's not. This could be trouble.

But these sensible concerns gave way to protocol.

It would be rude to refuse this, I thought, especially with all these lads looking at me. Besides, they are all drinking it, so it must be OK. I picked it up.

'What's this called?'

'Robbery,' or a name that sounded like that, one of them said.

That's a strange one, I thought, still vacillating a decision. Ah so what? I concluded, taking the first sip. It was a milk-shake for sure, mildly sweet, and I remember thinking to myself: 'You know, this stuff is all right.'

❅ ❅ ❅ ❅

Saturday morning, 6 September. I woke up in foul order; weak, sweating and nauseous. My innards were in turmoil. It was as if a grenade had exploded inside me. My eyes hurt and my head felt as if it was jammed in a compactor. I was consigned to bed for the day, shivering in a heap and only stirring when the rumbling volcano inside threatened to erupt, with little warning. I soon wore a track from the bed to the toilet. That damned Robbery. I cursed myself for taking it and being so foolish. Clouds of anger and disgust built up and spilled over. Here I was again in an incapacitated state and in a kip of a hostel. The dormitory had six beds and no windows — no air and natural light. Was it night or day outside? I couldn't tell. Paint peeled off the walls, insects ran about and Allah only knew what lived in the dark corners. I was fed up with the sub-continent now. Sick of the noise, grime and chaos. I'd had enough of the uncleanliness, the culinary minefields, the sprawling cities, the pollution and the ugliness. I was tired of the dangers crossing the streets. Tired of the hordes of faces staring at you and fed up with the continual interference of beggars, hawkers and others looking for something off you. I had reached a new low. My mood sank further as the morning wore on. I considered giving up. To hell with this travelling, I thought, if I'm not better tomorrow I might just take a plane home.

I persevered. Early in the afternoon I crept out onto the roof terrace for air. Malik the Inn-keeper was there. Pitying my state, he fixed a concoction of Kalash mixed herbs, added bottled water and handed it to me. He swore it would cure all ills.

Gingerly I sniffed it. Hesitant, I thought it might be no better than Robbery. 'Are you sure about this stuff, Malik?'

He was adamant. 'Yes. I know. Believe me, it is good. It will work.'

'All right then.'

Slowly I raised the cup and took a sip. Just one … before vomiting for Ireland.

Word of my condition spread around the Inn and a knowledgeable French-man made a diagnosis, suggesting a legitimate drug of a name I can't recall. Pascal went to a chemist and got it for me. I have to say one good thing about travelling around and staying in cheap communal hostels is the consideration you get from near total strangers. Everyone is in the same boat, a long way from home, family and friends and having to look after themselves. An unwritten code of assistance exists: look after yourself, but give the next person a hand if he or she needs it. At some point that next person will be you. Hence this was my day. I felt it didn't matter so much if the tablets worked or not. It was comforting enough to know there were people around who were willing to do what they could to help.

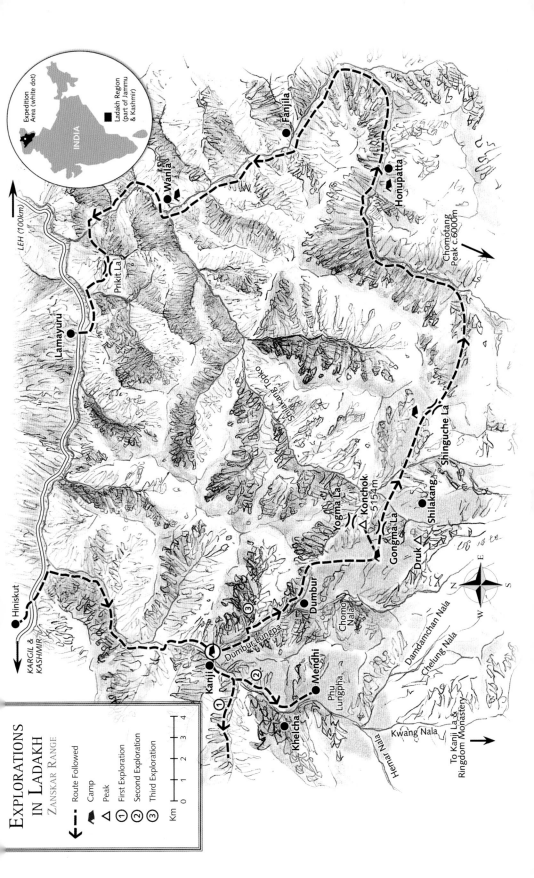

EXPLORATIONS
IN LADAKH
ZANSKAR RANGE

Route Followed
Camp
Peak
First Exploration
Second Exploration
Third Exploration

Km
0 1 2 3 4

Expedition
Area (white dot)

INDIA

Ladakh Region
(part of Jammu
& Kashmir)

LEH (100km)

Hiniskut

KARGIL &
KASHMIR

Lamayuru

Prikit La

Wanla

Fanjila

Honupatta

Chomotang
Peak c.6000m

Shakkang Topko

Konchok
5154m

Yogma La

Gongma La

Druk

Shilakang

Shinguche La

Dumbur

Dumbur Lungpa

Kanji

Mendhi

Khelcha

Phu
Lungpha

Chomo
Nala

Hemar Nala

Kwang Nala

Damdamchan Nala

Chelung Nala

To Kanji La &
Ringdom Monastery

N E W S

1

2

3

1 Monks, busy on a mandala. Lamayuru monastery, Ladakh.
2 Spinning prayer wheels and fingering beads. Local pilgrims at Lamayuru monastery, Ladakh.
2 'No rupee, no photo.' Sadhus of sorts, Kathmandu, Nepal.

1 Women on the march; The Free-Tibet demonstration, Leh, Ladakh.
2 On the same march, the lone Tibetan monk making his stand.
3 Ladakh. The view from the Shinguche-La, westwards over the Zanskars. In the middle-distance, L to R, Konchok, the Yogma-La and the serrated South Ridge of unclimbed Peak 5470.

1 Gerry retreating from a cloud topped Damavand, Iran.
2 Iran, old and new. Mehdi, seated on the right, beside the last guardian of Iran's Towers of Silence, Yazd.
  Also in the shot, Gerry (white cap) and Emilio Xaus. Photo: *Victor Castro*
3 Smoking the strong stuff at the Sufi festival, Pakistan.

1 The Sufi.
2 Alby and his landrover 'Stumpy,' Yazd, Iran.
3 The retired traffic cop — baton at the ready. Quetta, Balochistan.

1 All kinds of everything inside the wall of death; ladies (and ladyboys) at the Sufi festival, Pakoti, Pakistan.
2 Dancing ladyboy, at the Sufi festival.
3 The cripple spinning to the hypnotic beat. Sufi festival, Pakistan.

1

2

1 Göreme, Cappadocia.
2 Card seller, Kathmandu.

1 Tower of Silence, Yazd, Iran.

2 Sam, Nepal. Photo: *Sam Wales collection*

3 Le 28 Juillet. *La Liberté guidant le peuple* (28 juillet 1830). Eugène Delacroix (1798-1863) — © Musée du Louvre, Dist. RMN-Grand Palais/Philippe Fuzeau.

FOUR

The Sufis

Sunday 7 September. The tablets and group karma worked. I felt a lot better. I remained in bed for much of the morning but was up and about by early afternoon. During the night, fewer visits were made to the toilet. However one thing had changed: my attitude to food. Paranoia had taken over. I resolved not to eat anything presented to me by anyone for the rest of my time in Pakistan. From now on, self-reliance ruled. I would only eat basic things that came out of a package or tin, that were sourced in the supermarket and cooked by my own hand. Unlike 1.8 billion other bodies surviving on the sub-continent, there were limits to what this body could stand.

On the bus from the border Pascal had told me about the Sufi festivals and he recommended I experience one while in the country. The previous night he and the French fella had been to one in Pakoti, a town not far from Lahore. I was disappointed I hadn't been able to join them. However, as the festival was a three-day event, several others from the Inn were planning to go this evening. So despite my weak state I didn't want to miss a second chance. I convinced myself I was good enough to go.

Originating in Persia in the 7th century, after the death of Mohammad, Sufism is a mystical branch of Islam where followers diverge from the letter of the Koran and seek out physical, experiential and poetic means of worship. Mystics, usually men, like the Christian apostles, abandon all ties to home, family, friends and material possessions, choosing to become men of the desert. They live simple lives with no recourse to alcohol, drugs or relations with women. Their most celebrated activity is dancing, which allegedly induces a trance-like state that brings them closer to Allah. In earlier times Sufis held regular jobs, but today many live off alms and practice their faith, moving between the shrines of earlier Sufi saints. Some sleep next to, above, or inside the actual graves. Sufism is esoteric and liberating, quite unlike orthodox Islam, and because of this it is has a powerful appeal to many Pakistanis. Festivals are regular events held at these shrines where thousands flock to see their holy men dance. Some are very large, attracting hundreds of thousands, others much smaller. But they all share a common recreational ethos, with carnivals and circuses springing up around them. The Sufis themselves may be devout, clean-living men, and their immediate followers something similar. But the vast majority of followers are harmless pleasure seekers who view the festivals as appealing distractions; places to meet, places for drug-taking and leisure. Pascal's stories of these festivals drew my interest. I wasn't sure what to expect. In cultural terms the closest thing I could imagine was spending a weekend with The Grateful Dead. Thus I had to experience this Sufi business for myself.

At six o'clock a small group of us got a minivan from the Inn. Escorting us was Sajjad, a local lad who worked for the Inn. We made our way through rain and traffic-choked streets to the main road out of Lahore. Everything looked dreary; the industrial suburbs a sea of grey and brown. But there was one exception: the trucks. In Pakistan lorry drivers take an unabashed pride in their vehicles. Every inch of bodywork is decorated with pictures and designs in bright, bold paint. Usually the busy detail obscures any theme, but the overall effect is of intricacy, much like the rich mosaics that cover the walls of prominent mosques. Looped chains hang from the bumpers of these old Bedfords and large canopies jut out over cab roofs, not for extra storage space but to enhance the decorative effect.

Sundown, we reached Pakoti. Evening prayers accosted our ears, delivered by a wailing muezzin. Sajjad took us to see his fixer, a tall, brooding man with a thick moustache and a commanding presence. Baba Akhtar. Baba seemed to know his way around and everyone seemed to know him. He moved through the crowds much like a military general. Deference was invoked. He didn't say much, but when he did people around him just did what they were told. I had thought he must be some kind of bigwig, the mayor or a high-ranking civic official perhaps. But then Sajjad explained it.

'Baba is a very famous man here in Pakoti.'

'Really? How come?'

'Because he is the man who brought cable television to this area.'

First stop was a visit to Baba's house. We sat around in a circle on his living room floor and talked. Not that much was said. Two of Baba's associates came in. Chai and apples were served.

'Hashish?' Baba offered.

No one responded.

We watched him, intrigued by his method of rolling a joint. 'Roll' being the inoperative word. He took a standard cigarette out of a packet and carefully squeezed out the tobacco, without tearing the paper. Then he produced a small block of hash, heated a corner, crumpling a measure and then rubbed it evenly into the leaf. Deftly he inserted the mix back into the cigarette. Filter and paper remained intact. It was quite a piece of craft. He lit it. Only for the smell anyone would be fooled into thinking it was a normal cigarette. Around it went.

Baba led us to the festival. We walked through muddy streets with no lights and piles of rank, decomposing rubbish scattered about. It was disgusting and I found it hard to accept how people could live in such a filthy mess. But I had seen enough of this in India and Nepal by now and once more, I had to wonder about the community's sense of priority. Was cable television more important than public health?

We heard the drums then saw the crowds. The Sufis, we knew, danced to an energetic beat. The festival was spread over several acres around a shrine, a roofless series of courtyards and arches. Strings of party lights hung on the walls and over our heads. People milled about. We followed Baba into a tent — the first Sufi dance area. A thick red carpet lay on the floor and around it a crowd gathered. Being guests, we were given the best spot. Shoes off, we hunkered along one edge of it. Within minutes trays heaped with chapatti and dal were offered to us. Others ate but I dared not touch it. Two drummers came in and with them a chap with a pair of maracas. They took position and started to play; the drummers with barrel-like dhols hanging from their necks, both ends of which they beat with hooked sticks. They kept a steady rhythm, warming the atmosphere. A Sufi in a black robe stood by. He was talking with others. We watched him, thinking he would step out onto the carpet, but no, he slinked off into the night. We waited some more. The drummers kept going.

Out of nowhere a crippled midget appeared. He jumped into the middle of the carpet, faced the drummers and spun around on his hands. His limp, skinny legs were folded around his backside. Round and around he spun. A human ball. His arms did it all; lifting him up, springing him forward, catapulting him sideways. He worked the floor, spinning himself clockwise, then anti-clockwise and then hopping up on one hand. He would do this until he got tired. Then he would stop momentarily and get his breath back before spinning off again. It was bizarre. It made me think of a crab scurrying across a flat beach, determined to find rock or water. But he seemed to enjoy it and so did the people. Rupee notes were thrown out and he snapped them up. Then in an instant he disappeared into the crowd.

Baba got up, clapped his hands and summoned us on. Through the shadows he led us into the courtyard, the main part of the shrine. A decadent scene confronted us. Hundreds had flocked here, all men, in various states of dishevelment. Fires burned every few metres with groups of people sitting around, cooking food and smoking dope. Small clusters had collected around bubbling water-pipes. Old men with henna beards and missing teeth lay about semi-comatose. Other, younger fellas stumbled around, ebulliently stoned. A fug of charcoal and drug smoke filled the air and the deafening boom of Sufi drums echoed out. Thin holy men lounged on cushions in the midst of their followers. One Sufi waved, calling us over. He was bare-backed, with sharp green eyes and long, ragged hair. At his feet were a jumble of heavy steel cowbells which he wore while dancing. How he managed I couldn't tell, they must have weighed a ton. Nearby, I glimpsed the midget, squatting with his mates, blissfully sucking a hookah.

We garnered attention. Working our way through the crowd, many people were keen to meet us and shake our hands. Smiling, they asked us where we came from and if we liked Pakistan. We were quite a novelty to them. This was hardly surprising given the country's large population and minute tourist trade. Other than Afghan refugees, rural Pakistanis seldom get to meet visitors, especially the likes of us Europeans.

Following Baba in his immaculate white kameez, we passed busy food and sweet stalls and out into dark muddy alleyways, stumbling through flooded potholes. We didn't know what we would see next. But Baba did. Across the main road and into a field, a carnival was going on. Crowds flocked. There were roundabouts, wooden ferris wheels, the hum of generators, tacky signs, garish lights, toffee-apples and candy floss. The sights and sounds of childhood returned. We climbed some steel steps. What is this? A wall of death? We peered over the rim. Down in the pit was the warm-up act; a collection of women dressed to the nines, preening, posing and blowing flirtatious kisses at us. Were they showgirls? For what? But something seemed odd, something not quite right. I looked again. Was it their faces? The heavy make-up? The height of some? The wide shoulders of others or the way that they stood? Then it dawned on me. They were all men. Trans-sexuals and transvestites. Sajjad chortled.

'Ladyboys,' he beamed.

Ladyboys? I hadn't expected this. Not here. Not in Islamic Pakistan.

'They're not just dancers, Sajjad, are they?' I asked.

Sajjad grinned impishly. He shook his hips, bent forward, pointed to his backside and said: 'This is ladyboy's credit card machine.'

Enough said. We both fell about laughing.

The ladyboys made way for a bloke with a car. He started it, drove around the pit a half-dozen times, then onto the ramp and up the wall of death. After several revolutions he circled back down, stopped, got out and hopped on a motorbike. The same thing again. Only the bike was more of a visual and audio spectacle. A small, standard Honda, like countless others in Asia, except this one had its exhaust doctored for added sound effect. Kick-starting it, the thing roared into life. Man and machine made their way up the ramp, gaining speed and height with each revolution. The next minute both were at ninety degrees — a flashing, ear-splitting centaur. The wood planks that made up the walls rattled violently as he barrelled by. He was at touching distance now. On reaching his highest speed he took one hand off the bars. Then the other one and held them both aloft. This was a creditable stunt, one that required a good deal of guts. But the funny thing was the way it all looked. Here was a fella flying around in circles at break-neck speed, half upside-down with no safety helmet. Gritted teeth were his main protection, along with a grubby pair of sandals and a wind-whipped salwar kameez.

After him, the ladies came out. Only real ones this time. Beautiful girls full of grace and glamour. Men paid them individually to watch them dance. But behind their glitz none of them smiled.

'Prostitutes as well, Sajjad?' I asked.

'I believe so,' he replied.

Next, Baba hauled us to the circus. Inside the big top we saw a variety of acts: a strongman, fire-breathers, jumping lions, acrobats, a Russian gymnast, a knife thrower, clowns and a joker on a bicycle doing tricks. None of it was in any way flash. Certainly not Cirque du Soleil standard. More like Fossett's circus, Letterkenny 1960.

By now I had seen enough strangeness. The night was passing and I needed a spiritual experience. One of us had to say something.

'Baba, take us to a Sufi,' I said.

So it was back to the shrine and the mob. Baba led us to a section with a canopy and carpets, accommodating a Sufi he knew. Our mystic was a heavy-set man of around my own age, with thick black hair and a long, bushy beard. He wore a green velvet robe, a glittering red headband and, on his lower legs stitched to his dhoti, were scores of golden baubles that rattled when he danced. He had a sidekick, another Sufi, though more an aspiring one. This fella was shorter, with dreadlocks and a purple robe. Around them sat a handful of loyal followers, and around them, lounging on cushions, a horde of stone-head delinquents. Baba had words. The Sufi would oblige. Drummers were called.

Four drummers this time, plus a lad on maracas. They began beating and kept a steady tempo for several minutes. A standing crowd gathered. Once more we were given the best view, seated at the carpet's edge. The sidekick got up and started to dance, twirling clockwise then anti-clockwise, his dreadlocks and robe spinning out with centrifugal action. He kept this up, a complementary movement to the beating drums. Minutes later the Sufi stepped out. The crowd moved back. Barefoot, arms outstretched and eyes closed, he rolled his head from side to side, flailed his arms and moved backwards and forwards. Thrusting his head back, he stomped up and down, freeing his baubles to jangle in tune with the surrounding percussion. He stomped and stomped, moving around, twisting and turning, drawing us in. We watched his eyes. They were dark and wide — prisms of soulful exploration. Alongside, the escort kept twirling, regularly changing direction to avoid dizziness. The Sufi continued the gyrations, stomping faster then slowing, while waving his arms and bending and stiffening his fingers. Head forward, head back, mouth ajar, his torso writhed around. Small concentrated beads of sweat formed on the drummers' brows. The sound hammered on.

Our shaman's pace intensified. His head rolled. His arms kept flailing. His body continued to turn, to the right, then left. Rapidly so. He appeared to be winding up. The eyes still had it; projecting beyond the temporal, beckoning a union with the holy one. And then take-off. A line had been crossed. He was swirling like his cohort. Two whirling dervishes getting closer to God. Around they went, spinning like tops, with the karma of their acolytes urging them on. The drums beat louder, frenetically hypnotic. I too felt I was in a trance. I wasn't alone. Around me everyone sat and stood, absorbed. The whirling continued for a while, shifting direction and then slowed, easing into graceful turns. This was followed with more head-rolling, arm swinging, stomping and bowing, to be wound up again into another series of whirls. The pattern repeated itself. There was no mistake, our mystic was beyond us now, free-wheeling with the angels of Allah.

I looked over at his small band of unquestioning followers. More enthralled faces. One of them was so moved by what he was seeing he could remain still no longer. Rapt, he stumbled onto the floor and began swaying his arms and torso, in a vain attempt to emulate his master. But he only lasted moments. Another devotee stepped in and embraced him as if he was about to fall. They stood clasped together momentarily until the inappropriateness of the situation registered with them, whereby they shuffled back to where they belonged. It was hard not to empathise with them, such was the magnetic power of the dance.

Meanwhile as all this was going on, the crowd half-watched. Like Romans at an orgy they languished on their cushions, blithely toking. I glanced around, then had to take a second look as something bright caught my eye. A glowing ball. It was an apple, with a hollowed centre and a dozen burning joints sticking out of it. The thing looked like a miniature sea mine from the Second World War. One lad handled it, carefully, much like a priest with a host. He went from one to the other, offering it to open mouths. Twelve burning ends lit up with each pull, and a pall of thick smoke enveloped each celebrant. And, just like those sea mines, I noticed it had a detonating effect. Kaboom. Cerebral explosions. All around I had never seen such mental disorder, not even in the most dissolute parties of the West. I scratched my head, wondering, trying to make sense of everything I had seen so far. There didn't seem to be any. Not to me. Not yet anyway. Here I was in a sacred place after all, with a circus outside, a few oddballs up dancing and a thousand and one others hopelessly stoned.

The Sufis kept dancing and the irreverence went on. On the fringes another dancer appeared. A tall slender woman in a silk dress with long brown hair. She was an opportunist, seizing the crowd's attention and feeding off the ambient sound of our Sufi's drums. From where I sat she looked beautiful and I wondered if she belonged to the dancing troupe we had seen earlier. She was lithe and exotic. A Salomé. I found myself being captivated by her and paying less attention to the Sufi. Could a man like me meet her? I wondered. Could we take off on a carefree adventure together and drink from the cup of love? Or is that pure fantasy? But wait, things aren't all as they seem. I turned to Sajjad once again. He wasn't near me this time but was aware of what I had seen. He was looking at me and I could tell by his expression and grin what he was thinking. The penny dropped. 'Ah yes, the ladyboy and his credit card machine.' Suffice to say, I returned to my senses.

The Sufi kept at it for over an hour. I tried to imagine what it was like to him as he danced. It must feel extraordinary, with the corporeal world flashing by — lights, fires and dark faces — all in the charged atmosphere of hemp smoke and thunderous drums. It had to be electrifying. The irony wasn't lost on me that these abstemious men were drugged in their own sense, with faith, movement and imagination tripping them to another world.

In the early hours Baba insisted on taking us to the home of one of his relatives for a nightcap — a chai and a toke — before he crammed us into a minivan for home. Mentally it was impossible to switch off from the festival, what with the sensory overload. I hadn't known what to expect when I came to Pakistan. My presumption had been one of a conservative place, not a strict Sharia state, but one where the spirit of Islamic law applied, and where transgressions do not go unpunished. Instead I was pleasantly surprised to find this is definitely not the case. Quite the contrary. I know it's a cliché to say, but Pakistan is a land of paradoxes. Islamic laws based on Sunni interpretations of the Koran form the basis of civil law. Alcohol, drugs, homosexuality and prostitution are forbidden, and women in public, for the most part, must be segregated. But in practice, society behaves quite differently. In Lahore for example, the buses are segregated, yet male conductors patrol the women's section collecting fares. Also the driver sits openly in this section. And later, while on a cross-country sleeper train, I saw no evidence or enforcement of segregation. Furthermore, what I saw at the Sufi festival said volumes. Displays of homosexuality and vice are tolerated as conventional, and drug-taking is expected. No one seemed to care if any of it was illegal. What's more, I saw no policemen. Sufi festivals take place all over the country and some, as I said, are very large, attracting hundreds of thousands. Yet I learned there is seldom any trouble at them and never any police clampdowns. Sufism is part of religion after all, and, by this association, is part of accepted law. Today there are opposing forces working to shape Pakistan. There are political groups campaigning for secularisation. There are extremist ones pressing for increased islamisation and threatening the state's fragile democracy. There is violent sectarianism, in the cities especially, with deep divisions along ethnic, religious and social lines. Then there is a powerful military elite unwilling to cede power and who are pre-occupied with external affairs. But from what I could see, deep down, the majority of Pakistanis are amicable, tolerant types who care little about politics and unrest and the limitations of their laws, religious or civil. They just want to get by, enjoy their liberties while they can and make the most out of life.

FIVE

Across Balochistan: Cameras, Camels and Guns

Monday 8 September. I was feeling better. The following two days were spent exploring Lahore. I went down the Mall. I inspected Zam-Zammah, the heavy brass cannon, captured and used among warring parties from Afghanistan to Amritsar in the 18th and 19th centuries. Ranjit Singh coveted it most. The gun became a symbol of power during these times, epitomised by the saying: *He who controls Zam-Zammah controls the Punjab.* Later this gun was to be immortalised as 'the fire-breathing dragon' in Kipling's novel *Kim*. Across the road is the Lahore museum where Kipling's father, John Lockwood, served as curator. The museum houses a fine collection of artifacts from the religions, empires and civilisations that swept through the sub-continent down the ages. For me a few objects stood out: stone-carved panels in relief illustrating Buddha's life-story being one. Another, a haunting statue of a fasting Buddha; his body emaciated, his veins, sinews and bones protruding through his skin and cloth, and his eyes sunk deep in their sockets. The most poignant object was a porcelain plate commemorating the golden jubilee of Queen Victoria in 1887. It boasts a map of the world with emphasis on all the colonies of the British Empire: Ireland, Canada, New Zealand, Australia, Hong Kong, Burma, Bangladesh, Nigeria, much of East and Southern Africa. Below this, a list of statistics — imports, exports, population and land areas — and below that in proud livery, the ill-fated, hubristic declaration:

The Empire on which the sun never sets.

How impressive, and how ephemeral, I thought.

The streets of the city are noisy, congested and thick with dust and fumes. There's the usual mass of mechanised vehicles in various states of disrepair, and a good proportion of the more traditional means of transport — wooden carts, overloaded with foodstuffs and junk drawn by maltreated horses and mules. Their hard-headed masters are often barefoot men in turbans, standing upright wielding the reins — a far cry from the lives of the well-tended animals of Ladakh and McLeod Ganj. Women, few in number, can be seen in the streets, usually in twos or threes, some in purdah. In the quieter backstreets young fellas can be found avidly playing cricket.

I visited Badshahi mosque, a giant, marble and sandstone edifice, reputedly built by 75,000 slaves over two years in the 1670s. It is the fifth largest mosque in the world with a courtyard that can hold 100,000 people. Its internal domes are acoustically perfect and its 53-metre high minarets are constructed to tilt slightly outwards. The reason? To prevent catastrophe in the courtyard should an earthquake strike. It is quite a feat of Mughal engineering.

There's hardly room to swing a cat in the streets of the old city. I noticed, and not for the first time while travelling, that each street caters for a given area of trade. For example, one street is given to the manufacture and sale of musical instruments. Another for the sale of kitchenware. Another for shoes. Another for electrical and white goods, and so on. I thought this odd at first. Initially you would think it wouldn't make sense to try and sell your wares when you are surrounded by competition. Isn't it preferable to ply your trade in another street or another neighbourhood where there is none? But I had to accept people have been trading this way for centuries. They obviously know something and the arrangement works for them.

Two days earlier the country got a new President, Asif Ali Zardari, husband of the assassinated former Prime Minister, Benazir Bhutto. Earlier in March a new civilian government had been formed by opposition parties with Yousuf Raza Gilani of the Pakistan Peoples Party installed as Prime Minister. Both President and government replaced a nine-year military rule led by Pervez Musharraf. Since partition Pakistan has endured political instability and military rule for much of the period. Neither military or democratically elected governments have been effective, marked by corruption, censorship, meddling in the judiciary and the self-serving interests of elites desperate to retain power by whatever means. The Pakistani people have been poorly served. With a population of 172 million, health, education and welfare are hugely under-served, and investment in public infrastructure is abysmal. The literacy rate is low at 54 percent. Infant mortality is high. Also there is widespread gender and minority discrimination. Wandering around and seeing the outward signs of neglect, it is shameful to think that this country is a nuclear state. Also, since partition, Pakistan's leaders have given greater attention to external matters, namely squabbles with India over the control of Kashmir, than they have to domestic affairs. But in recent years new threats have emerged with the country being brought into a US-led war on Al-Qaeda and the Taliban in Afghanistan. The rise in jihadism and sectarianism has brought about terrorist attacks on government, civil and religious targets. I was curious to know what local people thought of their world. On the street I met Bashir, a teacher in his mid-fifties. Bashir had lived in the United States for several years and spoke English well. I asked him what he thought of the new Zardari presidency and Gilani-led government, and how he felt about the future. He was hopeful and happy to see the end of the Musharraf era, believing that a lot of local taxes and foreign aid went into the pockets of the General and his cronies.

'We've had too much of that. It is time to move on.'

Equally he was critical of the American government, seeing it as needlessly meddling in Afghan and Pakistani affairs.

'America is only pursuing its own agenda in Afghanistan, in order to protect its own interests at home, and they are using Pakistan to do this. We should look after our own affairs and they should go home.'

'But would you not think the Americans are needed in Afghanistan?' I countered. 'The Taliban is a brutal, destructive force and there is no one else of substance to oppose it. Don't you agree they are a threat to Pakistan as well as Afghanistan?'

Bashir's response was, to me, surprising. I held my tongue to prevent an argument.

'The Taliban are not bad people. Only extremists are bad, and few people in Afghanistan and Pakistan are extremists.'

I got a similar view from Mohammed, a young tour guide at Badshahi mosque. He believed 99 percent of Pakistanis were against Islamic extremism, such as that espoused by the Taliban. However he also believed all Pakistanis were against American influence in the region, especially given US-led raids on suspects on Pakistani soil, leading to the deaths of innocent civilians. He, like Bashir, was critical of his politicians, yet hopeful of what a new government might bring. But he was in no doubt that regardless of who was in power, Pakistan's future would be difficult as its economic problems are great.

'I think the biggest problem facing Pakistan right now is inflation.'

He was right there. I had read in the newspapers the country's general inflation rate for the year was 12 percent, with food inflation running above 17 percent. This didn't augur well. Rising inflation meant factory closure and job losses. Home produced goods would be more expensive to make and less attractive to sell. Imported goods would be more competitive than exports, increasing the balance of payments deficit. The currency would weaken also. The effects of all this would be felt by the ordinary person.

Back at the Inn I considered this. The price of a tin of baked beans, a safe food I had recently come to depend on, was 55 rupees. This was about the same price I had been paying, after haggling, for short auto-rickshaw journeys around town. Extrapolating this further, I estimated the average auto-rickshaw driver would do three of these runs an hour. Thirty over a ten-hour day, which meant an income of 1,650 rupees a day. Factoring daily fuel costs of 400 rupees and maintenance of 50, this leaves approximately 1,200 rupees to live on per day. That's equivalent to 21 tins of beans. Subtracting rent and the cost of feeding and educating a family, your average rickshaw driver isn't left with much. Perhaps a half-dozen tins at most. And let's not forget when he is sick, there is no income. Also, index-linked pay rises are uncommon in this part of the world, so when the cost of living escalates, the vast majority suffer. Thus my fears for the country and its stability are manifold. If the economic woes continue, life will get tougher. If the new civilian government fails to address living standards then people will become disillusioned, heightening a level of discontent with democracy. Sectarianism may rise. What's more, should the situation in Afghanistan remain unresolved and controversial US operations continue, the likelihood of anger and resentment grows. As squabbles with India have shown, Pakistanis do not like foreign powers interfering in their affairs. Compounding this, many Pakistanis cannot afford a state education. Instead many attend madrassas, which are informal religious-led schools, many reputedly good, offering a balanced, healthy education. But others are known to be less salubrious, being nurseries of fundamental extremism. In short, Pakistan faces a worrying future.

Tuesday 9 September. I bought a train ticket to Quetta and checked emails back at the Inn. Darach sent me a note. He had made it to Greece and was currently lazing on a beach. Tiredness had caught up with him. A case of travel fatigue. I knew how he felt. Usually travelling is interesting but sometimes it can be a drag. The hassle of constantly being on the move, hauling a bag, working out logistics, dealing with hawkers and having to engage in small conversations everywhere with new people can be wearing. Occasionally homesickness can lessen the travel experience. But we can't complain, For each of us it was our own decision.

I also got an email from Sam. 'I'm in India,' it read, 'And all the men are at me again. God, why did I bother coming back here?'

Exasperated Sam. There was only one way I felt I could reply and that was to give her some encouragement.

'Sam, have you considered setting up your own school? You could educate Indian men on Western women and how they could lure them. You could teach them about the virtues of subtlety and gentlemanly behaviour, and you can explain how listening to women, putting them at ease and complimenting them pays dividends. Trust me, you could be rich in no time, and in the minds of some you will be elevated to that of a god.'

❄ ❄ ❄ ❄

Wednesday 10 September. I boarded the 11.20 a.m. sleeper to Quetta. I had been travelling so long on buses by now I had forgotten what a comfort train travel could be. Here there were no broken roads, no blasting horns, no death-wish drivers, noxious exhaust fumes or insufferable Bollywood films. I re-discovered the possibility of reading and writing while journeying and to have conversations with people, or being able to get away from them if preferred.

We trundled through Lahore, passing its suburbs and satellite towns, stopping at the occasional station. There was activity at each stop, but the train never got crowded. The odd colourful Sufi stood out on platforms. Sadly though, what struck me most was the litter and squalor by the trackside; the impoverished living in makeshift tents, with dogs and buffalo roaming through the mess. Once more I thought of the political and military elites who govern this country and how they have failed the people. The refuse and dirt, a sight so common in India and Nepal also, prompted another discouraging thought; that few people in any of these countries give a damn about the quality of their environment. But they're not the only ones.

The thoughts, like the train, rolled along. We stretched out into open country, passing bullock carts waiting at crossings, and riotously painted lorries speeding along. Re-acquaintance was made with two rivers, the Indus and Satluj, both tamed from long meanderings. Green sheets of algae floated on stagnant pools. Men drove goats along farmland tracks and women hunched over, tending crops in fields.

The day wore on. We made Multan and the first palm trees appeared. Barrela camels were also about. Two lingered at a man-made pool, another was at work, hauling a cart laden with grass. Normally you would expect to see a smaller animal, a horse or a donkey at this task. Instead, the odd spectacle of an oversized draw-beast, with its long neck and head towering well above the handlers and cart.

The evening crept up and a lowering sun softened the earth's colours of green and brown. Workers filed home from the fields. A class of children assembled in a ruin for evening lessons. Gravel and scrub marked the onset of the Balochistan plateau. Everything was warm and calm. As we headed towards the sun, a sense of tranquility prevailed that made you think might spread out over every village, district, town and city in Pakistan. It was one of those rare golden evenings that dared you to imagine, however briefly, that all might be right with the world.

I was sharing a sleeping compartment with five other men. All were from Quetta. They were polite, middle-aged, Urdu-speaking types. One of them, Mohammed, had English. I had spent much of the day seated in the corridor, in conversation with him. Our discussion was broad. Every now and then I took out my camera to film the passing countryside.

Mohammed was 57. He had worked for most of his life as a chemical engineer at the Merck plant in Quetta. That was until recently, when he was picked for early retirement. The culling axe of globalisation and cost reduction was alive and well here, I noted. Anyway, Mohammed left with his severance package and a reduced pension. But now he was worried about his future. Life at Merck had been comfortable. The job had purpose and the company offered security. He didn't have to worry about anything. But now it was a different story. He had to look out for himself and his family, and he had to decide what to invest his money in. But there were too many options: property, the stock market, leaving the money in the bank, or investing in a small business. Now wasn't a good time to invest in property. The stock market was too volatile. The bank paid little interest and a business was too uncertain. He had much to learn and wasn't comfortable with all the risk, regardless of which option he chose. As a risk manager I felt compelled to offer advice.

'Mohammed, take your time and think things through. Write down all the options and the positive and negative aspects on each. Then if you're still not comfortable, spread the risk. Invest in a little of each. But may I say, if you're looking to start a business and you don't know what to do, one idea I can give you is to get into solar panels.'

He looked at me quizzically. I continued.

'I have noticed there is a dire need for electricity in this country. In Lahore there are blackouts all the time. And yet, outside there is an abundance of sunshine. This could be used. I have not seen one solar panel anywhere,' which was true. 'You could be the first in the market to supply and install them. You might do very well.'

I studied him, trying to divine the way he was thinking as he looked out of the window.

Solar panels? Yes it was an idea all right. Maybe a good one. But I know nothing about these things. It is too risky. I wish I was back in Merck.

Observing Ramadan's obligations, the men ate at sundown. They insisted I eat also and Mohammed bundled me a chicken leg and chapatti. I appreciated the gesture but was loathe to go near it. I couldn't trust anything I didn't cook myself or that hadn't come straight out of a packet or tin. Although refusing food was bad custom, I was fortunate. The lads ate behind the closed door of the sleeper, while I remained in the corridor. Surreptitiously I chucked it into a waste bin. Darkness fell and we all retired to our bunks.

❄ ❄ ❄ ❄

Thursday 11 September, 9 a.m. I wasn't long awake when we pulled into Quetta. A starkly different landscape met us now — one of parched earth, dusty hills and hard, blinding sunlight. An auto-rickshaw ride got me to the Muslim Hotel. On the way I reached into my bag for the camera. It was gone. I checked, rummaging through the pockets, and double-checked, while recalling the movements of last night and this morning. I hadn't mislaid it. It was stolen. It happened during the night in the sleeper and could only have been one of the men. Which one? I thought about each, but there was only one suspect; Mohammed, his behaviour gave him away. This morning he had said little, averted his eyes whenever I spoke and coyly shook my hand when we parted. Plainly he wanted to leave the station quickly. I was annoyed but I took it into perspective. It was only a camera after all, an object that was wholly replaceable. Luckily I still had all the footage I had taken. Nevertheless I couldn't help thinking it hypocritical that a devout Muslim could fast and pray diligently for Ramadan, offer food to a non-Muslim stranger at sundown, and then rob him before sunrise. With a final accusatory thought, I shrugged the affair off:

'Mohammed, if it was you, you're a bollocks. I hope it breaks on you.'

I dropped my gear at the hotel and went to look for breakfast. I read the best place to eat was the Serena Hotel, which happened to be the poshest place in town. When I found it I was surprised by its appearance. It looked less of a luxury hotel and more of a military compound. Surrounding it is a high wall with steel gates. Armed guards stand at entrances and corners. Bag scanners are in operation at each door. A road block exists inside the main gate, and brass plates with pictures of AK47's and the words *Arms Prohibited* are mounted on walls. I got the message all right ... Quetta isn't the safest place on earth.

After eating I strolled downtown. On Jinnah Road there was all kinds of commercial activity, but one thing stood out. The proliferation of gun shops. At home we've got more pubs than needed in every town. Here it is somewhat similar, except pistols replace pints. Curious, I went into one of these shops. The place was filled with rows of shotguns, handguns and rifles. Swords, machetes and knives hung from the ceiling, crossbows lay next to the counter and boxes of ammunition were stacked up the walls. All of it sinister looking and enough to start a regional war. What was the need for so many shops? Three long-nosed, turbaned men sat on a bench. I put this question to them.

'Hunting,' was their only reply.

'Hunting? That's all?'

'Yes.'

'But what is there to hunt around here?' It was hard to imagine anything, the place is practically a desert.

There was a collective pause before one of them piped up. 'Ibex, markhor, python. Many kinds of snakes. And birds.'

'And what about these,' I asked, pointing to an evil-looking array of handguns. They weren't your standard weapons for game hunting. 'What are these for? Target practice? Protection?'

'Yes,' they chimed. 'Target practice. Protection.'

'I see.'

Somehow what they weren't saying suggested a lot more. As for buying a gun, it was easy. According to them all I needed for a licence was a letter from my embassy.

A letter could be faked. It was too easy. I got a better insight on things at the camera shop when I went to buy a temporary replacement for the rest of the trip home. I learned there were turf wars between various Pashtun clans in the city and across Balochistan. Also being close to the Afghan border, there were arms and drug smuggling, and clashes with government forces.

'Don't leave town after dark. It's not safe,' I was told.

I picked a camera and to see if it worked and took a photograph of one of the shop's customers on the street, an old Balochi bloke. The old boy made quite a sketch, having sunglasses, a long grey beard, a ring on each finger and a mound of a turban. It was interesting to note he carried a wooden baton. The reason? To direct traffic. He stepped on to the middle of the street and proceeded to swing it about, snarling and barking at passing vehicles. He was good at this. Moreover he appeared to relish it. I was told afterwards he used to be one of the city's traffic policemen but had long since retired. However no one seemed to have told him this. Personally I concluded he was one of the few lucky people on the planet who consider their job a lifelong vocation.

Camera problem solved, I wondered what the main attraction of Quetta might be, so I consulted my notes from the Inn. The main recommendation was the British Military History museum, which apparently houses a fine collection of antique guns.

That's wonderful, I thought. Who needs to see that when the whole town is a living arsenal?

I wandered around, taking photographs. A plain-clothes policeman stopped me at one point and I thought I was in trouble. Not so. He, like many Pakistanis I met, was genuinely happy to talk to me. Doubtless he regarded an encounter with a foreigner such as myself as something exotic, possibly in the same way as we in Ireland would have felt meeting an African or Asian forty years ago.

I mentioned my surprise at seeing all the gun shops and hearing about Pashtun unrest. Abdul told me about the wider strife that exists in the region. Balochistan is the poorest, most neglected province in Pakistan with low standards in health, education, water provision and sanitation. In 2007 the World Bank noted an illiteracy rate of 60 percent. Not surprisingly, this has created much resentment and disillusionment with central government. In recent years an insurgency has grown, with several para-military groups such as the Balochistan Liberation Army waging a violent campaign for an independent state. These groups have been responsible for assassinations of politicians, government officials and police. To further instability, attacks have been made on critical infrastructure: roads, bridges, energy pipelines, power and communications lines. More disturbingly, there have been killings of non-Baloch settlers, Punjabis, as well as minority Shias. It is also known that Balochi separatist groups have co-ordinated attacks on government targets with the Taliban who, while waging war in Afghanistan and areas of Northern Pakistan, share similar tactical objectives against central government. In addition there is drug smuggling out of Afghanistan, through Pakistan and onward to Iran, Saudia Arabia and the West, as well as the illegal arms trade both ways. Then there is the situation of 220,000 Afghan refugees in Balochistan; some so desperate they become pawns in both trades. Drawing this unpalatable picture, Abdul like the camera shop men, warned me:

'Be careful, especially at night. It is not always safe. Don't travel around so much.'

That night I ate in the Serena and afterwards I got a taxi back to the Muslim Hotel. The streets were dark. The city mood tense. Armed police patrolled the streets and junctions. Soldiers remained on watch and both forces manned checkpoints at road-blocks. I thought of my friend from earlier, the cranky old traffic warden. Was he out there with his baton in the dark, lurking around?

❄ ❄ ❄ ❄

Friday 12 September, 6.30 p.m. I took a night bus to Taftan, the nearest town to the Iranian border. It would be a long, hard night on a broken desert road. The bus was full. It was an unusual set-up, with two drivers working shifts, and two others, a mechanic and a lackey helping out. The drivers had a bed up at the front, positioned lengthways down the aisle, which looked odd. What with the crowd on the bus, the bed in the centre of our world and the drivers in charge, I was reminded of Rembrandt's *The Anatomy lesson of Dr. Nicholaes Tulp*.

The journey itself wasn't short of colour. At sundown we stopped for a pee and a prayer, and at each subsequent stop the bus was jacked at the front for our mechanic to do running repairs. I had a seat at the front. The bloke next to me was heading for Qom, a city in Iran. Qom I knew to be the centre of Shia Islamic theology in Iran. It is where all the country's top clerics have studied and has a reputation, rightly or wrongly, for being a hotbed of rabid Islamic thought. He looked the mature type. I asked him what he was doing there.

'I am a student, studying Islam and the Koran.'

It transpired he had a few years to go before graduating.

'And what do you intend doing then?' I inquired.

He smiled, telling me he did not know. Frankly, considering what I knew about Qom, I didn't really want to know either.

It was hard to sleep, what with the craters in the road, dodgy suspension and the inevitable blaring horns, but the night was pitch black and I managed to nod off at one point. It wasn't for long. I woke with a start to the shrill blast of our horn as we made to overtake a truck. Typical of most Pakistani trucks, its bodywork was an explosion of colour. Lights all over it made me think of Christmas and the beams from our headlights only intensified the psychedelic effect. Dreamily I turned to see this and, as we sailed by, a camel's ugly head sticking out the side bore down on me. For a few seconds I thought I was drugged.

The sun came up as we neared Taftan — a ramshackle desert town smacking of frontier lawlessness. My eyes widened to another unusual sight. On the way in we drew up on an old battered passenger bus. Chugging along, it struggled under a collection of tall blue drums tied to the roof. Black smoke billowed at its rear. From behind I couldn't make out what was inside, though I knew there was life and assumed it might be a crowd of migrants, all asleep and heading to the border much like ourselves. However as soon as we were alongside I got the real picture. It wasn't what I or any of us expected. It wasn't even human. The thing was jam-packed with goats. Goats in a passenger bus — what next? Some windows were open. Pale beady eyes and bony snouts poked out. I wondered, where else would you find this?

SIX

First Impressions of Iran

Saturday 13 September. Iran. A new country, a new day. The body felt good and I hadn't a care in the world.

'You'll know when you've left the sub-continent,' Pascal had told me. 'The roads will be excellent.'

He was right. Once in Iran I found the road from the border to be near perfect. Later I was to see that every main road in the country is built to the same standard. However, the roads of Southern Iran contain one threat: kidnapping. Foreigners make lucrative targets. Earlier Pascal told me of his border crossing experience when he was leaving Iran. A Belgian couple he met in Zahedan had a car and were intent on making a crossing. They offered him a lift and he initially accepted. But when they told him they were planning on leaving at night he changed his mind. Daytime suited him better. He would take the bus instead. As it turned out, the Belgians were kidnapped not far from the border. Weeks later, after much media attention and diplomatic wrangling, they were released unharmed. Pascal made it through without a problem.

Because of incidents such as this, the Iranian authorities, not wishing to appear remiss, took measures to improve security. At customs I was ordered to take a taxi with a police escort from the border to Zahedan. There was no choice, I wound up sharing with three Koreans. It was a joke. The four of us in the car with the driver and one cop. There was no other escort, the car had no radio or phone and the cop had no gun. Some security. At Zahedan we did a relay around four police stations, where our passports were bandied from cop to cop. More nonsense. I asked to be taken to the bus station; Zahedan didn't look like much of a place and I was eager to make the next city north, Bam. The only sight of any note was a graveyard by a roundabout, with a thousand Iranian flags set among headstones and a myriad of photographs of young men killed in the Iran-Iraq war. Martyrs all.

At the bus station we met our last cop — a young pup with a Kalashnikov. He was civilised at first and shook my hand on inspecting the passport. But he had a motive. Mohammed our driver tipped me off.

'This man will try to make money. He will bring you to his ticket agent so he can get a commission. Do not follow him, even if he orders you. There are other agents and you will not pay more. I will show you.'

We entered the station, into the main ticket office and sure enough, Kalashnikov tried to lead us out again toward his man. I ignored him, following Mohammed's advice. Promptly I paid for a ticket and marshalled the Koreans to do likewise. When the cop realised, he blew a gasket. Eyes blazing, he pushed his way towards me, pressed his face into mine and roared at me. The abuse spilled out. All Farsi, a language unknown to me, but the way he expressed it had an invidious effect on me. All around went quiet as people averted their eyes, pretending nothing was going on. I got an earful, nothing physical, but enough to whip up base animal instinct.

Hit him. A fist in the stomach, then a kick in low. Get him round the head and bring him to the floor. Dig him with the gun and make him squirm. The crooked, power-crazed little shit.

I kept the head. Just about. There was no knowing what price would be paid for having a go at him. Still enraged, he barked more orders: I had to pay Mohammed. Mohammed had to declare the fare was correct. I had to show the bus ticket and get the Koreans to do the same and pay Mohammed. Then he stormed off. I thanked Mohammed, slipped him a few extra rials and we all broke up. However I could still see the creep waiting for me outside. Fortunately the station was big and busy enough. I waited a while, saw him grow impatient and then move off. Sharply I found my bus, timed my exit and slipped away. As a first taste of Iranian authority, it was nasty. I thought, If that's the kind of thing ordinary Iranians had to put up with each day, then God help them.

Pascal was right on another point. I would know when I was off the sub-continent. Only it wasn't the road quality this time, but the quality of the transport. Iranian buses are superb. They are modern, bright and spotlessly clean. This one had everything: air conditioning, a carpeted floor, comfortable seats, clean curtains and headrests, water to drink, snacks to eat and a fresh smell of flowers. What's more it had an attendant to cater for everyone's needs. It was the epitome of order and civility. All the passengers, men and women, were clean, neatly dressed and some very stylish. They were well behaved also. I was the odd, scruffy one now, with my weather-beaten looks, sweaty clothes and grimy bags that might have spent weeks on the backs of some far-flung mountain donkeys.

Sorry Trigger, sorry Dozy.

Nightime on the outskirts of Bam. The bus pulled into a lay-by and everyone got out. In this country where bus stations exist they are usually on the outskirts of cities, rarely in the centre. But there was none in this case. I had planned spending the night in Akbar's Hostel, a place Darach had recommended and also the only spot where foreigners are allowed stay in Bam. Anyway, the people dispersed in taxis. Some cars were marked, others weren't. I noticed people doubling up. A young bloke called me towards his motor.

'Taxi?' I asked.

'Yeah yeah.'

'Akbar's Hostel?'

'Yeah.'

Not convincing answers, I thought, but we'll give him a go.

Within seconds there were four of us in the car: myself, the driver and two other young fellas. Was this a shared taxi? They all seemed to know each other. Soon we were tearing down the main road. At first I thought it odd for a taxi to be travelling so fast. However as we clocked 100mph I suspected something worse. This wasn't a taxi. Not with the speed and not with the boys jabbering away excitedly. A horrible thought occurred to me. Was I being kidnapped? Instantly I felt sick. Sick with myself. Why did I let myself walk into this? It was so easy. So bloody stupid. And now what? Down the motorway we went, barrelling along in a clapped-out Peugeot. Then a stroke of luck. Red and orange lights flashed on the dashboard and the engine sounded like it was losing power. The lights wouldn't go out. Then came a grinding mechanical sound. The driver was forced to slow down. He pulled in. The engine stopped and it wouldn't restart. Meanwhile I grabbed the bags, got out and took off, back down the motorway. The boys called out, something about getting a motorbike and gesturing me back. I kept moving. My only focus was to get away from the lot. I looked around. It was pitch dark. The odd car speeding by and the city somewhere out there. I'll walk a few miles and doss in a ditch if have to, I thought.

Minutes later another bit of luck. A taxi — a marked one this time — with just the driver, on a slip road. I flagged him down and checked him. He was a mild-mannered old gent who knew Akbar and the way to the hostel. A legitimate operator. Fifteen minutes later I was safely there.

In retrospect having spoken with Akbar, I don't think the youths were kidnappers, most likely unemployed lads out joyriding and I just happened to be a novelty to them.

Akbar is 66 years old. He is tall, contemplative, has perfect English and is a genial host. He also has a broad view on people, the world and life.

'I love foreigners. I always have, every since I was a child. And so I am happy to run a hostel here, where we get all kinds.'

A French couple were staying the night, as were two Spanish architects, Emilio and Victor, who were on a busman's holiday, seeing the sights. In 2003 Bam was hit by a massive earthquake. It destroyed 85 percent of all buildings and flattened the prominent Agh-e-Bam, a 2,500-year-old fort which was an influential citadel of commerce in the time of the old Silk Road. It is estimated of Bam's population of 120,000, one third perished. Akbar's place was destroyed and two of his visitors were killed. He has since rebuilt his premises and business, crediting the help of his guests.

'I have many people who have stayed here. Foreigners, mostly, and they were wonderful after the earthquake, rescuing others. They brought medicines and money from their home countries, and physically helped me and others in reconstruction. Without them, we were lost.'

❄ ❄ ❄ ❄

Sunday 14 September. Mid-morning Akbar took myself and the Spaniards to the Agh. It was an incredible sight to see such a prodigious mud-brick city destroyed. Presently it is under UNESCO control and parts of it are being slowly rebuilt. We padded down the narrow, dusty alleyways where once stood orderly houses, balconies, arches and courtyards but was now a pile of rubble. Not one structure remained intact. Broken bricks and bits of adobe scattered everywhere. The atmosphere was strangely quiet. Was this Iran's Pompeii? Walking around we climbed steps to its highest point on a wall and looked out. Beyond, the land was flat and dry for miles. Hazy mountains stood in the distance. Nearby, in an oasis of palm and in a mixed state of repair, the newer city of Bam. I tried to imagine what life in the Agh was like at the height of its powers. I could picture the bustle: food merchants, bakers, tanners, potters and weavers at work, with people milling about. Animals scampering through alleyways and soldiers standing guard on the battlements. Outside, camel-trains making lengthy desert crossings, to and from other cities like Yazd, Mashhad and Herat.

The Agh; so many people clustered in such a remote spot, but where did they get their water? There were no rivers, the mountains were too far away and the surrounding land was parched. Looking at the palm trees around the city, it could only have been from underground. Full credit to their engineers and their ingenuity for harnessing a source, pumping it to ground and distributing it around the Agh. Mighty once, but all obliterated now.

Earlier, in the quiet of the morning, I had tea with Akbar. He seemed a bit melancholic, so to get a conversation going I plied him with a few questions I had on politics and religion in Iran. But he wasn't interested in these things, his mind was elsewhere. Gradually he told me he had been thinking about his wife, of whom he had been married to for forty years. They had a family but in recent years he felt they had grown apart.

'She is a good woman, but she has less energy than me now, and our interests are different.'

There was a tone of resignation in his voice and I got the impression he harboured regret.

'Was she the love of your life, Akbar?'

He shook his head. 'No. There was another woman once. A Dutch girl … a long time ago.'

I listened attentively. Somehow politics and religion were of little interest to me now. Akbar told me things about his past; about how he met this woman in Bam when he was in his early twenties. She was passing through, travelling around. They got on well together, had similar attitudes and outlooks on life and shared the same wry sense of humour. Soon they were in love. She stayed a while.

'Did you consider marriage?' I asked.

He nodded. 'Yes, of course I did. We were both very much in love. But … it was not allowed. Not in those days. My mother said no — "You shouldn't, it is not the proper way. Find yourself a Muslim girl and settle down."'

'And so?'

'And so my Dutch girl went back to Holland. And afterwards my mother, like all mothers in Iran, helped arrange my marriage.'

It was hard not to feel for him. I asked if he ever saw the Dutch girl again.

'Once. It was thirteen years later. I was in Belgium on business and a friend said to me, "Hey, you're not far from Holland. Why don't you go and see her?" I thought about it. "Go on," he urged. Now I was married with children, and so was she. There was no way we could get back together and besides, I thought we would both have changed. I was reluctant to visit. But I found the courage and I did. And Oh God, when I did — I was overcome. We both were. The same feelings of love we once had poured out. It came straight from the heart. Thirteen years apart and it was as if we had never left. But of course, there was no going back. We couldn't change things. I came home to Iran.'

We sat for some moments in a heavy silence, each of us in our own worlds, mulling over loss. Tea was sipped and Akbar in a nonchalant way, made a comment so universal and simple it summed up his mood and the essence of what we were talking about:

'Marriage is like a castle. You get people outside clambering to get in. And people inside desperate to get out.'

❇ ❇ ❇ ❇

Midday I moved on, planning to take a bus to Kerman. But Akbar had a better idea. He knew the Spanish architects were heading the same way, so instead of the bus he arranged a taxi to take us there. Sharing one was quicker and cheaper. It also meant we could stop and visit sights along the way.

Full credit to him. If ever a man understood good customer service it was Akbar. And just for good measure he drove us out reciting verses of 1,000-year-old Samanid-era poetry.

A hot desert drive followed. Flat earth, dried scrub, harsh light and pale colours. At Rayen we visited another Agh, a much smaller one, lifeless and dusty, but fully intact unlike Bam. Next to Mahan, to the garden of an erstwhile prince, and in the same town a visit to the mausoleum of a famous Sufi of an unpronounceable name. We examined his tomb and the tiled room where he used to pray. Although artistic and venerable, what really caught my eye was out in the courtyard where, barefoot and seated on the ground, were two women and a man, all calmly smoking a water-pipe. I found this intriguing. Iran, like Pakistan, is an Islamic state where religious doctrine determines society's rules. Only more so here. Iran's Shia interpretation of Islam is reflected by Sharia law, with harsh penalties for disobedience. These laws cover everything from the taking of life, insulting Allah, theft, promiscuity and so forth, right down to the way a person should dress. Of this dress code, women compared to men, fare worse, having to live their lives beneath hijabs and chadors. However I noticed over the coming days that despite Sharia law, Iranian women enjoy greater freedom and opportunities than their sisters in Pakistan. I saw many women working in all kinds of jobs, in banks, hotels, restaurants, post offices and bazaars. They can move freely and alone from place to place, and they can drive. They can talk to strange men. For instance, while in a Yazd bazaar, I was openly questioned by three curious women as to my nationality and reason for visiting Iran. Iranian women can enter politics. Many women hold positions on local and regional governments, and a number sit on the Majles — national Parliament. But perhaps the most impressive thing about women in Iran is their level of education. I came across several who were qualified, functioning professionals — scientists, engineers and teachers. Notwithstanding politics and law, something progressive must be declared about an Islamic state where 66 percent of students at its universities and colleges are women.

These two women were enjoying their smoke. They allowed me to photograph them. I couldn't imagine seeing the same thing in Pakistan.

❋ ❋ ❋ ❋

Monday 15 September. I could feel the shift in culture. Moving further away from the sub-continent I could sense a closer bearing to Europe. Unlike India, Nepal and Pakistan, Iran is much more orderly place. There is less of a wild, indeterminate element. The cities are cleaner and services such as electricity, water and sanitation function well. Essentially life in Iran appears stable. However it is by no means perfect. Poor urban planning has brought about sprawling cities and traffic-choked roads, particularly in Tehran. But given all of these things, good and bad, one impression I made is that the whole country seems locked in a 1970s timewarp. The streets are full of old Hillman Hunters, and their native copy, the Paykan. Long distance hauliers drive curvy Mercedes lorries of a similar design vintage. But most noticeable of all is the distinct lack of billboards and advertising; something we in the West have allowed ourselves become plagued by. I found this refreshing. Few tacky signs or garish lights, and of course, no messages laden with sexual imagery. Whether as a consequence of the Islamic revolution and its ideals, or isolation from the West since then, it made me think I was living in the past. This I have to say, has a nostalgic appeal.

No crass, American-inspired, cultural imperialism here, I thought. Iranians have something to be thankful for.

We strolled around Kerman. Returning to girl power, my first encounter with it was after breakfast. No sooner had we left the hotel and were crossing a street when I looked up to see four chador-clad women in an ancient Hillman tearing round a bend, gunning towards me. Veiled assassins. I had to leap out of their way.

The day was sedate after that. The Spanish architects were busy with their cameras. We moved through the bazaar which led to an open air market. It was hot. Temporary respite was found in an underground teahouse. Still being Ramadan, I felt mildly guilty indulging in tea and cake around fasting locals.

Outside there was only so much heat we could bear. After a few hours I got the idea of a trip to the Jameh mosque to cool down. It was a clever move. With thick walls and high ceilings, this mosque like many, remains cool and comfortable. Fans rotate overhead and soft Persian carpets cover the floor.

The recorded hymns of a mullah filled the air and a handful of men were scattered about, kneeling in prayer. The three of us lay down and dozed — a siesta of sorts. We weren't the only ones. Other boys were doing the same, ironed out on the carpet, or seated, or slumped against marble columns. Comfort was the only importance. Other than the mutterings of those in prayer, no one said a word. Nobody cared. Outside Christendom, the deportment of worshippers in mosques, temples and shrines can appear casual and inattentive. But as I had seen, many non-Christians such as Buddhists, Sikhs, Hindus and Muslims, actively live their faiths by praying, obeying commands and following rituals throughout each day. Unlike Christians, they don't merely observe a disciplined sermon on Sundays. Religion is at the forefront of their minds much of the time. That said, I still found it odd to be barefoot, lying on the floor of a holy place, asleep and not having a care. What were the chances of getting away with this at home? Not much. And what if I felt like having a smoke? No chance. At least here they have Sufi shrines.

Seven

History and Revolution

Iran, formerly known as Persia, has a turbulent, breath-taking history. It starts 100,000 years ago with evidence of human habitation on the Iranian plateau. By 5000 BC the first agricultural settlements existed in the Zagros mountains. Around 1000 BC the religious thinker Zoroaster, developed teachings that historically hold similar importance to that of the later prophets, Jesus and Mohammed. In the centuries that followed, Zoroastrianism became the region's pre-dominant religion. In the 6th century BC an Achaemenid, Cyrus the Great, became Persian king. Under his rule, by violent and non-violent conquest, a huge empire grew, stretching from the Aegean to the Indus. This empire was strengthened by a later Achaemenid, Darius I. Zoroastrianism, with its emphasis on equality meant that conquered tribes were not only permitted to follow their own religions, but given powers to conduct their own affairs. Complex though this was, it worked, and the empire remained strong. Its undoing was the march of an expansionist Macedonian in the 4th century BC, Alexander the Great.

Greek domination didn't last long and a revival of a kind came a century later with the Parthians, a tribe of skilled, horse-mounted warriors from east of the Caspian. They established superiority over other Persian tribes but were careful not to antagonise the Greeks, who were major players on the Silk Road trade route. At that time it was in everyone's economic interest throughout southern Europe and the Middle East to maintain the flow of goods to and from the Orient. After the Greeks, successive Persian kings — Shahs — fought wars with the Romans, who were creating their own empire. Territories were won and lost from the Oxus to the Euphrates.

In 610 AD in the hills around Mecca, Mohammed experienced his first revelations from the angel Gabriel. A new religion, Islam, was born and by Mohammed's death in 632, most of the Arabian Peninsula had been converted. Shortly after, emboldened by the unifying power of this new faith, the Arabs conquered Persia.

Their rule was one of restraint. Islam replaced Zoroastrianism and the following two centuries was a period of renaissance in the arts and sciences.

Next came the Seljuk Turks from Central Asia and an age of relative calm from the 10th to the 12th century. This period was to be associated with the rise of poetry and Sufism. The great Persian poet Ferdowsi lived during this time, creating his epic Shahnameh. This historical tale about Persian kings, love, war, heroism, and morality awakened a sense of Persian culture and identity which had lain dormant since the Arab invasion.

The 13th century saw the arrival of the Mongols of Ghengis Khan, and with them a time of massacre and upheaval. The scale of their cruelty was without precedent. In 1221 after an assault on Merv, the city lay under siege. When the siege was over, all of its inhabitants — one million — had been killed. Remarkably though, after a short period of time this invader's grip on power weakened with the rise of Persian administrators and scholars to positions of influence. Not for the first time in Iranian history was the indomitable Persian character recognised, with its ability to adapt under alien subjugation. The pagan Mongols had been assimilated and many subsequently converted to Islam.

In the 15th century a coalition of tribes rose to form the Safavid dynasty. Through them Shia Islam became the state religion. Notably they left a legacy of creativity and craftsmanship in textiles, ceramics, carpet-making and most prominently, architecture. The best examples remain in the magnificent blue mosques of Isfahan's Imam Square. The Safavid influence extended as far east as Delhi, but ambitious wars with Indian Mughals and the ever-advancing Ottoman Turks, brought their demise and crippled the economy.

Then came the Europeans. The spread of British and Russian imperialism of the 18th and 19th centuries, wars with both and naïve political and trade agreements resulted in the loss of territory, subservience and economic stagnation.

In the early years of the 20th century the British Navy ruled the seas. Mindful of growing German threats, the Royal Navy switched from coal to oil to power faster, more efficient ships. Although Britain had plentiful coal, oil had to be sourced, hence their interest in the newly discovered oilfields of Southwest Iran. The Anglo-Persian Oil Company, a majority British-owned enterprise, was set up and they moved in to secure the supply.

In 1926, facilitated by the British, a new leader, a former army sergeant, Reza Khan, came to power. He was an able Shah who achieved some success improving the country's transport infrastructure and expanding the educational system. He ruled with an iron fist, alienating all influential groups: the bazaaris, clerics, liberals, intellectuals and leading politicians. But it was his associations with the Nazis at the start of the Second World War which led to his downfall. The Allies couldn't accept this. Also, their interest in securing a supply line from the Gulf to Russia, led to British and Soviet forces invading in 1941. The Allies kept control until the end of the war, and the Shah's son, Mohammad Reza Shah Pahlavi was installed as a puppet monarch.

In 1951 after democratic parliamentary elections, a lawyer, Mohammad Mossadeq, became Prime Minister. Mossadeq's main aim was to nationalise Iranian oil, taking it out of the hands of the British. Unsurprisingly the British resisted, enforcing blockades which affected exports. Then they set about Mossadeq's removal. The Americans, concerned about rising Communist sentiment at that time, conspired with them in a CIA-led coup. Mossadeq fell and was allowed to live out his days under house arrest. The coup was a shameful episode in US and British international affairs. Here was a democratically elected leader forcibly ousted by vested foreign powers. But perhaps most significantly it damaged Iranian perceptions of the US. Like the British and Russians and centuries of invading foreign powers before, America could not now be trusted. The ramifications of this would be felt in future years.

Meanwhile the Shah remained an American proxy, taking control of government. The American influence deepened. The terms of the Anglo-Persian Oil Company's agreements were altered. 50 percent of profits remained in Iran, with 40 percent going to the US and 10 percent left to the British. An oil boom in the 1960s and early '70s generated huge revenues. Initially Iran did well. But the economy overheated. Inflation rocketed and the national purse was raided and squandered on fatuous military and civil engineering projects. The young Shah had delusions of grandeur and set about creating a 'Great Civilisation.' However state theft, cronyism and corruption were endemic. The people suffered. Unemployment and poverty grew. What's more, the lavish Western-orientated life-style of the Shah generated widespread resentment. He became deeply unpopular. Like his father, his rule was autocratic and ruthless. Dissenters were imprisoned, tortured and murdered by his notorious SAVAK, secret police. Eventually the people took to the streets, to be faced by army and police violence. This only caused further dissent, the flames of which were fanned by anti-Shah rhetoric from an outspoken cleric in exile, Ayatollah Khomeini. Anarchy and blood flowed in the streets and state forces became increasingly powerless to contain it. Mass desertions swept through the army and the people called for the Shah's head. In a sense they got it. On 16 January 1979 he fled into exile and died of cancer eighteen months later.

Out of this revolution came the new leader, Khomeini. Ruthlessly he took control, executing all senior figures of the Shah's administration as well as his own adversaries. Then he established his own regime. This was an Islamic one, with no monarch, a secular government, a re-written constitution and a president responsible for day to day affairs. All of it overseen by a cleric-dominated power structure answerable only to himself. Khomeini as Supreme Leader would have ultimate power. In the blink of an eye Iran moved from two extremes: a profligate, terrorising, Western-style monarchy to a theocratic, repressive republic founded on Sharia law. Press freedoms, civil rights and particularly the rights of women, were curtailed. This is broadly how Iran stands today.

However the new order was still in its infancy when a cataclysmic event began which was to have a devastating effect on the lives of all Iranians. In 1980 Saddam Hussein's armed forces invaded. The Iran-Iraq war was to last eight years. An estimated one million Iranians were injured and killed. The origins of this war are unclear: maybe Hussein saw an opportunity for territorial gain during Iran's vulnerable period of change, or maybe Shia propaganda during the Revolution incited Shi'ites in Iraq to rebel, forcing Hussein into action. Regardless, one unquestionable truth remains: the Iraqis were heavily aided and abetted by the US and other powers, prolonging the war and leading to the enormous loss of life on the Iranian side, not to mention the damage caused to the national psyche.

Thus, throughout the ages Iranians have endured wars and invasions, tyranny, conquests and re-conquests. They have had foreign laws, languages, religions and cultures foisted on them. But they have absorbed all these pressures, cleverly re-casting them to their own benefit. Moreover, they have kept their ancient Persian identity; an identity forged before the Arab invasion and the coming of Islam, and tempered long before today's clerical-led authority. They have a dignified belief in themselves. The impression I formed was of a people able to withstand all kinds of hardships, be it war, terror, famine or penury at the hands of any regime, domestic or foreign. What's more, they have the ability to see every regime out, including at some stage, the current, home-grown one.

We had cooled and rested sufficiently to move on. Beneath the entrance arch outside the mosque we met Reza. He was a mathematics lecturer who approached us in order to practice his English. I was curious to know how he felt about life in Iran — namely what was it like living under Sharia law and under a government controlled by Ayatollahs? So far, like most outsiders, I had little idea of what this was like and could only imagine it. Yet it came as no great surprise when he told me life was all right for most people. There was no war, no food shortages and no SAVAK secret police to terrorise anyone. Most people had work, public services such as hospitals and medical care ran well and the educational system is excellent. He acknowledged there were problems such as a weak economy, high unemployment, particularly among the youth and a drug problem in the cities. Nothing unique there, I thought.

He was of the view that some laws were draconian, for crimes such as adultery and blasphemy, but they affected few and most people tolerated them. He accepted the government censors all media. 'Everyone knows and puts up with this also.' The general feeling was, you can have a grievance against the authorities and you can grumble. That is OK. Just don't go around broadcasting it.

So why was I not surprised to hear all this? On the surface, daily life in Iran appears normal. Other than the low risk of kidnapping near the Pakistan border, the countryside is quite safe. Order reigns in the cities. There is little evidence of any crime and most people go about their lives freely, without any apparent threat. What's more, I found as an outsider and Westerner, I and others like me weren't just tolerated but treated with utmost respect.

Returning to the notion of Persian self-belief and sense of identity, I noted Reza exuded both. Strongly so. By drawing a metaphor from Ferdowsi's Shah-nameh, he confirmed my impression that these attributes are inherent to Persians. Ferdowsi describes the tyranny Persians faced while under Arab rule. Having been corrupted by a demon, Zahhak an Arab prince, kills his father to assume the mantle of King. He then makes plans for world domination. Earlier in his youth, Zahhak had been transformed by this demon into a three-headed monster, with snakes on either shoulder. Their appetite was ravenous, satisfied only by feeding them human brains daily. A failure to do this meant they would turn on Zahhak. Understandably he was tormented by this.

Zahhak was a creature of great vanity. One day he attempted to coerce all his subjects into signing a declaration confirming his greatness in order to prevent them rising against him. Most complied, but one, a blacksmith, Kaveh, whose two sons had been sacrificed to the snakes, refused. He tore up the declaration and raised his leather apron in an act of defiance. This struck a chord with many of his compatriots and emboldened, he led an assembly of tribes to the Alborz mountains. There they sought the leadership and support of their rightful Persian king, the young Fereydun. Fereydun listened and agreed to their request. Upon this they mounted an army and marched on the capital. Zahhak was away and when he returned he tried to reclaim what was his, but Fereydun struck him down with an ox-headed mace. Instead of killing him, Fereydun bound him in chains and brought him to the Alborz where he imprisoned him in a cave on Mount Damavand, Iran's highest mountain. There, starved of human brains, the snakes turned on Zahhak. So ended Arab rule and the restoration of Persian order. The underlying message is a powerful one — one not lost on modern Iranians. In the words of Reza:

'We were a great nation once, and a great empire. We still are a great people. We deserve to be treated as equals among other nations. To trade freely, to develop ourselves and be involved in international affairs. To contribute to the world.'

※ ※ ※ ※

Tuesday 16 September. We took another shared taxi north, to Yazd. Much of central Iran is scrub desert, largely flat with a few hills. To the west lies the Zagros mountain range, while to the north above Tehran, the volcanic Alborz mountains hem the south coast of the Caspian Sea. Predictably the journey was hot and the surroundings featureless, other than some farms with wide desert fields of pistachio. Like Bam's Agh, I was once more impressed by how the locals could harness enough water from such arid earth to irrigate the crops.

Venturing through Iran I met a number of foreigners. Some were doing trips around Turkey and the Middle East. A few like myself were travelling east to west, but many more were going in the other direction on much the same route. Given the shared Iranian leg linking the cities, several meetings wouldn't be uncommon. Stories and experiences get swapped and tips passed on. Much talk focuses on shelter. Once a good hostel or hotel is known about, word quickly spreads. As a result it is easy to meet the same people in different places at different times. One such popular place is the Silk Road Hotel in Yazd where, with the Spaniards, I spent a few days. I found its atmosphere convivial and its comforts homely. So much so I found myself hard-pressed to leave. I also found myself advising those heading east to savour the luxury while they could.

There were some curious people travelling east. I met four middle-aged fellas — two Germans, an Aussie and a Brit — motorcycling to Kathmandu. I felt they were doing the right thing; travelling as a unit, physically and psycho-logically supporting one another over such a long, demanding journey. Their bikes were modern and well-equipped, BMW boxers and Africa Twins. As to their reliability, there was no question. Comparing the approach these men were taking to my original plan, namely a solo run on a second-hand Bullet from Nepal home, made me think I was daft. Once again I was glad that idea had been scrapped.

Then there were Ben and Sylvie, a French couple cycling from the UK to China. Nothing extraordinary there, you might say. The thing was their bicycles weren't the conventional upright ones, but recumbents, where you're lying on your back, low down, with your legs out in front of you. They both had panniers and drew a compact trailer. In order to help being seen, both had small tricolours flying from antennae sticking above their back wheels. I had seen such machines once or twice at home but I doubted if anyone east of the Bosphorus ever had. One thing was certain, this couple would soon be the talk of every town and village from Iran to Beijing.

They wouldn't be the only ones. Weeks later while in Istanbul I met a 24-year-old English lad who was also heading east, on a solo world trip. Only he was riding an even more unlikely bike: a small-wheeled, Brompton fold-up commuter type. Mad dogs and Englishmen, I thought.

Another interesting character I met in Yazd was Alby, a long-haired photographer and scuba diver from London. He and a pal were journeying from England to Nepal on an indirect route via the deserts of North Africa. Their vehicle was well suited for the purpose, being a boxy Landrover that had a previous incarnation towing Rapier missiles for the British Army. Alby had a name for it: 'Stumpy.'

'She's more used to carrying weapons than people,' he claimed.

'There's plenty of room in her all the same,' I said as I admired it. Stumpy was part-tank, part-house, part-Tonka toy. I asked him if he found himself picking up many passengers, fellow travellers, along the way.

'Oh all the time. I've had lots so far. The thing is most of them get quite attached to her. They tend to stay a long time and never want to leave. Once or twice I've had to park up for longer than I intended, just so as they get the message. You know what I mean?'

❄ ❄ ❄ ❄

Wednesday 17 September. One of the most interesting things about Yazd is religion. Not Islam but one of the world's oldest — Zoroastrianism. It is a monotheistic faith which influenced the development of Judaism, Christianity and Islam. Its doctrine is simple. There is good and there is evil. A follower should aim for the former to please god, Mazda. Direction for salvation is summed up in the oft-quoted phrase 'Good Thoughts, Good Words, Good Deeds.' Zoroaster's teachings are documented in a sacred text, the Avesta. Prayer ceremonies led by priests are held at fire temples. Fire is not worshipped but seen as symbolic, a representation of Mazda. A temple's flame is never extinguished. On a tour of Yazd's temple I learned its fire, glowing in an urn fuelled by pomegranate wood, had been burning for over 1,500 years.

Like Buddhism, the natural elements of earth, fire, wind and water are associated with divinity and purity.

However this faith is under threat and has been for some time. It is thought there are only about 140,000 Zoroastrians in the world today. The majority of them live in India. Persecution in the 10th century drove them out of Iran, whereupon most settled around present-day Mumbai. Today the number in Iran is estimated to be 30,000. Although tolerated by the Islamic regime, many choose to emigrate. This causes a problem as it disconnects social bonds and reduces the chance of marrying within the religion. Sharia law doesn't help as it propounds conversion to Islam. This causes more problems as relatives of former believers find themselves denied of inheritance. Only Muslims may inherit. Worse, apostasy, by way of reversion to the former faith, is punishable by death.

One of the unusual aspects of this faith is its funeral rites. Upon death a corpse is kept in a room for three days. A dog is brought to visit it five times a day and a fire is kept in the room after the first day. Priests conduct purification ceremonies. Then it is carried to the summit of a designated hill outside the town. This hill is known as a Tower of Silence. Tower guardians remove the clothing and place the corpse onto a wide circle on the ground. There are three circles, one each for men, women and children. There, exposed to the elements, in the same manner as Tibetan sky burials, the corpse is eaten by vultures. The remaining bones, dried by the sun, are swept into a central stone pit. The reason for all this is to prevent defilement of the earth, which is considered sacred. Traditionally Zoroastrians avoided burying their dead. However, as is often the case, over time traditions change. After visiting Yazd's Tower of Silence we inspected a nearby graveyard. It wasn't old and most of the graves had uniform headstones. But the interesting thing was how the plots were made. All remains laid to rest were encased in concrete. By this measure Zoroastrians accept that the surrounding soil remains unblemished.

Mehdi, a recent university graduate and tour guide, had been showing us around. Near the Tower the Spanish lads took photographs of him alongside the Tower guardian. Both men were on the same level sitting down. The contrast they made was remarkable, representing two different types of Iran, old and new. The guardian was an elderly gent of sun-beaten complexion, dressed in worn clothes and a loose turban. His education was little and he had worked as keeper of the Tower all his life. Translating, Mehdi told us he was the last Tower guardian left in Iran. Mehdi on the other hand, was young. He had a business degree, spoke English, ran his own tourist business and was very familiar with the internet and communication technologies. Also, he dressed sharply in Western-style clothes and drove his own car.

Mehdi and I chatted at length. I was still interested in getting a sense of life in Iran. As it turned out he had roughly the same opinions on his country and its governance as Reza. He verified the positive aspects of peace, education, health and the dissatisfying nature of a poor economy, high unemployment and living under strict laws. Both credit and blame lay with the government. He also stressed the responsibility that lay on foreign governments for prohibiting Iran from trading freely on international markets, importing and exporting. He was referring to UN Security Council sanctions which had been in place to varying degrees since the Revolution.

We discussed Iranian youth and I expressed the view that their numbers are great, many seemed well educated and have no fears of war or state terror. I noticed they are exposed to foreign influences, through satellite television and the internet. Hence, from all this they would have high expectations for themselves. However one thing perplexed me. If people were dissatisfied with how their country is managed and the way they were being led, then surely this mass of youth would be agitating for a regime change? If so, then why weren't they, or why hadn't they before now? After all, this same stifling, dictatorial admin-istration had been in power, with negligible change since the Khomeini-led revolution of '79. Mehdi's response was frank but sadly deflating:

'But most of us young Iranians were born after '79. This is our normal. We don't know anything else.'

EIGHT

A Question of Rights

Thursday 18 September. We took another day-tour with Mehdi. This time to Meybod, a town north of Yazd. We visited an old governor's house containing ornamental stained-glass windows and well-tended gardens. This house failed to impress me, knowing its purpose and the privilege associated with its former occupants. However one feature did — its air-conditioning — developed by the Persians centuries ago. Here, above the foyer, stands a tall, square wind-tower. Slits angled at the top, catch the prevailing winds which sink to the tower's base, cooling as they go. They stream across a pool of cold water, cooling further before dispersing around the house. The simplicity and practicality is brilliant.

Aquatic innovation could be found elsewhere. Mehdi took us to an old ice-house; a thick-walled, mud bricked dome, around 25 metres high and wide, with a small round hole at its apex for light. Inside was a large pit and outside, a canal. Again, the idea was simple. In winter water in the canal froze. Chunks of ice were carried from here into the house and thrown into the pit. Once full, the pit was covered by a layer of adobe for insulation. Incredibly the ice would remain for up to a year, throughout long, hot summers where temperatures can reach 40° Celsius. Who would have thought in the days before refrigeration, ice could be found in Iran?

Best of all was the pigeon tower. This was another old mud-brick and adobe construction, 20 metres high, 15 wide, and round like a Martello tower. Like the ice-house, it had long been out of use. Inside there were three levels of circular walls, the entire area made up of pigeon holes. There were entry and exit points on the roof, plus air vents for cooling. Its purpose was to attract as many pigeons as possible in order to collect their droppings from each hole. This was then used as fertiliser by farmers growing vegetables. Pigeon dirt is far superior to that of camel, horse, donkey and sheep, and therefore highly prized. I would never have known.

The tower had two clever features that impressed me and my Spanish friends. Once more, they were both very simple. Outside, the roof and upper section were painted red and beige to attract the birds because these are the typical colours of their nests. Also, a very smooth band of adobe plaster one metre wide and halfway up the wall, encircles the outside. Above this, the wall's gradient changes to a slight overhang. The reason? To prevent opportunistic snakes slithering up the walls and into the tower. If the lack of friction didn't repel them, then gravity did. Ingenious!

The only drawback I could see with the tower lay with the farmers who had used it. They had to climb inside and go from hole to hole, scraping out the dirt. This couldn't have been easy, especially in the heat and with birds flustering all around. And did I say how many holes there were? From what I could see, at least two thousand.

Friday 19 September. Another daytrip out of Yazd. This time to the Zoroastrian holy site of Chak Chak. Legend has it during the Arab invasion a local Sassanid King, fearing for his children, gave each of them a torch from their temple's eternal flame and ordered them to flee. One of them, a princess, made it to the hills with the Arabs giving chase. Not wishing to be captured she disappeared into a cave, never to be seen again. In her place a stream emerged at the cave mouth which has been dripping down the entrance ever since. The name Chak Chak means 'drip drip.'

We arrived to find a glass conservatory covering the cave exterior, a symbolic fire burning at the entrance and a group of women preparing for a feast day. There were very few men.

Contemporary princesses, I thought. Still keepers of the flame.

While here I was to learn that this religion promotes gender equality. Women can become high-priests, wielding the same powers as men. This helped to form my view that throughout Iran the influence of women, though far from ideal, was greater than I had expected. They can, as mentioned, hold high positions in all areas of society. They can choose their husbands or get a divorce. Also traditionally, by meeting other women in communal places such as bazaars and bath-houses, they have arranged marriages for their sons and daughters. They have, and continue to be, the understated architects of Iranian society.

Saturday 20 September. The Spanish lads departed for Tehran. I left for Isfahan. It was tempting to remain in Yazd. I was getting known, enjoying the craic and the Silk Road Hotel was too comfortable a place to hang around and doss. But sometimes a man must have purpose. It was best to move on.

Word from the grapevine suggested I doss at Isfahan's Amir Kabir hostel. But when I got there my occasionally felt mood of indifference came over me. I'd had enough of meeting new people for the time being; of having to introduce myself and give my story, while at the same time asking and listening to others on theirs. That's the nature of travel — moods can change — and it's not always motivating. All the more so when bonds, quickly formed, get quickly broken. So this time I didn't fancy a dormitory or a shared room. I wanted to be alone so I asked for a single room. But there were none. The best thing available was a twin to share, or I could pay double and have the whole room to myself. I considered this and was very tempted by the latter. It meant more freedom, physically and psychologically. More peace of mind. After all, who normally likes sharing a room with a complete stranger? But something told me not to do this. Two things, actually. For one, the hostel would be full and someone might need that bed. But the bigger reason was for the sense of the unexpected. Who could tell what kind of person might take that bed? They could be the greatest bore, or perhaps the most interesting person on earth. I would never find out if I kept the room to myself. Curiosity got the better of me again. I took the room, choosing to share.

Was I glad I did? If I hadn't I would never have met Klaus Peter. Otherwise known as KP. He was a German in his mid-thirties who had been travelling throughout Asia alone on his motorbike. Originally he had set out from Hamburg to ride to Australia, however after two years, he got as far as Indonesia then had a change of mind. He had grown so accustomed to life in Asia that the thought of a return to the West, with all its affluence and cultural blandness, became anathema to him.

'I thought if I went to Australia it would only be the same as everywhere else. I might as well have stayed in Germany,' he said.

I knew what he meant. Travel in Asia is a journey of experience, not a mindless, quick commute. So what does he do only turn the bike around and ride back across Asia again. It had been four years since he left Hamburg and now he was making his way home.

We stayed up late, exchanging stories of our travels, of life in India and of our lives at home. For KP, his adventure had been life-changing in part. In Germany he had trained and worked as an electrician. But once he reached India he learned how to be a tattoo artist, making enough money to keep himself and the bike. He would travel for a while, then stop in one place for a few weeks or months to ply the new craft. He enjoyed this work, preferring the traditional, slow method of Indian ink and bamboo needles, as opposed to using an electrical device.

'The hardest part was starting out and getting my first customer,' he recalled with a smile. 'Fortunately for both of us he was happy with my design.'

Now satisfied with his progress, KP was determined to continue with his new-found career in Germany.

'Do you think you'll ever go back to electrical work?' I asked.

'I hope never.'

It was quite a change for him, or for anyone. But there were other more immediate things which he hoped hadn't changed; things at home which he had been looking forward to. Things that had crossed my mind also.

'Like my mothers cooking and my own bed.'

'Hear hear,' I said.

❄ ❄ ❄ ❄

Sunday 21 September. I helped KP to load his bike, before seeing him off. Then I wandered down to Imam Square. It was a hot, clear day and I was taken by the splendour of mosques, particularly Imam mosque with its huge turquoise dome, and the surrounding minarets of intricate floral and geometric patterns. The square is part of the city's bazaar, and walking through its arcades, I saw craftsmen at work. A cloth shop caught my eye. Stepping inside, I studied a printer at work. He was absorbed in his task of stamping paisley designs on a pale cotton cloth using a pearwood block. Different patterns and inks went with different blocks, whereby an overall design was built up. The job demanded patience and careful hand to eye co-ordination. One slip meant hours of work undone.

In this shop I met Mohsen, a well-spoken individual in his late twenties, who owned a business selling Persian carpets. I liked him. I knew he was scouting for business but he wasn't pushy. I asked him about life in Iran. Like Reza and Mehdi, he felt life was OK, but he wished he had more freedom and that young people in general had more freedom. He cited the taboo around personal relationships. If an unmarried couple are seen cavorting by the police or Revolutionary Guards, they can be detained, lectured and warned about the dangers of un-Islamic behaviour. Parents can also be informed. If found in a house together, the authorities can assume sexual activity to have taken place, even if not. Again, the couple can be detained and the parents told.

Pressure would then be applied on the hapless pair to get married, or face unending harassment from the authorities, the clerics and society. Given this, I asked Mohsen if he had a girlfriend. Perhaps wisely he did not answer, though I detected a smile.

Limits to freedom didn't appear to be confined to dalliances either. Mohsen described how he fell foul of the law once when he was seen with a Dutch woman on Imam Square.

'The police were suspicious. They thought I might be giving away political or security secrets to a spy. Me? What would I know about such things? And how could I do that? I was just trying to sell carpets.'

He was brought to the barracks, interrogated for several hours, then driven out to the desert and abandoned. With no shelter, money or food, he had to hitch home, returning in the dead of night. The experience frightened him.

'The police — they are hard on you. I was scared.'

I could believe him, recalling my own brush with the law in Zahedan — the Kalashnikov kid with hate-filled eyes and a crazed sense of power. I could well imagine the intimidation a lone Iranian might feel if several such blackguards ganged up on him.

Changing tack, I asked about married types and the implications if one or more have an affair. Mohsen explained. Should that happen, the offended partner has a right to a divorce and the offending couple must then marry. If the jilted one refuses to divorce or refuses a pardon, or if the offending couple refuse to marry, then they are liable to a punishment of death, often by stoning. The message I was getting here was of the immutable power of Sharia law, where religion and state know best, where mercies are few and individual freedoms must be curbed.

But the most absurd thing I was to learn was the authorities' view on prostitution. In Iranian law a man can be with a prostitute even if he is married. However he must get permission first. He goes to his mullah, explains his wish and if the mullah obliges, he is given a note granting permission to take another woman as a wife, temporarily. The mullah gets a commission for this service. Then if the man is found with this new woman by the police or Revolutionary Guards, he merely has to present the note and all is fine. The irony of it wasn't lost on me.

'So what if a woman wants a similar service, Mohsen, from a man or another woman? Can she go to her mullah and get the same deal?'

'No,' he implored. 'That is impossible.'

We made our way over to his shop. He had all kinds of carpets on the floor and walls. I was drawn to some tribal kilims woven by nomadic Kurds of the Caspian. They were crude and beautiful with small human figures and motifs of their natural environment: peacocks, camels, butterflies, birds and mountains. Some had curious S-shaped patterns which I assumed to be snakes. But not so.

'They are the lock to guard against the evil eye,' said Mohsen.

'Lock? Evil eye?' I said, wondering. 'Please, tell me more.'

He explained that in Iran if someone is jealous of you over something you have, they have the power to put a curse on you, causing you or your possession some harm. This is known as the curse of the evil eye. Earlier I had noticed small, round, glass ornaments, of the shape and colour of blue eyes for sale in the Square. The S-shaped lock, as Mohsen described, is a hook that symbolically pierces the eye, nullifying its curse. He gave me some stories of the evil eye at work. One was about the time he started a shop selling household goods. He was cleaning a pair of candleholders on display in the window when a neighbour, a competitor, called by.

'This is a nice shop you have,' said the neighbour, disingenuously. 'And they are pretty candleholders.'

Mohsen understood the caper. He knew this neighbour had wanted his premises, only to lose out as Mohsen out-bid him for it. Now he was jealous of Mohsen and wished him no good. Not long afterwards a light fitting in the window fell from the ceiling and broke both candleholders. The curse of the evil eye. However I wasn't convinced.

'Come on, Mohsen, that's all nonsense.' I said. 'All superstition. What happened there was just co-incidence.'

But he was adamant. 'No, it is true. I didn't believe in the evil eye until it happened. But now I do. It is real.'

Another story concerned his father who made a living driving an old Mercedes bus. Once again, a jealous rival passed by with a veiled remark.

'That may be an old bus but the engines in them are great.'

Within days, having run smoothly for years, the engine seized up. It cost Mohsen senior a small fortune in repairs and lost earnings to get it working again.

Later that night I wandered into a teahouse near the Amir Kabir. It was still Ramadan, though after sundown. People had eaten and men were inside smoking hookahs. I was still sceptical about this evil eye business. One man, Hamed, saw I was alone and invited me to share a pipe with him, which I did. Hamed worked in the catering trade. I explained the evil eye conversation I had earlier and the difficulty I had believing it. But he also held the same faith as Mohsen.

'The evil eye is true. It is written in the Koran. There is a verse which, if you put on the door of your house, will protect you from badness.'

'Just like the lock?'

'Yes.'

Then he described his experiences, or more accurately, his father's. This elder who lived in a village, had a valuable milch cow. One day he placed a bell around its neck to help him track it whenever it strayed. A woman from the same village met him with the cow and commented on what a fine bell it was. Shortly after, the bell broke into pieces. But in the greater scheme of things this event remained insignificant. Worse was to befall this man. When Hamed junior was fifteen his father, having moved to the city, embarked on a career in the hotel industry. He bought an old guesthouse and set about renovating it. During these works, as expected, neighbours, competitors and other parties came by. Most expressed support and approval, but there were critics. Generally though, Hamed the elder was happy. As a matter of course, he decided to get a medical check. His physician examined him and declared him fit and healthy. Everything was going well. One week later, he collapsed, dead. The evil eye at work again.

I had heard enough now, my scepticism had waned. Perhaps there was some substance in the curse. After all, many different cultures have their superstitions. Take Hoodoo in African-American communities for example. Or the Irish piseog. Or as I discovered earlier, the ambiguous power of Hadimba in Manali. Arguably if you live in a culture and you believe its superstitions, then they must carry an element of truth.

❋ ❋ ❋ ❋

Monday 22 September. A holy day today, commemorating the death of Ali. Ali was a cousin of the Prophet Mohammad and husband of the Prophet's daughter, Fatima. He was the fourth caliph — leader of the believers — hence the most influential being in the 7th century Islamic world. The deaths of his two sons, Hossein in battle and Hassan by poisoning, denied what many followers believed was the rightful bloodline to the prophet, and as such, the rightful leadership. These followers later came to be known as Shi'ites. The caliphate went to another, larger group, the Sunnis, and a schism emerged between both groups. The Arab invasions brought Shi'ism to Persia, where it grew, being declared the state religion by the Safavids in 1501. Today Shi'ites account for 89 percent of a 99 percent Muslim population of Iran.

I wandered downtown. Everywhere was closed. I crossed the long Si-O-She bridge, hoping to get a look at an Armenian cathedral, but it was also closed. I wound up near the bridge by the Zayandeh river.

The murals. They're everywhere, I thought.

Nearby on the gable of a large modern hotel was the austere-looking face of the country's Supreme Leader, Ayatollah Khamenei. Some nations are littered with statues of their rulers, usually wanton dictators with penchants for seeing three-dimensional representations of themselves. In Iran it is slightly different. Images work best. Everywhere I went I kept seeing Khamenei's face, or the dour mug of his predecessor Khomeini, plastered on outside walls or hanging up in offices, banks, hotels, post offices and bus stations. Often both faces can be seen together, put there by loyalists no doubt. I suspected before the revolution these same spaces were filled with portraits of the Shah, and possibly put there under duress.

The Shah was a monster. Using revenue from oil exports he attempted to impose his idea of a 'Great Civilisation' on his people. Essentially a feckless programme of modernity, it became one of colossal wastage. Vast sums were squandered on the armed forces — on tanks, planes and helicopters that no one knew how to use, let alone maintain. Money was poured into factories, power plants and machines that no one knew how to assemble. Mountains of imported goods lay idle and rotting in ports as no one had any coherent plan for them. Iran had no technologists — no specialists — to create this 'Great Civilisation.' So the Shah opened the public purse and imported them, by the plane-load. Engineers, architects, electricians, mechanics, accountants, chemical technologists, military experts and so forth, from the US, Europe and Asia now thronged the streets of the cities. His cronies joined the party, amassing fortunes out of hare-brained state contracts. Meanwhile the people looked on in disbelief, humiliated by their leader's arrogance and made to feel inferior by the presence of so many foreigners. On top of this they were subjected to the physical and psychological terror of SAVAK, the Shah's secret police. So the people turned to their mullahs and rebelled. They took to the streets in waves of demonstrations, shouting 'Death to the Shah,' while facing the army's guns. Massacres followed. But they won. The Shah's reign ended when he was forced into exile.

Out of this ferment a new leadership emerged in the form of Ayatollah Ruhollah Khomeini; a revered cleric and the figurehead of anti-Shah dissent. Through him a tyrannical monarch had been swept away, but a new era of autocracy under the cloak of Islam had begun.

Khomeini was cunning. In the early days he ruthlessly set about destroying all opposition to his rule. He re-created the Majles — national Parliament. Then he established an intricate web of public offices, councils and assemblies — most cleric-led — to impose Islamic order and to ensure that he, as Supreme Leader, held ultimate power at all time. This included his own private army, the Revolutionary Guards, plus a strong-arm militia, the Basij — the kind of thugs you need to stamp out dissent, particularly during an election.

'Dissent cannot be tolerated. Neither can liberal democracy. We must jail subversives, activists, journalists, reformists, insubordinators. There can be no threats. We must defend Islam. We must protect ourselves.' This has been the construct by which Khomeini led until his death in 1989, and his successor, Khamenei now leads. Thus since '79, a hard-line religious head of state, surrounded by ultra-conservative clerics, has ruled Iran. Efforts at reform were attempted by a liberal-minded President Khatami between 1997 and 2004. But they were snuffed out by the same ultra-conservatives determined to maintain power and keep the status quo.

Khomeini may once have been applauded in those heady days of '79, but few expected the kind of society he engineered. Neither did they expect to find themselves estranged from the world.

Meanwhile the day to day affairs of running the country fall to the President, currently the ultra-conservative layman and former Revolutionary Guard commander, Mahmoud Ahmadinejad. Since taking office in 2005 he has made sure the Iranian economy has remained in the doldrums. Cronyism and corruption is rife. Services are inefficient and underdeveloped. Wastage and monopolisation is common. Examining the socio-economics, the statistics are telling. In 2007 the rate of inflation was 25 percent and the unemployment rate 20 percent. Large numbers when you consider a population of 74.2 million. Many are forced to do two or three jobs to get by. As for private enterprise, given the iron grip of the state, with warped regulation and cack-handed economic management plus UN trade sanctions and political uncertainty, Iran has a hard time finding investors. As a country, its only saving grace is the chief export, oil. Iran has the second largest deposits of oil and gas in the world, which account for 80 percent of its export revenue. Yet incredibly, the country is forced to import 40 percent of its oil for its own consumption, as its capacity to refine what it needs is deficient. Compounding all this is a vast scheme of state subsidies, where oil revenue is used to keep energy and food prices down. This has had a vicious-circle effect, as cheap subsidised oil brings on increased demand, hence greater imports. In 2007 when government attempts were made to introduce rationing, there was widespread public unrest. Why? Because in the cities and towns, many Iranians depend on taxi-driving as that second or third job to make ends meet. That said, continuing with subsidisation is unsustainable. It uses up vital revenue which would be better served on energy reform. Also, should the price of a barrel of oil plummet, then the Iranian economy would be in serious trouble. Interestingly some analysts maintain Ahmadinejad *et al* choose to uphold a truculent stance on international affairs in order to maintain instability in the Middle East and a high price for oil. Other commentators claim Ahmadinejad's offensive rhetoric on Israel and the denial of the Holocaust, plus his insistence on Iran developing nuclear technology are attempts to distract from his domestic failures as well as sabre-rattling on greater regional domination.

Anyway, the stranglehold of Ahmadinejad's leadership, with his strings pulled by Khamenei, is a mismanagement of Iran's economy and disservice to the people. Today, of the 800,000 young people who enter the labour market each year, only half can expect to find work. Furthermore, an estimated 150,000 university graduates emigrate each year. And unlike the reciprocal flow of oil, educated émigrés seldom return.

Earlier, before seeing the murals, I was in a sandwich shop near the Armenian cathedral. I struck up a conversation of sorts with three fellas working behind the counter. A television sat in the corner and the news came on. Ahmadinejad appeared, giving a speech at the UN headquarters in New York. The three men stopped what they were doing to pull faces and make rude finger gestures at their puppet president. They wanted me to know how they felt. This was clear, and it seemed consistent with views others had expressed to me. It made me wonder. They, the people, can moan and complain all right. But how bad does an economy and a society have to get before they rise up demanding change?

Since '79 public, democratic voting rights are tokenistic. Candidates for Parliament are elected by public vote right enough. But any decision made by Parliament can be quashed by the Guardian Council — the Supreme Leader's men. The office of President is also open to public vote. However all such candidates are vetted and decided upon by the Guardian Council first. This eliminates liberals, reformists, opponents of the Supreme Leader or influential clerics. Thus with control of the law, control of the press, and a subservient militia enforcing its will, Khamenei and company have every outlet for self-determination and free expression stitched up.

In the teahouse I touched upon this with Hamed. We talked about Khatami, the liberal-minded president who tried to introduce legal, economic, social and political reforms between 1997 and 2004. He offered a ray of hope to Hamed and millions of others for change. But his efforts were blocked by Majles hardliners and he failed. Tellingly in the 2005 Presidential Election, all of his reformist candidates were barred from the race.

'Then we got Ahmadinejad,' said Hamed, cynically.

'But there were other candidates in that race, including the moderate, Rafsanjani,' I said. 'Was Ahmadinejad a surprise?'

'Yes.'

I pictured the Basji out in numbers, intimidating voters, stuffing the ballot boxes and manipulating the count.

'So tell me Hamed, do you think that election was rigged?'

'Yes.'

I guessed as much. Hearing this made me reach my own cynical conclusion: that Iran is a country where its citizens have a right to vote all right. But they've no say in who they wish to vote for, nor any meaningful say as to who gets elected.

Vive la Révolution.

NINE

Damavand

Tuesday 23 September. I took the night bus to Tehran. The plan was to get to the Alborz mountains and try and climb Damavand, Iran's highest peak. I still carried bulky mountain gear, such as boots, a sleeping bag and tent for this project, and I was looking forward to getting rid of it later by posting it home once back in Tehran.

It was black outside as we drove through the desert. Thoughts came and went. All kinds of things. I imagined how Mohsen must have felt after his police grilling — cold alone and frightened. And then an unrelated picture; Joss Lynam stuck out here with a broken vehicle on his way home from India in 1958.

Back in those days, before air travel became common and cheap, expeditions to the Himalayas by Europeans were long, arduous affairs, with people and supplies freighted over land and sea. In September 1958 Joss, having made the first explorations of the Gyundi valleys in Spiti, was on his way home in a four-wheeled drive Austin Gypsy. Only four hundred miles south of Tehran a spring broke in the rear wheel assembly, immobilising them for a week. Joss and another passed the time with the vehicle, while the others went to get a tow-truck in Tehran. From his notes he describes his experience of living off the last of their hill food: *tea and bully beef in a semi-liquid condition,* and fruit and bread given to them by passing lorry drivers. It was no picnic. Then when they got to Tehran they spent another week waiting for a part to be air-lifted from England. There he describes being almost penniless and dossing in the cheapest of places, eating *cornflakes, milk and doughnuts.* Further on, the road wasn't kind to them either. He mentions the unmetalled kind, of *corrugated gravel, a series of hollows and ridges, where shock absorbers are almost useless,* and where party and vehicle are *rocked around like a dinghy in a choppy sea.* European standards fare little better as he describes *rutted tracks and roads that looked as though shelled.* As for rest, he mentions *sleeping in ploughed fields.*

Now here was I, exactly fifty years to the month later, re-tracing his steps in an air-conditioned coach on a perfectly smooth road, and with plenty of food. The lap of luxury. I wondered what Joss might say if saw me. I pictured him in his study, grumbling:

'Spoiled is not the word … '

❄ ❄ ❄ ❄

1958. Another era, another world. The rise of atomic weapons. The Cold War. It can be said a cold war still exists between the US and Iran. Presently Iran is trying to develop its nuclear capability. Ahmadinejad and company maintain this is purely for peaceful purposes, namely securing an energy supply for the future. There may be some truth in this. However I can't help thinking Iran doesn't need expensively produced nuclear energy. It has enough oil to power itself indefinitely. It has endless solar potential. There is enough empty desert to fill with solar panels that would generate enough electricity to power the Middle East. As for wind and geothermal options? Having seen the brilliant air-conditioning and water-management systems built by ancient Persians, I am convinced modern Iranians can be world-beaters in such fields if so directed.

For me, on the nuclear question, the Khamenei-Ahmadinejad pretence is just that. A lie. That said, why wouldn't they build the bomb? One could argue, with some justification, they do so to guard themselves. Their near neighbours have it: Pakistan, Israel, Russia, and the other power that stays in constant, close proximity, the US. If they have it, then why shouldn't Iran? After all, which of those countries has the right to deny them? Moreover, which of those states has a right to have it? The answer on both counts, is none. But given this, one has to ask why is the US in particular so determined in denying them? They do so by imposing economic sanctions on Iran, and by using their clout at the UN Security Council to force other countries to do likewise. In other words by choking Iran's ability to trade internationally, they prevent it gaining the technological means for nuclear activities. These measures also prevent Iran from doing business for legitimate economic reasons. Hypocritically though, exceptions are made for the export of goods considered important to the US or its allies, like oil. Personally, I don't agree with Iran getting hold of nuclear weapons, in the same way I don't agree with other states having them, but neither do I agree with the US and its policy on Iran — be it now or in the past. I strongly oppose it. The US will do whatever it takes to protect its own interests and hegemony. If that means surreptitiously or otherwise, by manipulating or exploiting a country, then so be it. If that means installing a proxy like Shah Reza, and propping up tyrants, then so be it. Or worse, invading a country like Iraq and destroying it, then also be it. The end justifies the means.

It is understandable that Iranians feel enmity towards the US, or more precisely, enmity towards successive US governments. The fact is the US has behaved abominably towards Iran. For a start, during the Second World War, Roosevelt allowed Churchill and Stalin invade a non-aggressive Iran, in order to secure a supply line from the Persian Gulf to Russia. Then in '53 the CIA led a coup to remove the only democratically-elected Iranian leader, Mohammad Mossadeq — a lawyer of integrity. His unpardonable act was to retrieve Iranian oil from US and British control. Once he was dealt with, the US and British took back the oil, with the Americans increasing their stake. They then made sure a now unpopular Shah remained head of state. But their finest performance came in the 1980's with Saddam Hussein's invasion. For eight years the Americans aided and abetted Iraq in a war costing the lives of one million Iranians. The war ended in a stalemate. Meanwhile, since the Revolution, the US has been the main champion of UN sanctions to keep Iran politically and economically isolated. And to cap it all, in 2002, while planning his own invasion of Iraq, George W. Bush described Iran as being part of an 'axis of evil.' A fine compliment to pay any people. With such an illustrious record, is it any surprise today that comments decrying the US are heard from Iran's leaders, and anti-American demonstrations take place on Tehran streets?

❄ ❄ ❄ ❄

Wednesday 24 September, Tehran. The Naderi Hotel was a recommendation I heard through the grapevine. The plan was to spend the night here and set out for Damavand the next day. But when I got there two grumpy old men in string vests fobbed me off. They, the staff, had been sleeping on lobby couches and I had the impertinence to waken them. Instead I had breakfast at a neighbouring hotel and made off for the Alborz straight after.

Damavand (5,621 metres) is a free-standing, active volcano, although its last eruption is little known. The bus snaked through the mountains. Coming out of a bend, as if a curtain was raised, Damavand appeared. It is a perfect cone, brown, with minor, crease-like, ridges. A dusting of snow covered its upper reaches and a thin plume rose from its summit. Only this wasn't cloud, but sulphurous gas. The simmering volcano. The highest in the Middle East and Asia.

My expectation was that this would be my last mountaineering project for the summer. Like Konchok, it wouldn't pose any technical difficulty.

Nonetheless, it would be a new place, a fresh experience, a chance for exercise and a change from the road. Also I was hopeful I might get a view of the Caspian Sea from its summit.

The village of Reyneh lies a couple of miles from its base. I walked into a guesthouse owned by two middle-aged brothers, Ahmad and Reza Faramarzpour. There was no grumpiness this time, only welcoming arms and smiles with dollar signs. Both men worked as guides, bringing tourists up the mountain. Their father had been a guide before them and their guesthouse had been in operation since 1966. Ahmad showed me the guest-books. Both men were very proud of all those who had availed of their services down through the years and who had left complimentary messages. Leafing through, I noted many nationalities: Japanese, Czech, Slovak, German, English, French, Canadian, Pole. But there was one noticeable omission:

'You haven't had any Americans here for a while, have you?'

'No.' They smiled.

Hardly a surprise. The books were of historical note, with incidental references to the 'Iron Curtain' and a 'Free Shah Iran.' There were scribbles by European travellers and hippies from the late '60s and early '70s on their way to and from the sub-continent, and notes from climbers on their way home from Himalayan expeditions. One stood out. It was by a Polish team from October 1971 who, having made the first ascent of Kunyang Chhish (7,852 metres) in the Karakoram, climbed Damavand on their home journey. Six names were listed. What they said was little. Of greater significance was who they were. Two names registered with me. One was Krzysztof Cielecki who, in 1968, put up a new route on the Eiger's North Pillar. The other, Zygmunt Heinrich, was a giant in world mountaineering. Heinrich was part of a band of tough Polish climbers of the '70s and '80s who made the first winter ascents of several of the world's highest mountains. He was a member of the team that climbed Everest in the winter of 1980 and, in the winter of '85, partnering with Jerzy Kukuczka, established a new route on Cho Oyu. He partnered with Kukuczka again that year to make the first ascent of Nanga Parbat's Southeast Pillar. But then tragedy stuck in '89 when he was killed in an avalanche back on Everest. These were extraordinary men who rose above the hardships of life under Communism to do things no one else dared to dream of, let alone attempt. Financially and operationally, how they did so was remarkable. With no money and the zloty being almost worthless on international markets, they raised funds, legitimately and otherwise, through importing and exporting. They loaded cheap Polish crystal, whiskey and cameras onto their lorries to sell in the Asian bazaars as they made their way to the Himalayas, while return journeys saw them bringing back piles of silk from Delhi, sheep-skins from Kabul and jeans from Istanbul. All this stuff served European demands and generated a handsome profit. Their climbing equipment was mostly improvised — car parts being the prime source — as wheel nuts and pinions made acceptable chocks, while seat belts cut up and tied made workable harnesses. Once on the big mountains, they tackled them with extraordinary stoicism, persevering through unimaginable cold, storms and high winds, as well as overcoming the usual hazards of avalanche, crevasse, serac and rock fall, low oxygen levels, dehydration, sickness and oedemas. Therefore it's not surprising they earned a reputation that endures today ... no one does pain like the Poles.

Spurning their offer of guidance, I asked the brothers if they had a map. They produced one. It was laughable, being a child-like stick drawing of a hump, with hap-hazard lines indicating a track, the standard route, and boxes showing a hut midway and cars on the road below. Nevertheless, by looking at it and asking questions, I got what I needed to know. I would rest for the night and set out the following day.

❄ ❄ ❄ ❄

Thursday 25 September. I assembled the gear: stove, gas, food, water, sleeping bag, bivvy, among other bits and pieces. Over breakfast, Ahmad arranged a taxi to take me the few kilometres to the base of the peak. The day began clear, with a full view of the mountain. An hour's trek had me passing Gosfand Sara, a small golden-domed mosque where, beyond it, I stopped for a drink. A gaddi with a flock of sheep and goats went by. I was glad to be out in the hills again, detached from the frenzied, urban world.

Progressing, I met a party of Swedes making their descent. Most had made the summit. Then I met three young Iranians, a woman and two men who had also summitted.

There is something different about this lot, I remember thinking. The woman appeared to be leading. Briefly we stopped for a chat. She was articulate. A bright girl. Interestingly, she was the first adult woman I had come across in Iran without a hajib or chador, choosing instead to wear a practical woollen hat in keeping with the environment. Anyway, we chatted about the mountain and weather before moving on.

I walked a good while, making good height but my thoughts remained around her. It was interesting not to see the headscarf. There's nothing like the mountains to restore human parity, I mulled. Nature has no regard for obligatory dress code or religious tradition. But developing my observations further, I came to the conclusion she was confident and capable, most likely university educated, and not afraid to speak out on any topic with her own views or representing the views of others. There are probably a lot of women in Iran like her, I reasoned. I had met some along the way and I knew they held influential roles in all areas of society. As to the future, could it be that an inspired movement of women is the force that does away with the clerics?

I reached the hut at 4,200 metres, a basic concrete and steel Nissan-type shelter. A bigger, more comfortable Alpine-style one was being built nearby. Inside there were a dozen others, all Iranian and all men staying the night with the same plan as myself to make a summit attempt the following day. Most were firemen with Tehran city council. Once more, being the foreigner I was the novelty attracting attention. Numerous group photographs with their brigade flag were taken and they made sure I was in all of them.

The evening closed in. I cooked a meal, lent the firemen my stove and went to bed. I lay in the bunk with torches flashing all round, listening to the different voices, unable to comprehend a word. Outside the wind piped up. I felt I was back in the Alps.

Friday 26 September. It was a cold night. The wind strengthened as the night wore on. I slept off and on.

Around the hut I could hear loose, rattling sounds. Ferdowsi's Shahnameh came to mind. I could picture the beleaguered Zahhak, tied up in chains and facing the snakes, about to be rendered brainless. That was probably his ghost out there now, cursing his life and how it all went wrong.

At 5 a.m. I got up and went outside. A gale was blowing, the temperature was at zero and the mountain was draped in cloud.

This doesn't look good, I thought. If it's cold down here, it'll be Baltic up there, what with the windchill. Also the poor visibility might be a problem. There were no defined features or ridges to follow and not much sign of a track. It would be easy to drift and wind up on the wrong side of the mountain, lost. Yesterday would have been the day to do it, I mused. Less wind, warmer temperature and clear visibility. I went back to bed thinking, I'll wait and see if it gets any better.

Around seven I got up again. Although brighter, there was still no change in the weather. If anything it seemed worse. Grey cloud streamed around the mountain and next to the hut, a large Iranian flag on a pole flapped violently.

Storm force, for sure. I wasn't going any further. It just wasn't worth it. Moreover, if I got to the summit I wouldn't see anything. It would be quite miserable. I would pass on this one. Instead, I went back inside and fixed up a brew. There was no hurry now.

Around eight I packed up and watched eight firemen, poorly dressed in jeans and light jackets, purposely set out. Off up the hill they went, buffeted about. Hypothermia candidates there, I thought. Moments later I slung my pack and was off. On the way down I stopped every now and then to look back. Nothing had changed. I had made the right choice and wasn't disappointed. It has been a great summer and now I am ready to go home, I thought.

Back at Ahmad's I had a shower and lunch. He was eager that I stay so he could make as much money as possible out of me. He offered me excursions to other mountains, extra nights in the house and stays at his other house on the Caspian. Ahmad was a masterful salesman; identifying a need, creating a desire, up-selling then cross-selling, while all the time being persistent and polite. But he got no luck from me, I declined everything.

Before I left, I had another browse through the guest-books. I noticed another Irish lad had passed here in 1967. One Rory Mac Con from Galway. It seemed he had a better time on Damavand than me. But I wasn't the only one that had failed. In fact I was in good company. In April 1971 a Tyrolean party experienced the same fate:

We reached near the summit, even if we could not see it, their message read. *It is very disappointing having being defeated by Damavand, in a very stormish day.*

Five signatures were below this. One belonged to a fella known to have tackled a few mountains in his time. Reinhold Messner. Good company all right.

A taxi to the main road followed by a bus, saw me back in Tehran. The old boys at the Naderi let me in this time. In the foyer I met the French cycling couple, Ben and Sylvia. They were packing their recumbents for the next leg of their trip east into Turkmenistan. We chatted until they were finished and then I saw them off. Awkwardly they mounted their bikes, lay back and made tentative U-turns on the busy city street. Tiny French tricolours fluttered over their heads. I had to hand it to them; Tehran is a fast-moving, dangerous place, where traffic at any time is merciless. But these two with their odd-looking bikes had the effect of making drivers slow down for a double-take. This suited them, they were given way. China is a long way off, I thought, but more pedal-power to them.

Saturday 27 September. After a lie-in and breakfast I braved the traffic and found the Central Post Office, where I sent half my belongings home. It was a relief to be free of the load.

Mid-afternoon I took a bus out of town. I wasn't hanging around, being more interested in making my way north towards Tabriz and the Turkish border. I fancied staying in Tabriz for a couple of days to investigate the cave-houses of Kandovan.

It seemed to take forever to get out of Tehran. Its sprawling outskirts are testament of the worst kind of urban planning possible. Somehow I managed to make a connection to another blight — the ribbon development at home along the west coast of Donegal. Thankfully though, my thoughts didn't dwell on either for long.

Reflections turned to the Iranian state and its people. Like most outsiders I had known very little about either before coming here. But that had now changed. I had come to admire the Iranians for their patience and tolerance, the hospitality towards strangers such as myself and for their many abilities. I have less admiration for their rulers, but that is nothing new. How enamoured was I to the country overall? It was difficult to say. The best thing I could do was compare it subjectively with another country, another culture I knew about. Which one?

Why not its adversary, the US? I thought. Why not. This proved interesting.

For a start, leadership and governance in both countries is appalling. The clerics and Ahmadinejad stand in one corner, George W. Bush and his neo-conservative Republicans in the other. Little difference there. There is a lack of civil liberty in Iran; whether on free speech, freedom of religion, freedom to protest, women's rights and democratic voting rights. There are too many liberties in America, noting military and financial lobby power, gun control and white collar crime. Both have prejudicial legal systems, rife with inhumane punishments including incarceration without trial, torture and the death penalty. Both are police states. Iran has one state-imposed religion and a limited tolerance of others. The US has an excess of religions, cults and individual fundamentalist nuts. The economies of both countries are in disarray. The US is at war. Iran is not. Iranians are proud, dignified people, as are many Americans. Iranians are modest. Many Americans are also, but many are not. America has a strong literary history and is recognised as a pioneering nation in modern science and technology. Iran has an ancient history of poetry, carpet making and a stellar record in civil engineering and architecture. Iran has a censored media. America has a depraved one. Iran has good healthcare and education which is readily accessible.

Much of America's education and healthcare is only available to those who can afford it. In Iran everyone is relatively equal. There are few displays of ostentation, unlike America, which is a deeply unfair society with gaping differences between rich and poor. There is very little crime in Iran; guns are principally held by agents of the state. America is a world leader in violent crime. Guns are everywhere.

So as an outsider, if I was given the choice of which country to live in — America or Iran — which one would it be? I had no hesitation here, and I still don't. Iran any day, hands down.

After a few hours we stopped for something to eat. It grew dark and I dozed off. Around eleven the bus reached the outskirts of Tabriz. I looked out. It was raining heavily and unattractively dark. Large puddles filled the roadside and soaked people stood about.

This is miserable looking, I thought. Here I am in a warm, comfortable bus, enjoying a good kip. I don't want to get off.

The thought of having to find shelter so late, in the rain, while still on the outskirts of town was too much. I knew the bus was heading northwest to Maku, a town close to the Turkish border. I reasoned if I stayed on it I would at least get another few hours sleep and could probably doss the rest of the night at the last stop. Then it would soon be morning. Tabriz and the cave dwellings quickly lost their appeal. I stayed put.

The hours passed. Prods from the attendant woke me up. It was almost four and I was the last on board. Both driver and attendant had been talking about me. I attempted to explain the recalcitrance but they weren't bothered. Neither had more than five words of English but that didn't stop us communicating. The driver was a sociable type who was interested to know what I thought of Iran. Naturally everything I said was complimentary and I meant it. Both men nodded in accord.

Maku was up ahead. We travelled slowly and discussed football. Roy Keane got a mention. Not by me, them. Like many Iranians, they were passionate about soccer. I was getting on well with them now. As we drove I expected us to make straight for the terminus once we reached town, given this was the last stop. However, events took a different course. Quietly we rolled through the town and then out, past the final street lights, for a few kilometres into the black beyond. Then we made a left, up a narrow gravel road, up a hill. The engine laboured.

What's going on? This can't be right, I thought.

Further up the hill we found a clearance, made an awkward three-point turn and rolled slowly back down, pulling up next to a small, dimly lit, house. The engine was switched off.

What now?

Both men stepped out. A conversation started when another man came out of the house. Minutes later the driver and attendant re-boarded. They rummaged at the dashboard, assembling lunchboxes, cups, foil packages and flasks, while their associate busied himself outside. Then they tucked into a breakfast of cucumber, salt, bread, honey and tea. They insisted I join them and I was happy to. After all, it was be rude not to. Everything was going well, but I was still mystified. It took the smell of fuel to draw me outside. Then I twigged what was going on. A PVC pipe stemmed from a barrel on a wheelbarrow to behind the front wheel, into the organs of the bus. They were siphoning what was left in the tank. Diesel robbers. I had to smile. No wonder they were forgoing the terminus for the back of beyonds. I looked at the pair munching their breakfast. There was no need for interpretation, we all knew what was going on. It transpired their mate with the wheelbarrow was a taxi driver who ran his business on this spare fuel, and the boys got a cut for the supply.

Although I couldn't condone what these fellas were doing, I couldn't condemn them either. At best I felt I understood them. They were just tiny cogs in a great Iranian machine. If their lives were made difficult and the state didn't support them, then they were going to look after themselves. Stealing a little diesel was their two-finger salute to those at every level of society who make up the rules.

Job done, we rolled back into Maku and the terminus. We spent the rest of the night in the yard, sleeping on the bus. The driver in a caboose next to the hold, the attendant ironed out on the backseat and me in the centre, stretched across the aisle next to the exit. The boys had blankets, but not enough to go around, so they offered me a discarded chador. I took it and wrapped myself in it. I discovered it was useless for warmth but perfect for blocking out light. Would I care to be an Iranian woman having to wear it every day? No thanks. I lay there in the dark, reflecting on the night's events. The evening hadn't turned out anything like the way I expected. Come to think of it, it was absurd. Here I was on a bus wrapped in women's clothes, hanging around with a pair of thieves. Unconventional I know, but I couldn't think of a better way to leave this fascinating country.

TEN

Transitions, Turkey

Sunday 28 September. It began raining before dawn and continued into morning. Around nine, with the day still grey and drizzly, and snores emanating from the backseat, I slipped out and was gone. I took a taxi to the end of the road, changed the last of my money and walked across a dull, barren and windswept border into Turkey.

I would spend the night in the next town, Doğubeyazit; a hamlet situated on the plains below another volcano, the five-thousand metre high Mount Ararat. The mountains of Ararat are mentioned in the Book of Genesis as the place where Noah's Ark came to rest. However, being overcast, I couldn't make out the mountain, let alone remnants of any ark.

Doğubeyazit looked grim. It's a town of ugly buildings, rusting aerials and satellite dishes. Its main street is pedestrianised. Along it there are shops selling gaudy clothes, smelly kebabs and mobile phones. Unfortunately the grey day did little for the mood of the place. Being market day, there were people about. Lots of teenagers and their elder brothers, smoking in two's and three's. Most were weedy and olive-skinned. They had slim moustaches, slick-backed hair and wore shiny, creased suits, with pointy, buckled shoes. These fellas, their fashion and the look and feel of the whole shabby town had me placing it somewhere between Palermo and Carlow town, 1984.

I checked into a hotel and wandered around. After visiting the remains of a palace outside the town, I met Bertil, a Dutchman who runs a hostel and campsite. Over a coffee he told me this part of Turkey is often neglected by Ankara. It is remote, has no industry of any significance and very few jobs. Government support is directed more to the Mediterranean coast — the money-making tourist resorts.

'That explains the large numbers of men loitering around,' I said.

'The men ... they dream of leaving,' said Bertil. 'To Ankara, Istanbul,

Germany. And many do. They get married then have no reason to return.'

It added up. The groups on the streets. The chatter in doorways. The full teahouses. The ennui. The smoking. I was reminded of home; of every city and town, twenty, twenty-five years ago. The armies of unemployed men, the dole queues, the absence of power and purpose. This was a time when the most common subject of conversation was emigration. 'Where do we go? London or Boston? Can we get visas for America? Do you know anyone who'll give us a start?'

Sauntering back to town I passed the army barracks. Outside among tanks, stood young sentries, in ponchos and helmets, looking miserable in the rain. Doubtless they also harboured dreams of getting away.

❄ ❄ ❄ ❄

Monday 29 September. No tide lasts forever and this day was no exception. The weather had changed. The sun was out, the sky was bright and a sense of optimism filled the air. At breakfast on the hotel roof, the town's drab architecture didn't appear quite so offensive. Beyond the buildings, a gleaming white Ararat stood out. It was awe-inspiring: a monolith of such bulk it defined the town and at the same time, over-powered it. I felt it was so close I could touch it. Small wonder it drew Biblical affiliation. However there was still no sign of the ark.

The light and positive energy could be felt on the streets. All the more so given the end of Ramadan, and the start of three days of celebration, Eid. Again there was much activity. People were walking around with large bags, stocking up on food. Women, young and old, milled around bakeries. Others congregated around vegetable carts, haggling. Cliques of young fellas still loafed about. And old fellas, a lot of them, sat on wooden stools on the pavements, drinking chai from small glasses. Their suits were well worn. Their faces wrinkled and unshaven. But their expressions were very much alive through animated conversation. One sensed the town had been transformed overnight. No more fasting. No more dreariness and rain. There were good times to be had. Any sullen thoughts about leaving could be put to one side.

A transformation of place and culture was noticeable to me now. Asia, in all its spontaneity and wildness, now seemed very distant. The deserts of Pakistan and Iran had given way to the gentle, vegetated hills and plains of Anatolia. Other changes stood out, like raised bread, or women abandoning Islamic dress code in favour of Western garb. Or the warm lounge of the hotel, with leather couches and widescreen television. I have to say, I enjoyed watching the Inter versus AC Milan game last night.

An overnight bus journey took me to Ankara and a shorter one got me to Göreme, a hamlet in Cappadocia. Pascal had spoken of this place. It is famous for its fairy chimneys; pale volcanic rock known as tufa, formed into hundreds of spires. They resemble many rows of capuchin monks or, to those of crude mind, lines of giant phalluses. The tufa is very soft and easy to carve, to such a degree that Cappadocians have excavated the spires to make cave dwellings. Many are cleverly carved, with latter day ones having multiple floors, windows and staircases. People have used them as shelter since Neolithic times and today, many have been converted into comfortable guesthouses. Naturally Göreme is a quirky looking place and on first sight you might call it a fairies playground. This hobbit came, liked the look of one cave and stayed for a week.

I wandered aimlessly. I drifted through valleys, inspecting the flora and rock formations, and passed hours reading and sleeping on warm outcrops. I visited a cluster of tiny Christian churches carved into rock walls up to 1,500 years ago, admiring their simple, faint, frescoes. I investigated the troglodyte city of Derinkuyu — a labyrinth of tunnels and caverns created by the ancients as a refuge against marauding invaders. I drank coffee and tea. I watched hot air balloons float over the tips of the chimneys in the mornings. Their size and sounds made me think of breaching whales.

This is the life, I thought. I have little to worry about, and it's great being a strolling player.

Göreme, being a pretty place, is a popular tourist destination. However, like many tourist spots, it has its share of problems. I met Lauren, a Canadian and Göreme resident of fourteen years. She told me about what happens to many foreigners, Britons especially, when they come, hoping to create idyllic lives for themselves. They arrive with high expectations. They start businesses, usually hospitality-related, buying cave-houses and running them as guesthouses. Some marry locals. Some get by. But others are city types who find it hard to adapt to village life. After a while they pine for the suburban lives they once had of middle-class comfort and familiarity. Of shopping malls and 4x4s, dinner parties, golf club outings and hob-nobbing with their peers. They begin to wish for a European-style education and upbringing for their children. They start to feel different to the locals — a tad superior. They grow aloof and smug. This is picked up by the locals, who come to feel jealous and disgruntled. Jealous of these blow-ins with their attitudes and money, who buy all the available property and push up prices, forcing them out of the market. Then they're disgruntled by the competition they bring — there's only so much business to go around. Very often these effects and the cultural differences are too great for the expatriates.

They give it time. Things don't change. Then they leave, dreams broken.

Tourism brings ambivalence. It creates money and jobs in a community but these come at a price. On my walks I noticed a great many fields had been left to waste. It was a sad sight seeing once-healthy vines, apple, apricot and plum trees now ragged and overgrown, their fruits rotting. All around, agriculture seemed to be suffering. What was going on? Lauren explained the problem:

'Young people nowadays don't want to work on the land. It's hard work. It's unexciting and there's little reward. It's much easier to take a soft job in tourism, in a pension or in a shop. The money is better. You get to meet people and its more fun. Also, people here are more educated these days. And women have more rights. They see better opportunities in the cities, in professional and semi-professional work. So they go there for better, more comfortable lives.'

She highlighted another problem. Water. The demands of tourism has been a strain on supply. This, and a change in climate, has led to a lower water table. The consequence being an increase in well-drilling and an increase in costs, making farming less viable and appealing.

'Ask the old folks around here, they'll tell you there was a time when the fields were green — full of crops — and no lack of water. Back then everyone worked the land. Things were very different. But it's not like that now. And most likely never will be either.'

Tourism. The serpent in the Garden of Eden.

❄ ❄ ❄ ❄

I moved on, taking night-buses to Istanbul where I spent another couple of days. It was great to be near the sea again. All that open blueness, onshore winds and fresh, salty air.

Once more I went walkabout. I had never been in Istanbul before but had seen pictures of it. As a maritime place, it was what I had expected. Dozens of passenger ferries hurried across the strait linking Europe with Asia. They dodged freighters trickling down the Bosphorus, a funnel-like passage connecting the Black and Marmara Seas and a danger facing all skippers. With such heavy traffic during the day, the water is constantly white, churning. Foghorns blow. They blow across the Marmara where, on the horizon ships remain anchored, waiting for the night and the ferries to stop. Then it's their turn to navigate the bottleneck. Up they go into the Black Sea, to old ports with alluring names and renowned histories: Sevastopol. Constanța. Odessa.

The city's fishermen were no surprise to me either. All middle-aged and elderly types, short and swarthy, with brush moustaches and cigarettes dangling from their mouths. They surrounded themselves with buckets, plastic bags, tinfoil, and tupperware containing weights, hooks and bait. Among all this, sometimes four-inch sardines — the spoils of patience and time.

Some things don't change, regardless of place, I thought. Old boys go fishing, not for the catch but to get out of the house and away from their wives. Succour is found being alone or being among their own kind.

The mosques with their minarets were as I thought they would be, sketching Islam across the skyline. The spread of the city with its palace and museums, its crowds, its shipping and full bazaars, confirmed my preconception that Istanbul is an important trading city today as it has been for empires through time. The locals know this and the city displays it. The national flag, a sharp red banner with a white star and crescent, flies everywhere. Its presence seemed to suggest 'Istanbul is big, Istanbul is strong,' and by extension, 'Turkey is big. Turkey is confident.' This is all very well. But emblems and national matters aside, this wasn't the kind of Istanbul I was hoping to see. Certain things were missing. I wanted to see an old-world city. A city displaying little wealth, with dusty streets and crumbling buildings. A place of heaving bazaars, smoke-filled cafés, hash dens and secretive alleyways. A town bustling with exotic people: shifty characters, hustlers, merchants, fixers and sailors. Of skull-capped men, veiled women and errant children. A place hinted at in the film *Midnight Express*. A place of mystery and intrigue. The Istanbul I imagined would be one of excitement, uncertainty and flux; a historical stage-post for traders of the Orient heading west and a dispatch point for beatniks and adventurers going east.

I went searching for this place. I searched in vain. I could see no shifty characters, no miscreants or wheeler-dealers. There were no hash dens, smoke-filled dives or speakeasies. Instead I found clean streets — safe ones — and shiny modern buildings. I found general order and law-abiding locals. Everyone was tidy and orderly in appearance. Disappointingly, the city looked and felt like any other place in today's Western world. Bland commercialism had crept in and spread. The soulless enterprises of consumer formulae, eye-battering advertising and neon lights. I looked everywhere for that old place. I went around Sultan-ahmet with its Blue Mosque and museums. But there was little to see here, only gimmick shops and elderly American tourists with baseball caps and cameras. I went around the bazaar quarter. Although colourful and busy, it lacked the lively precariousness of those in Asia. I took a ferry to the Asian side, hoping for better. But walking along the seafront with its tacky commercialism felt like being on a New Jersey boardwalk. Up Beyoğlu hill and around Galatasaray it was the same story. The modern world had taken over. It struck me that in our unquestioning drive to appear wealthy, sophisticated and fashionable, or to use that sinister term 'progressive,' governments and societies chip away at the very charms and characteristics that make their towns and cities unique. Sometimes this is done innocently, other times it is not. Usually in any city or state, powerful business groups get preferential treatment. Laws can be changed. Spaces move from the public to the private. Pet projects are trumpeted and dissenting voices are silenced. A price is put on everything and small businesses and communities get pushed around. Old atmospheres die. Small changes are barely noticed, but over time they add up. One decade your sense of place reflects your history and identity, the next your town has become a corporate franchise. Perhaps this is inevitable. But with today's world of capitalism, inequality, flawed governance and ideology, maybe in the future all cities on earth will look and feel the same. And of culture, there might only be one.

Disappointed, I retreated to Sultanahmet. To the Pudding Shop, a café where, in the '60s and '70s, legions of hippies and wanderers would gravitate to meet like-minded souls travelling to or from the East. It was a place where you could get a cheap feed, listen to music and people's stories, smoke a bit of weed and hit on a lift some place. Any place. Famously it had a message board where connections were made and vehicles were bought and sold. It was so well-known on the hippy trail that a stop for a few hours, a few days or a few weeks, was considered obligatory. This having been the case, I wanted to investigate to see if that old communal spirit remained. I was hoping to find a roughness, a warm, nostalgic dinginess, with a liberal air and maybe a few drifters.

Physically, I found it. But once more, I felt let down. This former bohemian hang-out had been infected also. First off, the place was practically empty, except for occasional, middle-aged, tourists poking their heads in. There were no longhairs, no cushions, no incense, no beads, no tatty furniture and no acoustic-folk sounds. Instead, a pallid interior of clean lines and organised tables, set menus and self-service, sport on the television and a hurrying waiter service. Now The Pudding Shop looked and felt like thousands of other insipid bistros in today's modern world. Hippydom had been purged — replaced by a vibe of conservatism. The kind of vibe where, if you took a guitar out and started playing it, the police would be called.

'Where's your old message board?' I asked an old waiter.

'Gone,' he answered. 'It's not needed now. People use email and mobile phones now.'

'When was the last time you had a hippy in here?'

'1975,' he replied, before adding his own lament. 'People were happier back then.

They may have been poorer but they were freer and happier. They would come in here and eat a plate of beans. They couldn't afford much more, but they didn't need anything more. But now the world has all changed. I'm afraid money is all that's important now.'

I was heartened to find I wasn't the only one with such thoughts. Still, in one sense I had to give up. The past couple of days had been spent trying to find an elusive past. The Istanbul of my imagination was no more, and this waiter was right … the world had moved on.

He also touched on a bugbear of mine concerning today's world; namely many people's fascination with modern, electronic technology. It seems to me we are pathologically drawn to gadgets like moths to candles. This particularly struck me back in Lahore at the Inn, when I was stuck in bed sick. A young South Korean bloke occupying the bed next to me, hardly left it the whole time I was there. He was immersed in his laptop computer and zoned out with his headphones on. He may have left home to travel and experience other cultures but I got the impression he wasn't aware of it. Back home I know many people who would find it hard to live without a mobile phone. Others can't sit still or walk around unless they have their headphones with music on. And there are other distractions. Home lives also are diseased by all things technological and non-essential: alarm systems that, when raised, often go ignored; television sets of a thousand mind-numbing channels; gadgets that make life radically better, like helping you brush your teeth. And I won't mention cars. The point is, whenever these things break, more often than not, they're too complicated and considered uneconomical to repair. Usually they are thrown out and replaced by the next model or upgrade. And the technological fetish continues.

Of all recent technological creations, the mobile phone is the most vulgar. It has reduced our ability to plan and manage our affairs, and it coarsens our diction. The more we use it, the more we have to use it. I confess I have never had a mobile phone and I don't know how to text. I hope I never will. My work, ironically in the IT industry, forces me to use a computer. I can happily live without electronic communication such as email or the internet. I'm not an outright Luddite and I will freely admit, some modern technology has its value. But frankly, in order to live a simple, fulfilling and stress-free life, much, if not all of it is irrelevant. The thing is, I believe many of us choose to forget this.

Eleven

Europe. Another World

Thursday 9 October. From here on I would take the train home. In the afternoon I bought a ticket for the night-train to Sofia. My last few hours were spent in the Pudding Shop drinking coffee and writing my journal. When it came to pay, I realised I was short. I had changed the last of my lira earlier and had nothing smaller than a one-hundred euro note. The waiter looked at me, looked at the note and shrugged.

'Don't worry, pay next time.'

'Thanks, man.' It was a small gesture but to me it was an important one. Perhaps the old hippy spirit in the town wasn't dead after all?

Four of us formed a group on the train: myself, a young Belgian couple who had been travelling from China, and Peter a geography student from Poland who had been wandering around Eastern Europe all summer. All were heading home.

The rocking motion of the train put us to sleep. All would have been fine only for the passport checks and having to disembark at the Bulgarian border at three in the morning. Rail travel often comes close to therapy, but sometimes, such as now with the unavoidable bureaucracy, it can make you feel like an animal shunted about with the herd. However, we mustn't complain.

Daylight awoke us. We kept rolling, passing through villages and wooded hills. The leaves were changing colour. A sense of autumn filled the air.

We made Sofia at midday, with a nine hour wait for the connection to Belgrade. Peter and I spent much of that time in a city-centre park, lounging on benches, soaking up the sun. We weren't bored. Not with the sights on offer. The park was busy — all kinds of people were using it. Yet we couldn't get over the numbers of jaw-dropping, beautiful women parading by us. They were a never-ending stream. Each was just like the next: tall, leggy and bottle-blonde, with tight jeans that showed off their figures, high-heeled boots and enormous sunglasses.

What is it about Sofia? I wondered. It's not so much a city as an urban catwalk.

This was quite a change for me now, having travelled through Islamic countries where society and religion decree that women and their figures be obscured by cloth. I had grown accustomed to such practice but now I wasn't quite ready to face such contrary norms. Nevertheless I felt I could adjust without too much trouble, and so could Peter. Only nine hours wasn't enough.

Back on the train we slept without hindrance overnight to Belgrade. At the station we had a coffee before going our separate ways. I had time to kill and moseyed around the streets. I was struck by the bleak civic buildings, some eerily quiet and boarded up with weeds growing in places. Others lay in seriously damaged condition, having been shelled by NATO forces in 1999 as part of an operation to remove Milosevic's Yugoslav army from Kosovo. Everything looked dark here: the streets, the buildings, the people dressed in black and greys. Trams rolled by. The air was chilly. A real sense of having made Europe now.

Mid-morning and the sun was out. Next stop Ljubljana. I climbed on-board and the train pulled slowly away from the station. It eased across a bridge spanning the Danube. Houseboats were moored on the left-hand side. Next to the right-hand bank, within eyeshot of clean, concrete and steel buildings, stood a gypsy encampment. Here were clusters of patchwork huts, with packing wood for walls and strips of corrugated iron for roofs — tyres flung on top. Mud tracks lay between them and detritus was everywhere. Half-naked children ran about. For a few moments I thought I was back in India.

The sun streamed through the carriage all day and the train never got full. I spent most of the time gazing out the window at the Serbian countryside. The fields were flat and most crops had been harvested. Here and there lay rows of decaying corn stalks. Hedgerows were few. Unsightly power lines stretched overhead. We moved through towns and villages. Red-tiled roofs sealed most of the houses. Most homes had sizeable back gardens. I noticed each one was put to good use by the growing of vegetables. Drills of cabbage, potato, carrots and onion. There were fruit trees and bushes and the odd sunflower. Occasionally their owners could be spotted bent over tending to all. I thought, This is the way home life should be — gardens cultivated to feed ourselves. This was the way it used to be but in the Western world we're too wealthy and lazy to bother now. Supermarkets and convenience life-styles have taken over, and often we trade our valuable, private green spaces for petty vanities like decking and patios. I consider this sacrilege. All of us need to work with nature and to see it around us. It is vital for our nourishment and necessary for our souls. I suspect as the economies of the Balkan states grow, people's living standards and expectations will rise. Their life-styles may change and the importance they place on their gardens might fade. I hope not.

Nightfall in Ljubljana. It was hard to find a bed as a World Cup qualifying game was on: Northern Ireland versus Slovenia. There were plenty of green shirts about. I avoided the crowds. Walking around town, I spied a quiet building site to doss in and was half looking forward to it when a phone call to a hostel on the edge of town yielded a spot. The thoughts of a hot shower and comfortable bed won out.

I hung around town for a couple of days. Like Istanbul, I had never been here before, but unlike Istanbul I had no expectation as to what I would find. Yet I was surprised. I got an overwhelming sense of having returned to a wealthy, highly organised, Europe. For one, the streets and buildings are all immaculate. I could see no litter or any signs of municipal negligence. The cars are mostly expensive, German types, silver and gleaming. The people look prosperous and fashionable, and their pets, pampered collies and poodles, seem born into luxury … a far cry from their Asian counterparts. On the streets small things stand out; like cycle lanes, fresh road markings and how everyone obeys traffic laws. Basically I could see no hardship in Ljubljana. The place oozes affluence and by association, the country does too. This intrigued me. To think that Slovenia was until recently, part of a Communist Yugoslav state. However unlike other Communist states, Yugoslavia had a better, more open economy, with regional autonomy and no restrictions on travel. This was due to Josip Tito, a visionary leader who managed to distance his country's affairs from the clasp of Moscow. I must admit, like most Western Europeans growing up, my limited perception of life under the hammer and sickle was of nations of forsaken people, their lives filled with drudgery, their aspirations and freedoms trammelled upon and their creativity blunted. For many this was the case and when I think of the likes of Stalin, Honecker and Ceauşescu with their barbaric rule, the perception remains. But here, looking around, I could have sworn the blight of communism and dictatorship never existed. Slovenia seemed very different. It is very different. I investigated further.

Up at the castle overlooking the city, I learned of the country's past; how Ljubljana had once been a city-state, having developed through various empires and regimes: Roman, Frank, Habsburg and latterly Communist. Its bankers, merchants and industrialists traded with Austrians and Germans to the north, Italians to the west, Balkan states to the east and south. Such international contact led to its citizens becoming influential in business, the arts, technology and sciences. The city-state grew and prospered. Over time the city-state became a small country, as it is today, and the fruits of that vibrant, outward-looking, entrepreneurial culture can also be seen today. I had noticed the difference in prosperity between it and its ex-Yugoslav neighbours from my view on the train. I discussed this with Sandra, a pretty receptionist at the hostel. What were her thoughts on this?

'Slovenia has always been different,' she claimed. 'We never fit into Yugoslavia and should never have been Communist. We were too used to trading with Europe and too much part of it to be anything else. In fact we were the strongest part of Yugoslavia. Yugoslavia would have been nothing without us.'

On the face of it, you'd need a strong argument against her, I felt.

Some indulgence now. In the town's flea market I bought a warm shirt. I went to an Impressionists exhibition at the National Gallery. I sat by the river drinking cappuccinos, observing and thinking. I watched the football game in a pub in the evening and ate a steak dinner. I tried to chat up Sandra — failed — then hopped on a train to Innsbruck.

❄ ❄ ❄ ❄

The landscape through the mountains was more familiar to me now. Alpine valleys, rich, green farms and thickly, wooded slopes. Copper-toned leaves and the fresh smell of pine. Austrian houses of broad pitched roofs and wooden balconies. Cold, tumultuous rivers.

I had been looking forward to Innsbruck. The city was now home to Paulie and Barbara who moved here after their Indian trip. It was great seeing them again — the first familiar faces in months. I was fed well and I dossed on their living-room floor. We spent hours re-living our adventures — experiences shared in the mountains and independent journeys around the sub-continent. Despite being one of the few pale-skinned, blue-eyed blondes in India at the time, Barbara enjoyed the adventure.

'I liked it. But there are things I don't miss about India.'

'Such as?'

'The lack of personal space. People are everywhere. And all the stares.'

I smiled. 'It's a different world, isn't it?'

'You can say that again.'

The next day was a gloriously indolent one. Barbara went to work. Paulie and I got up late, had breakfast and sauntered downtown. We did a little business in the internet shop. I booked a ferry ticket and a bed in Paris. Then we spent the rest of the day sunning ourselves outside a bar next to the river.

'Another rest day at Thwak Debsa base camp,' I remarked.

'Yeah, it's a hard life,' said Paulie.

❄ ❄ ❄ ❄

I took the 8.24 train to Stuttgart the next morning and had a seven minute connection for a TGV to Paris. Wandering across the platforms of Stuttgart station, it occurred to me I was slowly being re-acquainted with advanced European life and standards. Standards most of us take for granted, like orderly queues, traffic etiquette, strict timekeeping and a clean environment. Everything works here and works smoothly, I remember thinking. I can breathe the air. And look at this floor — you could eat your dinner on it — it is spotless. Here in Europe, all our needs are catered for. It's as if we have nothing left to improve upon. Half of my head was still in Asia and appropriately, I could recall Samten's words: 'Europe is like heaven. You have everything you need.' I wouldn't use the same analogy but given that as I was seeing things anew, I understood exactly what he meant. We Europeans are indeed fortunate.

I boarded the TGV. In European rail terms, if heaven could be compared to a train then I had found it. The sophistication and technological advancement immediately struck me. I was taken aback. The doors had sensors to open them. The décor was first-rate. Each seat was digitally numbered and the carriages were meticulously designed and sound-proofed. The science didn't end there. All around me sat robots, plugged into iPods and laptops.

On the dot we eased out of the station and effortlessly gained momentum. The motion was smooth, not so much rolling as gliding, irrespective of speed.

All that technology, I thought. All that speed. This can't be a train, it must be a spaceship.

Unfortunately the wonder was short-lived. Twenty minutes out of Stuttgart we broke down. The proverbial 'technical fault.' And so, for an hour and a half, from the comfort of our ergonomic seats, we idled in a field, watching German grass grow.

How ironic, I felt, all this snazzy technology and the reliance and importance we place on it. Yet it fails in its fundamental objective of getting us from A to B. This was all the more ironic when I recalled all the modes of transport I had taken up to now. My experience in India, Nepal, Pakistan and elsewhere, other than one taxi ride in Delhi and a joyride in Iran, was of exemplary service. No vehicle, whether bus, car, jeep, motorcycle or train, had broken down. Some gave trouble all right, but were quickly fixed, such that journey schedules were always kept. This was all the more remarkable considering some of the machines hung together by a thread.

Le Train à Grande Vitesse eventually made Paris, hours late. However by the time we arrived, I was unequivocal in my belief that most high-tech objects in our Western lives are of little worth. They are fragile, expensive, unnecessarily complex and as I said earlier, a headache when they break down. The TGV may be our best example. I would have been quicker getting to Paris on an auto-rickshaw.

TWELVE

Looking Back

I had been long enough away — four and a half months — and was now looking forward to home. I had little desire to see any Parisian sights, except one. A prominent painting kept in the Louvre. Eugene Delacroix's 1830 masterpiece, *La Liberté guidant le peuple*. Whenever in Paris I always make a point of seeing it. Its political message resonates with me. It shows a near life-sized woman, barefoot and bare-breasted, storming a barricade of troops loyal to the unpopular Bourbon monarch, King Charles X. Defiantly she brandishes a tricolour in one hand, a bayoneted musket in the other and looks back as if rallying her mob. Around her are the ravages of upheaval: dead royalist soldiers, a pulverised barricade and a burning city. By her side are other, smaller, figures, equally determined and enraged. Among them, an armed bourgeois man and a young boy waving pistols in the air. It is clear she is their leader.

Delacroix was portraying the Parisian scene in July 1830 when, over three days, the people rose against the monarch who attempted to increase royalist powers to that of pre-revolutionary days of 1789. A time when France was governed by privileged elites, the nobility and clergy. The country was in debt. The middle and lower classes were heavily taxed to pay for wars in America. Food shortages were common, and the monarchy, with an extravagant court, was seriously out of touch with the people. Charles X tried to reduce government and electoral powers and strengthen the clergy. He imposed censorship and introduced laws indemnifying aristocrats for lands seized during the Revolution. Parisians of all classes — liberals and republicans — took offence and rebelled. This painting captures that revolutionary zeal, of how ordinary citizens, normally passive, could rise and sweep away hubristic powers in such a lightening, violent, way. To me, the painting is greatly symbolic. Delacroix's choice of gold for the colour of the woman's dress possibly signifies his wish for the dawn of a new order. She no doubt represents France, mistreated and in ruin. His choice of this figure being a woman leading the charge, with a boy at her side, may also be his desire for a transformed society where all people are considered equal and no one small, elite corp of men hold sway. Patently he had the welfare of his country and republican sympathies in mind. You can see his signature not in a lower corner like most paintings, but on a broken plank of the barricade in the midst of the scene. It's as if he was issuing a personal decree for the removal of the king.

This painting had been on my mind for days. I had to see it. Its significance goes beyond revolutionary France and can be applied to struggles everywhere. Thoughts and images seen over the summer came to mind. Associations were drawn: the impoverished and the disenfranchised low castes of India and Nepal. The river scene in Kathmandu. The mis-served peoples of Pakistan. And the savagery inflicted on Afghans at the hands of the Taliban. These countries — these people — could well do with some of the reformatory, if not revolutionary spirit and leadership of *Liberté*. I thought about the Olympic protest in Leh. Of those vocal, young Tibetan women at the fore, demanding an end to Chinese tyranny and rule. I could see the droves of emboldened monks with them, banners and flags in hand, and that lone, older monk making his stand. Might they, with their passion, purpose and with international support, reclaim their sovereignty and rights some day? And, like Delacroix's heroine, might they wave their flag in Lhasa in the same justifiable manner? In the same vein, I thought of the Iranians. In particular, Iranian women. Could they be the ones to overcome a male dominated, cleric-led power base and cause shock waves to reverberate throughout the Islamic world?

These may be wishful, audacious thoughts, which many might see as impossible. But in our generation we have seen profound changes. We have seen the collapse of Communism, the break-up of the Soviet Union and the creation of independent states in Eastern Europe and Central Asia. We have seen the end of apartheid in South Africa and peace in Northern Ireland. We are also seeing a weakening of American influence in world affairs and uneasily, the rise of other powers, especially China. And disturbingly, we are seeing new threats in the form of Islamic extremism. Major changes, good and bad. And who could have foreseen them? Thus positive changes may come about for the Tibetans, the Afghans, the sub-continentals and the Iranians, in time. Granted, they may be hard to imagine now but as Delacroix's painting attests, they are not inconceivable. Those turbulent days in July 1830 brought profound change. Charles X was deposed and France, for the first time, became a republic.

Saturday 18 October. In the morning I tried to get into the Pompidou Centre but was refused by a pair of bouncers. My rucksack was considered a security threat. My remonstrations fell on deaf ears. Instead I had a coffee and a nose around a bookshop on the Left Bank. Lunchtime, I took a sandwich at St. Lazare and got a train to Cherbourg.

There was plenty of time before the evening sailing. Plenty of time to reflect. In a few weeks I would be back at work at the corporate treadmill, poring over contracts and proposals, attending meetings and writing reports. A far cry from the kind of life I had been living all summer. But I'm not complaining. I am fortunate. My job as a Risk Manager is varied and interesting, and I have to do it to earn a living. That said, it was great to get a long break away from it. Often I think many of us, regardless of the work we do, can get too immersed in the daily grind of meeting our own or our company's demands that we lose sight of the wider world around us. By retreating every once in a while we allow ourselves space to think about life, our purpose in it and to question everything we see around us. We gain new perspectives and these can lead us in new directions.

The past few months had been one such retreat for me. It had been a fascinating, educational adventure and I enjoyed every bit of it. I got to live a Himalayan dream but equally, I learned a great deal about other cultures. Other worlds. Take the mountain world. In the remote, barren lands of Spiti and Ladakh I was able to see how small communities thrive by working closely and respectfully with nature. They live quite happily without money, modern technology or outside interference, and have done for centuries. Experiencing this has allowed me question the merits of our 21st century Western lives. My conclusions are mixed. We are lucky in the sense that we live in relative comfort, in societies with high standards of public services, especially healthcare. But not so lucky in the sense that virtually all of us have lost, or never had, the skills to live self-reliant lives. We are bound to a money-based system for our needs. We are dependent, directly or not, on markets for our jobs and incomes to pay for our needs. We are fearful of the relentless drive for economic growth — the competition, challenges and changes they bring. Our lives can be filled with stress. Generations ago, our forefathers used to live simpler lives, like the people of the Himalaya. I am not saying their world was perfect, but in many ways we would do well to regress.

The journey also reminded me of the futility of being enslaved to certain dreams. Dreams of status, power and material well-being. Life is short and can be extinguished in a moment. If there is an afterlife, you can't bring anything of this world with you. Such dreams are pointless.

I got to meet all kinds of great people. Most, friendly and hospitable. On the sub-continent their industry and ability to make, mend and sell anything, amazed me. In India almost everyone is an entrepreneur. In hot, crowded, dusty and dirty conditions, millions eke out a living. No challenge in life seems too big for them. They impressed me.

Across the sub-continent and through Iran I encountered several religions, and I found in terms of faith, there is a big difference between East and West. In Asia and the Middle East, people actively practice their convictions and beliefs. Particular characteristics were found: Muslims and their hospitality to strangers, Buddhists and their obligations to community and the co-operative well-being, Hindus by their adoration of various gods, and Sikhs by their care of the weak. Although I am well aware many of these same characteristics are found and practiced widely in our society, I can't help thinking the wealthier and more secular we get, the more self-absorbed we become and some of these virtues weaken. As individuals we are all free to follow or reject any religion but you have to ask, if every one of us chooses to reject, what will become of Western society in the decades ahead?

The journey opened up more. Much more. I got to see vibrant, colourful, life of humans surviving, thriving and others barely getting by. We tend to forget our Western world is only a tiny part of a much bigger, poorer world. Also I got fresh views on governance and justice, social and religious freedoms and human rights. The inequality conferred on weak, lower castes, minority religions and women in certain places stood out, and yet the high status conferred on women in Buddhist cultures such as Ladakh surprised me. Critically, we Westerners should never take the rights we have for granted.

To conclude, my travels have been revelatory. Originally I had intended a different kind of adventure — an exploratory mountaineering expedition, followed by a motorcycle trip home. But as we have seen, it didn't quite turn out that way. Not the bike part, although I discovered this was probably for the best. I would have missed out on what I did experience. I would never have discovered Ladakh and experienced its mountains, culture and people. I may never have met Pascal and witnessed first-hand the Sufi culture of Pakistan. Also I might not have had the energy and ease to learn so much about Iran. They are the things that stand out but there has been plenty more. It has to be said there is beauty in travel; plans may change and each day you can never tell what you might discover or what might happen next.

Soon my journey would end and my old life would return. Now I found as I waited for the boat, the tide of multifarious images and sensations of the summer returning. They were impossible to ignore. To start, the mountains: arenas of thin air and tiresome load-hauling. Of camp life, summit views, free-wheeling birds and cascading nalas. Of lonesome valleys, ink-black nights, endless stars, endless rivers of rock and ice. Of hardy gaddis and their flocks, chortens, mani walls and prayer flags. Of horse-trains, nimble donkeys and lumbering yaks. Wind-swept passes, rumbling skies and silence. The lower valleys had their own charms of muggy rainforests and powerful waterfalls, juniper, grasses, sweet-smelling flowers and colour. Further on, the deserts and plains offered their own treasures of tamed rivers and space, wandering camels, precious grain fields and blissful sunsets. As for the cities and towns, they harboured an intoxicating array of fascinations. Merchants and trade, holy men and Sikhs. Doped snake-charmers, orange kawarias and elegant women. There were elephants and dogs, unfazed cattle and acrobatic children. I could see the temples and mosques, shaven-headed monks, veils and turbans, henna-dyed hair and teeming dark skins. There was hemp smoke, whirling dervishes, the adoration of the faithful, darkness and festivals. I could hear unremitting Hindi music, the plaintive call for prayer, bell-ringing mendicants, chanting and drums. I could smell spices and incense. There were busy markets, crowded bus stations, cramped living spaces and hawkers everywhere. I could feel the stifling heat and monsoon rain. More noise and activity. The put-put of auto-rickshaws, the din of incessant car horns; traffic, decorated lorries, speed, endless movement, fumes and dust. Then flags and martyrs, glass evil-eyes and guns. There were waves of images, sensations and experiences orbiting my head; too many to recall, too many to quell. I felt they would be with me forever.

Darkness fell as the boat left the dock and the lights of the port receded. The land link to Asia is broken, I thought. Back to the island now.

With my sleeping bag I dossed on a seating room floor on the boat, among others. I slept soundly. The waves rocked the boat like a mother nursing a cradle.

❄ ❄ ❄ ❄

Sunday 19 October. I awoke, finding everything grey: a grey sea, grey sky, a dull grey day. I ate a fried breakfast in the dining hall. It was nothing exceptional, except the price. I had forgotten how expensive life at home could be.

I walked out on the deck, read, dozed some more and as land approached, contemplated the last leg home. Rounding Carnsore it began to rain. After the TGV episode I had bleak thoughts of hanging around Rosslare station for a train home.

Why not hitch? I thought. This made sense. The N11 motorway goes from

Wexford to Dublin. If I got a lift on it I could hop off at Delgany and be at home in no time. That would obviate any train hassle and save me a walk from Greystones station home.

Decision made, I asked around. There were bound to be people with cars on the boat who were going that way. I got some funny looks, several excuses and refusals and was beginning to have second thoughts, when the roughest-looking bloke on the boat obliged. Long-haired, unshaven, denim clad and amply tattooed, Mac cut a dangerous first impression. As well as that, his voice was gravelly from decades of heavy smoking.

'Yeah, I can give you a lift. I'm going that way.'

'Great, thanks.' Then I thought for a second. Customs. The two of us in his lorry. Contraband.

I had to say something.

'You're not carrying drugs, are you?'

'No. Are you?'

'No.'

'Right. See you down below.'

A Yorkshireman by birth, Mac had been living in Cork for years and was making a delivery to his depot in Dublin before heading home. Like me, he had been away months, hauling groupage all over Europe.

The boat docked, we rolled off, cleared customs and made our way onto the N11. Mac's Scania had all the trappings for a comfortable life on the road. A bed, fridge, cooker, plasma television and stereo, not to mention soft seats and a commanding view of the world. I had often thought the life of a long-distance truck driver to be an unhealthy and lonely one. But Mac didn't see it that way.

'Nah, I love it. Been doin' it all my life. On the road you're your own boss. You make your own routes an' there's no one looking over your shoulder. I sit here with my fags, my coffee an' my music, an' I don't worry about a thing. I get to see the world from up here an' I pick up cheap booze and tobacco all over the place. It's a great life. I wouldn't change it for the world. I don't wanna retire.'

'What about your family, Mac? Have you got a wife? What does she think?'

'I'm divorced. Being away from home for long periods was too much for her.'

'Any regrets there?'

'Nah. You've got to enjoy life while you can.'

I nodded.

We chatted away. I liked Mac and quickly realised the first impression he gave was misleading. He was sound and a good talker, with lots of interesting things to say about his life and life on the road.

'I was in the army when I was younger. On supply trucks.'

'The British Army?'

'Yeah. I did ten years. Got out just as Saddam Hussein invaded Kuwait. Good timing.' Mac liked to go fishing on his time off. This struck me as somewhat unusual. Not the activity but the choice. Here was a man who spent all of his work time alone. Now this solitary state applied to his leisure time. How come? He was no oddball. Quite the contrary. To me he appeared quite normal. I observed him as he talked, taking in his unconventional looks: the long hair, the rough beard and tattoos. The pot-smoking, ash-clad Shiva came to mind. It must be meditative aspects of each that draw him, I thought. Maybe this truck was his temple and the burning cigarettes his incense? And perhaps in another life, another world, Mac would be a sadhu or a Buddhist monk, eschewing the road for transcendent journeys of the mind and soul.

The rain kept up. All around the fields looked richly green to the point of being overpowering. It's always that way whenever you come home, having been away some time. Familiar names were on the roadsigns. Enniscorthy. Ferns. Gorey. Bottles clanked in the back when we went over a bump.

'What's that Mac?'

'Just some wine I got for my daughter. She's havin' an Ann Summers party on Thursday night. Her an' her girlfriends.'

'Ann Summers? Isn't that the crowd who make and sell kinky women's lingerie?'

'Yeah, that's them.'

We rolled on. Into Wicklow now, cruising by Arklow, Brittas Bay and Wicklow Town. My thoughts veered towards the local hills and the treasures they offer any walker. Fresh air, solitude and space. Blazing heather and fraughan-berries in summer, the coconut smell of furze in spring. Fauna and more. Being Wicklow and noting it was the sabbath, I couldn't but spare a thought for a temple close to my own soul. The white, granite cliffs of Luggala. I missed this place all summer. It's a captivating spot for any climber. The routes on its walls and buttresses are mostly hard, demanding a fight, and the airy situations they offer, overlooking Lough Tay and Luggala Lodge make you feel very much alive. I have spent some of the best days of my life here, wrestling with beautiful routes with seductive names like *Spearhead*, *Curved Air*, *Taktix*, and the sublime *All Along the Watchtower*. Most of the routes were pioneered by hard-chaws in the 1970s. Some of the names they gave them reflect the space exploration and rock culture of that time. Whenever I think of *All Along the Watchtower* I visualise Hendrix and I hear the cat-like sound of his guitar crying out as if a siren call. I can hear it now.

Mac pulled up at Willow Grove junction and I hopped out.

'Thanks for the lift, Mac, you're a star.'

'My pleasure, mate. Glad to have you, you're good company.'

'By the way,' I said, 'enjoy that Ann Summers lingerie party.'

He laughed. 'I will. An' did I tell you? I'm goin' as the model.'

Standing on the verge, I watched him go and waited for the swarm of headlights to fly by. A gap in the traffic emerged and I crossed to the island, stepping over the barrier and across the south-bound lanes onto the Delgany slip road. The rain spat down. I put up my hood. Conkers lay on the ground and I kicked them into puddles. I walked along, turned up into the laneway and made some height. Looking out, I expected to see the Sugar Loaf mountain through the Glen of the Downs but it was hidden in cloud. All around the leaves were changing colour to autumn shades and the last of the season's blackberries were over-ripening on the hedgerows. Home turf.

In logistic terms it had been an extraordinary journey home. I had covered 11,000 kilometres from the top of India to Delgany, by all manners of transport: jeep, bus, train, taxi, auto-rickshaw, boat, foot and truck. I asked myself, would I do it all over again? I probably would. Or maybe something like it in the years ahead. You never know. But first it was back to a regular life of work, exercise, domestic matters and writing this book. And perhaps the small matter of finding a woman prepared to put up with me and my adventures. But that would be another day's work. For now though, it felt good to be home.

Appendix I

THE RAMAYANA

The earliest known copies of this legend go back to the 5th century BC in the form of 24,000 Sanskrit verses within seven books. The sage Valmiki is credited as being its author long before then, with the story memorised by his acolytes and handed down by constant re-telling. As such, several versions developed in different parts of India and Southeast Asia. This much loved myth maintains its power among all Hindus today, as a lesson in leading a rightous life, not without personal suffering, in order to dispel evil for the greater, common good. The following is my interpretation and synopsis of the generally accepted story.

Gerry Galligan

Many moons ago in the northern Indian city of Ayodhya, there lived a good king, Dasaratha. This man had three wives but no son — no heir — so he petitioned the gods for one. Meanwhile in the heavens there was much apprehension. Ravana, an evil creature of ten heads, twenty arms and a plethora of scars from countless battles, was running amok across the universe. He was killing innocents and claiming the earth and cosmos as his. The gods convened and put a case to Vishnu, Lord of the Universe.

'You must stop Ravana,' they declared. 'He will destroy us and everything. You must enter human form on earth and do away with him.'

Vishnu listened and acted. It was improper to deny the request of any fellow god. Through his intercession, the wives of King Dasaratha became pregnant. They bore four sons. All were imbued with divine powers but of the four, Rama was the one who inherited the most. Vishnu had marked him as the one to overthrow Ravana. With his new sons, King Dasaratha was overjoyed.

The boys grew up, passing happy childhoods in the kingdom and excelling in their sports and studies. Two grew especially close; Rama and his younger brother, Lakshmana.

One day a local sage, Visvamitra, approached the king. He complained of demons causing havoc at his ashram in the forest and asked the king for help. Reluctantly the king agreed, granting him the services of the two boys in return for their education on the use of powerful weapons. Visvamitra took them away. Under his guidance Rama and Lakshmana trained in the art of weaponry and warfare. The pair were then tested. They were made to confront the offending demons, of which there were three, and they did so skillfully and successfully with a combination of bows, sabres, wind and fire weapons. Visvamitra was pleased and as a reward, he brought them to the festival taking place at the court of King Janaka of Mithila. For a while, all was well with the world.

King Janaka had a beautiful daughter, Sita, who had many admirers and suitors. No sooner had Rama seen her as he passed one of the king's gardens than he was smitten by her. Their eyes met and she also found herself taken by him. The question was, how could they be together?

Visvamitra took the brothers to meet this king. He told the king of the boys' exploits with the demons, describing their bravery and skill. The king was impressed and liked the look of them. So much so that he allowed them inspect his finest weapon, the great bow of Mithila, which once belonged to Lord Shiva. The weapon was large and heavy, being mounted on an iron chest with wheels. Hundreds of men were needed to move it.

'No man or god has ever strung this bow,' the king said. 'The first one to do so can have my daughter Sita. Come, Rama, see if you can string it.'

With that the young prince lifted the bow easily. He aligned it to fire, drew on the string and pulled to such an extent that the great bow snapped. All were astonished. Rama had done the impossible. By the king's word, Sita would be his.

There were great celebrations. King Dasaratha and his court travelled to Mithila and a grand wedding uniting the four sons of Dasaratha and four daughters of Janaka took place. Happily, Rama and Sita were now one.

The cavalcade returned to Ayodhya, to more feasting and celebration. Rama and Sita made a home together, as did his brothers with their new wives, and there was harmony in the kingdom.

The months went by. King Dasaratha looked at his sons. He was getting old now, he had done much for his people and all he could for his grown-up sons. There was little more for him to do — it was time to cede the throne. Reflecting deeply, he chose Rama as his heir. This decision was unwelcome in one quarter.

One of his queens, Kaikeyi, took umbrage. She was the mother of Bharata, Rama's older brother, and felt the kingdom was rightly his. Moreover, she was jealous. If Rama became king, then Rama's mother, Queen Kausalya, would have power over her. This was unacceptable. So together with her evil maidservant Manthara, they crafted a scheme to make Bharata king.

'You owe me two favours,' she told the king. 'I saved your life in a chariot accident once. Do you remember? You granted me two wishes which I never used and now I call upon them.'

'What are they?' he asked.

'That Bharata is made king and Rama is banished to Dandaka Forest, to live as a hermit for fourteen years.'

When the king heard this he was grief-stricken. This was improper. Only Rama would make the best king. Over several days he pleaded with her to change her wishes but she refused. Heart-broken, he had no option but to concede. Rama followed his father's orders without query or resistance and, together with Sita and Lakshmana, they went into exile. The kingdom of Ayodhya fell into mourning. The king himself was inconsolable.

One person was infuriated by these developments, Bharata. It had all happened while he was away and now that he had returned, he had no desire to be king.

'What right have I to sit on my father's throne?' he declared. 'It belongs to Rama. He is the rightful king. I will only serve to guard it until my brother returns.'

A short time later the king died, a broken man.

The forest of Dandaka was full of dark shadows, restless spirits and demons. On the advice of a sage, the trio found a home in the valley of Panchavati, a place plentiful in food, flowers fruits and water. Lakshmana constructed a bamboo and thatch hut wherein they assumed the peaceful life of hermits. However the tranquil life was short-lived. They were visited by a witch, Surpanakha, sister of Ravana. She became infatuated with Rama. When he rejected her advances she turned on Sita in a jealous fit and attempted to kill her. But Lakshmana intervened by chopping off her nose and ears. Then bleeding profusely, she fled into the jungle and told her brother Khara. In retaliation, Khara gathered an army of 14,000 rakshasas and marched to destroy Rama. The young prince stood his ground alone. He absorbed all their arrows, javelins, spears, and the blows from their swords, axes and clubs. Then, taking his divine bow, he fired a river of arrows, reducing Khara's troops to fragments and broken bodies which littered the ground. Khara was the last to expire, dispatched to hell with an arrow that tore through his heart with the sound of thunder. The disfigured Surpanakha fled the forest for the island of Lanka, home of Ravana. Here she told him what happened and of the indestructible force of Rama. Vengence coursed through Ravana's blood. He had heard of the reputation of Rama. Now he vowed to destroy him and claim Sita as his. So with his magician friend Maricha, they conjured a plan to kidnap her.

Together they entered the Dandaka forest where Maricha took the guise of a deer. He sallied across Sita's path and when she saw him, she was struck by his beauty.

'Rama, that is the most magnificent creature on earth. There is none finer. Please, capture it for me.'

Rama obliged and gave chase. He had been gone some time and Sita and Lakshmana became worried. 'Go and find him,' Sita said. Lakshmana was reluctant to leave her alone at first, but after a while she insisted he go. No sooner had he left when Ravana, disguised as a beggar, appeared. Sita was suspicious at first, but his soft words appeased her. She gave him food and water, all the while anxiously looking around, waiting for her prince to return. Then the monster revealed itself. Its ten heads, twenty arms, forked tongues and battle scars terrified her.

'I am Ravana, king of kings. Care not for Rama, he is worthless. I am taking you to Lanka and you will be my queen.' Then he grabbed her by her hair and dragged her screaming to his chariot. Sita cried out in vain but she was no match for the monster. Bundling her through his many arms he took off, skyward through the trees. Meanwhile the noble old bird, Jatayu, had been watching from a branch. He could not stand idle and allow this pernicious deed happen. Instantly he swooped on the chariot and tore at the monster's arms. But with each one he severed, another one grew. Ravana responded with fury and chopped off the bird's wings. Jatayu fell to earth and remained there, unable to move. As Ravana flew off, the gods in heaven looked on. Their prophesy was being played out. Ravana will soon be no more, they agreed. Nothing can save him from the wrath of Rama now.

The princes returned and looked everywhere for Sita but could not find her. They asked the animals and trees what happened. Flocks of deer gave a clue, turning to the south and raising their heads to the sky. They stumbled upon Jatayu who, in his last breath, told them what happened. With grace, Rama acknowledged the bird's sacrifice and when it died he gave it a cremation worthy of a lord. At Pampa lake they wondered what they would do next. Head south? But to where? The land was vast and there were just two of them. As they spoke, Sugriva, lord of the monkey tribes, came by, gathering fruit. He was impressed by what he saw. Two strong princes — fearless and well armed.

They may be useful but are they powerful enough? he wondered. Years earlier, Sugriva had been banished from his home kingdom of Vanara by his older brother Vali. Vali also stole his wife. Unsurprisingly, they became sworn enemies. Since then Sugriva wandered the forest, living in fear of his powerful brother. But one day he hoped to take back what was rightfully his. Could Rama be the one to help him? They met and exchanged stories.

'Show me your strength Rama,' he said.

Rama picked up his bow and fired an arrow which sliced through seven thin saplings in a row. They fell like dominos. The arrow then dived, submerging to the underworld, where it circled around before piercing its way up through the earth to land neatly back in Rama's quiver. It was an inspirational show of force. Sugriva was impressed. A deal was then made. If Rama assisted in the defeat of Vali, Sugriva would grant him the services of the monkey tribes to find Sita. Not only that but the head of this army would be the talented and resourceful monkey-god, Hanuman. But first, the matter of Vali.

The brothers arranged a duel in the forest. Rama with his bow, hid behind a tree. A ferocious, bare-handed battle took place between Vali and Sugriva. Feet, fists and arms flew. Boulders and trees were torn up and tossed in every direction. The ground shook with the collisions of animals and objects. Even the heavens were disturbed. Eventually both monkeys tired. With their slower movements Rama was able to take aim at Vali. It took a few attempts. But once he released a gold-tipped arrow, there was no mistake. Vali was hit in the chest, mortally wounded. As he lay dying, he looked Rama in the eye and said:

'What have I done to you to deserve this? I am but a mortal monkey.'

'You mistreated your younger brother and stole his wife,' chided Rama. 'These are grave sins. But fear not, upon your death as punishment, you will be absolved. Thus by the powers of my kingdom and the heavens, it is my duty to administer justice.'

And that was the end of Vali.

There followed much celebration; Rama had done his service, Sugriva was happy and the kingdom of Vanara was at peace. The monsoon rains came. Nothing was done for three months but once the rains had gone, the monkey army was assembled from all parts of the forest and Vanara kingdom, with Hanuman in charge. Sugriva gave them his blessing, while Rama took Hanuman aside.

'Hanuman, son of the wind god, go and find Sita for me. She is more precious than all the jades of the earth and the constellations put together. Here, take my ring, for when she sees it she will know you serve me.'

Hanuman took the ring, bowed and led his troops away. They headed south, over the mountains and deserts and fanned out to expand the search. At first they had little luck, scouring the plains for weeks until they happened upon the keen-eyed vulture, Sampati.

'You're wasting your time,' he told them. 'Neither Sita or Ravana are here. I know. I saw him take her on his chariot. They were heading to the island of Lanka. That is where his palace is. Poor Sita, she was in much depair.'

With great alacrity the army marched to the coast. But when they got there they were disappointed. The Indian Ocean was vast and the island was far away; how could they ever hope to reach it? Hanuman paused for thought.

'Brothers, there is nothing lost. Wait here. By the powers invested in me I alone can go. And I will return.'

The monkeys watched as he called upon the wind god. He rolled himself into a ball and grew to enormous size. The wind died down and the sea became calm. Then with a lash of his tail he catapulted himself over the ocean. Safely he landed on Lanka and, instead of returning to normal size, he made himself much smaller in order to escape detection.

Throughout this time Ravana had Sita imprisoned in a wing of his palace. He tormented her daily, demanding her submission. 'You are my queen. I can give you all the treasures of the earth. I command you obey me.'

But she would not yield. Her thoughts remained squarely on Rama and a return to her former life. 'You are not worth a curse with your threats and evil ways. I will never surrender to you. Rama is my only love. He is a noble, true lord. You are nothing but poison.'

'Very well,' said Ravana disdainfully. 'Have it your way. But be warned, I will give you one year. If by then you haven't changed I will cut you into pieces and eat you for breakfast.'

Hanuman found the princess mourning in one of Ravana's walled gardens. He explained who he was and the reason for his visit. At first Sita thought he was another ruse of the monster and was suspicious. But when he showed her Rama's ring her heart filled with joy.

'Oh forgive me dear monkey, you are who you say you are — a true friend of Rama. How I have longed for this day. Please, you must free me from the clutches of this devil. My only wish is to be with the one I love.'

Hanuman offered to take her away on his back to India but he had forgotten he had made himself so small. Sita laughed.

'My dear Hanuman, I can see you are a determined one but you are too small. We would never be able to fly such a distance and brave the winds and ocean together. No, it is better that Rama should rescue me and do away with the wicked one.' Instead she gave him one of her jewels as evidence for Rama, along with a message to hurry.

The monkey-god slipped out of the garden. He was pleased with his work so far. But he knew there was still much to do. If Rama was to come here he would have to take on Ravana and destroy him. But what of Ravana's army? How big and powerful was it? There was only one way to find out. Draw them out. He created a racket, uprooting trees, breaking boulders and shaking the earth. Ravana's demon troops filed out. One by one he killed them. Then successive waves retaliated with their arrows, club and spears. Thousands of them, but once more, Hanuman overpowered them. Next he felt he had to get sight of Ravana. So he allowed himself be captured. He was taken in shackles and put in front of Ravana. The monster looked him up and down. 'Who are you?'

'I am Hanuman, envoy of Rama. I command you release Sita at once. Be warned, failure to do so will lead to your annihilation. Of that I am sure. I know your power and I know the power of your army. Neither has any chance of overcoming a determined Rama.'

Ravana became enraged. 'Kill this monkey now!' he cried. But his brother Vibhishana took hold of his many arms and said: 'No. Let this monkey go. It is Rama we really want. Let him come here, we will destroy him once and for all.'

Ravana gave in and ordered Hanuman's release. But this was not before parading him in the streets as an enemy captive and setting his tail alight. But Hanuman didn't feel the flames. Moreover he got the last laugh. He hopped over every roof in Lanka, setting each one alight, including Ravana's palace. As he flew back to India, Lanka was ablaze. 'Victory to Rama!' he roared.

The flames couldn't harm Sita either. Watching Hanuman go, her heart lifted. Come, save me quickly, Rama, she thought. Another day without you is turmoil.

There was much celebration on Hanuman's return. He presented Sita's jewel to Rama who was beside himself with glee. Then Rama listened to the monkey's report. If Ravana was to be beaten it required a well-armed, committed force. A rescue campaign was mounted. Monkeys from all parts of India were called. They were given weapons and training and motivational lectures on the importance of opposing evil for the sake of their kingdoms, the earth and the universe. A giant causeway of boulders, tree trunks and reeds was constructed between Lanka and India, and Hanuman placed a standing force on either side to protect it. Food and munitions were gathered. Then Rama, Lakshmana and Hanuman led the army over the bridge into battle.

There were nervous utterances in the court of Ravana. 'Rama the indominatable is coming. They say he has a force of a hundred million. We may be doomed.'

They were right to feel this way. The first battle was a bruising encounter. The monkeys weren't used to the tactics of Ravana's demons and many fell. But the demons suffered their own losses by the deft club work of Hanuman's charges. Then Rama and Lakshmana got hit by the invisible Indrajit. His arrows penetrated their vital organs, leaving them writhing in the cleaved earth among the groaning and the dead.

The gods saw what was happening and dispatched their celestial bird Garuda to administer to them. This divine creature swooped down and hovered above the princes. All the island's snakes disappeared down holes, terrified of its presence. The arrows that were lodged in the men vanished. Their bleeding stopped and their wounds closed up. Simultaneously the brothers sat up, then stood up, shook themselves down and felt right again. Then Garuda, with its blue wings and long tail, flew back to the heavens.

On seeing this, a fuming Ravana sent in his other brother, Kumbhakarna. This demon was a particularly nasty piece of work. He had a reputation for devouring any creature of warm blood and his appetite was voracious. Into the battlefield he charged, grabbing at any monkey within reach, funneling it into his mouth and chewing it with nine-inch fangs and incisors. He was machine-like in speed and operation. A river of blood and guts flowed from his maw. He spotted the brothers and went barreling towards them, maddened by their scent. Rama took aim with a diamond-tipped arrow. He waited until he could see the back of the creature's mouth before releasing. The projectile found its mark. Kumbhakarna's head from the upper jaw was sliced off. A geyser of blood erupted from the remaining stump. The heavy-weight Kumbhakarna toppled and fell into a crater of his own making. It soon filled up with blood and he was submerged. He would never bother another creature again.

The battles ebbed and flowed for days, weeks and months. At one stage things looked grim for Rama's forces. Ravana himself had entered the fray and had whipped his demon troops into an extraordinary frenzy. Their kill count suddenly trebled. Hundreds of thousands of monkeys lay wretched and dying on the battlefield. There were few opportunities to tend to them. Corpses began to smell. One of the older monkeys, a sagacious veteran of many campaigns, approached Hanuman and said:

'Sir, this is not looking good. If we are to win this then we will need some of those potent herbs that grow on the side of Mount Kailash. We used them before and they worked, remember?'

Hanuman pondered this. 'You know brother, you are correct. I will go and get some now.' With that he took off into the air, flying north to the Tibetan

Himalaya where he found the mountain. He landed and marched several times around its lower slopes. There was flora of all kinds here, including all varieties of herb. What was he looking for? He knew the name but couldn't remember what it looked like. Moreover the flowers, with their overwhelming colour and smells, were confusing.

Blast this, he thought, I shouldn't have come here alone. I'll never find it.

There was only one thing for it — take many of them. So he took a deep breath and unearthed a whole side of the mountain. He put it on his back and flew off for Lanka. It was slower return trip but it was worth it. As he circled over the battlefield, the fragrance of that magical hidden herb wafted out. It drifted down, assailing the wounded and dead. What happened next was a remarkable sight — the stirring of hundreds of thousands. Miraculously the wounded began to heal. Arrows and spears fell out, flesh-holes closed, severed heads and limbs were re-set. A sea of monkeys arose, including those that had been dead. Within an hour Hanuman's army was back to full strength. The same could not be said of Ravana's charges. The magical herb had no effect on them. Confidence now surged through Rama's forces. They regrouped and embarked on the mother of all offensives. Line after line of demon resistance fell. Then the monkeys moved in on the palace. From his battlement, Ravana looked on in disbelief. If he didn't act quickly there would be nothing left. Into the maelstrom he went. With his brother Indrajit and their close guards, he pushed back. Then Indrajit fell — decapitated by one of Lakshmana's arrows. The guards and remaining demons did all they could but soon their numbers would dwindle. It came down to a duel: Ravana against Rama.

'No earthly or heavenly spirit can protect you now, Rama,' declared Ravana, though even he now felt these words to be empty.

'We'll see. Come on, try me with your sword, brute,' said a defiant, provocative Rama.

The titans clashed. From their chariots they slung arrows at one another for three days and three nights. Some inflicted deep wounds, many missed but none were of a fatal kind. Ravana switched to javelins and spikes. He catapulted fireballs and sent up clouds of smoke to obscure himself. Rama tried his mace but more often than not he just hit the demon's chariot. One by one the weapons ran out. They turned to daggers and sabres. Each time he lopped off one of the hydra's heads, Rama saw another one appeared. And it was no different with the arms. Every time the bodies collided there was thunder, and at night the sky lit up with flashes of light. The gods and monkeys looked on. After seven days, their bodies and minds were exhausted and their arsenals depleted.

Rama had only one idea left. He reached into his quiver. Brahma's arrow was still there. Of all the divine arrows he had, this was the most powerful. It had a shaft of ether, a tip of diamond and feathers belonging to Vayu, the wind god. Brahma himself had to use it once and he swore upon its efficacy. Rama put it to the string, offered a mantra, aimed carefully and released. It turned into a fireball as it flew, travelling faster than the speed of sound. Ravana was unable to stop it. It shot through his heart, cauterised his pulmonary vein and aorta and ripped his lungs, spleen and liver out the far side. He fell back to earth in a smouldering heap. One of the heads rolled back and forth for a moment and three of the arms managed to twitch, and then it was over. His adversary failed to move again, Rama had slain the beast.

And so the gods were pleased. Rama and Sita were re-united. There was much joy on the return from Lanka. Hanuman and his charges went home happy and well rewarded. The trio, Rama, Sita and Lakshmana, were welcomed as heroes on their return to Ayodhya. Bharata gave his younger brother the throne. Sita became queen and all was right in the kingdom. However this story does not have a happy ending. For two years everyone was content. But then rumours circulated about Sita — that she may not have been faithful to Rama during captivity. They were untrue of course, but they unsettled the people and caused Rama anxiety.

'The people think if Sita can be defiled by Ravana and you accept her back, then all men in the kingdom will have to tolerate infidelity from their own wives,' a sage informed him. 'Whatever a king does, his subjects will follow.'

Rama called Lakshmana aside.

'Brother, my people believe Sita has been unfaithful to me and yet I know this to be false. I have been thinking. This is not easy for me but my people must be served. Take Sita away from me, bring her across the Ganges to the ashram of Valmiki. Tell him to look after her, in my name.'

Though filled with grief, Lakshmana obeyed his brother's instruction. When Sita discovered her fate she was bereft. 'My life is nothing but sorrow,' she cried. What's more, she was now with child.

Valmiki and his cohorts looked after her and her twin sons, Kusha and Lava for twelve years. The boys learned about their father and his deeds by the stories Valmiki told them. Throughout this time Rama and Sita learned to live with their respective grief. Rama immersed himself in doing good works for his people. Sita remained busy with the boys.

One day the boys arrived at court and Rama recognised them as his sons. His heart now troubled him and those longings he had for Sita years earlier suddenly returned. Could he have her back? Would she come back? Lakshmana was sent to get her.

When she appeared in court a great crowd assembled. She spoke out.

'I have always been faithful to Rama. If the gods believe this as true, then let them take me from this mortal coil as one of theirs.'

Her words echoed between the many walls of Rama's palace. The ground shook and opened up. The goddess Mother Earth appeared and drew her towards her. They both sank down into the earth and it closed up. Rose petals fell from the heavens and the gods rejoiced. Rama was inconsolable.

The kingdom of Ayodhya prospered for eleven thousand years under Rama's rule. There were no wars, the harvests were plentiful, the weather was kind and demons were few. His sons were installed as future monarchs. When the time came, Rama journeyed with his brothers to the Sarayu river. They stripped to their dhotis and entered the cool waters where they returned to the realm of the gods. Finally, Rama and Sita were re-united forever more.

Appendix II

PEAK 6135, EAST UPPER DEBSA VALLEY, SPITI,
HIMACHAL PRADESH, INDIA

Co-ordinates: N 31º 57' 45" E 77º 53' 05"
Type of rock: Sedimentary shale & slate
Date of first ascent: 22 June 2008
Route: Southwest Ridge
Grade: Assez Difficile (AD)
Peak name proposed: Ramabang
First ascensionists: Gerry Galligan, Darach O'Murchu,
Paul Mitchell (all Irish)

PEAK C.5154, DUMBUR-SHILAKANG AREA, ZANSKAR RANGE,
LADAKH, STATE OF JAMMU & KASHMIR, INDIA

Co-ordinates: N 34º 10' 10" E 76º 40' 15"
Type of rock: Limestone
Date of probable first ascent: 18 August 2008
Route: Southwest Flank
Grade: Peu Difficile (PD)
Peak name proposed: Konchok
First ascensionist: Gerry Galligan (Irish)

Acknowledgements

There are many individuals and several organisations who I'd like to thank in helping to make this adventure and this book possible. Firstly, my family, for everyone's patience and support. The boys, Darach O'Murchu, Craig Scarlett and Paulie Mitchell for all contributions made. For research, advice and hospitality, Roger McMorrow, Sara Spencer, Sé O'Hanlon, Paddy O'Leary and the Lynam family. Also Harish Kapadia, Rajesh Gadgil, Sham Samant and The Himalayan Club; and the staff at the Alpine Club, London.

Sponsorship is a project in itself and I am grateful to the following for all their support: Kieran Kelly and the Irish Mountaineering Club committee 2007-8; Karl Boyle, Dawson Stelfox and Mountaineering Ireland staff and board 2007-8; Joe Cotter, Jim Leonard and Lowe Alpine; Hugon Simm, Colm McMahon and Glenwalk committee 2007-8.

In the field, the following must be acknowledged: Directors and staff of the IMF; The Rimo gang: Yangdu, Motup, Alka, Nima, Raj Kumar, Manbahadur, and all supporting staff for their care and professionalism.

Obviously the Vertebrate team in Sheffield for their skills, enthusiasm and professionalism in producing this book, and for making the whole process enjoyable: editors Jon Barton and Claire Carter; designers Rod Harrison, Simon Norris, Jane Beagley and supporting staff. Here at home I must not forget to acknowledge Sé O'Hanlon for his independent expertise and his time spent, particularly on map development and feedback on the text. Neither can I forget Anne Dempsey who helped me shape my writing style, many years ago.

There are many others who in no small way played their part in making things happen: Doctors John Duignan and Peter Staunton who kept us healthy before the expedition (and still do); Anthony McCourt, Maurice Gowen, Barbara Guenther, Nicholas O'Murchu, Fionnuala Morgan, Ron Kelly, Ciaran Dunne, Peter Langan, Anne Fitzsimons, John Scully, Jim Osborne, Rob MacCallum, Simon Yates, Lindsay Griffin, Victor Castro, Emilio Xaus, Sam Wales, Bénédicte Reau, Brian Neill. Pearse Street (Dublin) Library staff; Grant, Martin, Valerie and Co. at Grants, Baggot Street; Tadhg and Stephen at the Teachers Club, Dublin; the staff of Coffee 2 Go, Mespil Road and Caffè Parigi, Sir John Rogerson's Quay, Dublin.

There are many more. Finally, to all I came across in the mountains and on the road. Thanks all.

Select Bibliography and Sources

Axworthy, Michael, *Iran: Empire of the Mind. A history from Zoroaster to the present day* (London, 2008).

Bhaskar, Sanjeev, *India: One Man's Personal Journey Round the Subcontinent* (London, 2007).

Bonington, Chris, *Annapurna South Face* (London, 1971).

Chomsky, Noam, *Hegemony or Survival: America's Quest for Global Dominance* (London, 2004).

Craig, Mary, *Tears of Blood: A Cry for Tibet* (London, 1992).

Fleming, Fergus, *Killing Dragons. The Conquest of the Alps* (London, 2001).

Harvey, Andrew, *A Journey in Ladakh* (London, 1993).

Heim, Arnold and August Gansser, *The Throne of the Gods* (London, 1939).

Holmes, Peter, *Mountains and a Monastery* (London, 1958).

Kapadia, Harish, *Spiti: Adventures in the Trans-Himalaya* (New Delhi, 1999).

— *Across Peaks and Passes in Ladakh, Zanskar and East Karakoram* (New Delhi, 1999).

Kapuściński, Ryszard, *Shah of Shahs* (London, 2006).

Kipling, Rudyard, *Kim* (Oxford, 1998).

Klimburg-Salter, Deborah E., *Tabo Monastery: Art and History* (Vienna, 2005).

Kumar Bhasin, Sanjeev, *Amazing Land Ladakh: Places, People and Culture* (New Delhi, 2006).

Lama (XIV), Dalai, *The Four Noble Truths* (New Delhi, 2007).

Luce, Edward, *In Spite of the Gods: The Strange Rise of Modern India* (London, 2007).

Lynam, Joss, 'Exploring the Gyundi and the Bara Shigri Valleys 1958', The Himalayan Journal, Vol XXI, (1959).

— 'Overland from India', Newsletter of the Wild Geese section of the IMC, No. 9 (1959).

Mcdonald, Bernadette, *Freedom Climbers* (Victoria, BC, 2011).

Mehta, Soli and Harish Kapadia, *Exploring the Hidden Himalaya* (Kent, UK, 1990).

Murphy, Dervla, *Full Tilt: From Dublin to Delhi with a Bicycle* (London 2004).

Norberg-Hodge, Helena, *Ancient Futures: Learning from Ladakh* (New Delhi, 2007).

O'Leary, Patrick, *Servants of the Empire: The Irish in Punjab 1881-1921* (Manchester, 2011).

Prime, Ranchor, *Ramayana: A Tale of Gods and Demons* (San Rafael, CA, 2004).
Rashid, Ahmed, *Taliban: The Story of the Afghan Warlords* (London, 2001).
Scott, Chris, *Adventure Motorcycling Handbook* (Surrey, UK, 2006).
Shaw, Isobel, *Pakistan Handbook* (Chico, CA, 1990).
Shipton, Eric and H.W. Tilman, *Nanda Devi: Exploration and Ascent* (Bâton Wicks, a compilation of the two mountain-exploration books, *Nanda Devi* and *The Ascent of Nanda Devi*, London, 1999).
Simpson, Joe, *Storms of Silence* (London, 1996)
Smythe, Frank, *Kamet Conquered* (Bâton Wicks/The Mountaineers anthology, *The Six Alpine/Himalayan Climbing Books*, London, 2000).
Snelson, Kenneth, *'The Dibibokri Basin ... and Beyond,'* The Himalayan Journal, Vol 18, (1954).
Tammita-Delgoda, Sinharaja, *A Traveller's History of India* (New York, 1999).
Thubron, Colin, *Shadow of the Silk Road* (London, 2007).
Tomory, David, *A Season in Heaven: True Tales from the Road to Kathmandu* (New Delhi, 1998).
Twain, Mark, *Following the Equator* (Washington DC, 2005)

Newspapers and periodicals
Daily Times (Pakistan)
Iran Daily
Iran News
National Geographic
New Statesman
Newsweek
Peak Performance
The American Alpine Journal
The Economist
The Himalayan Journal
The Himalayan Times
The Hindustan Times
The Nation
The International News
The Times of India
TIME Magazine

Other (Guidebooks)
Insight Guide: Pakistan
Lonely Planet: Nepal; India; Turkey.

Internet sites
British Broadcasting Corporation, bbc.com
Buddhanet, buddhanet.net
Encyclopedia Britannica, britannica.com
Circle of Ancient Iranian Studies, cais-soas.com
Central Intelligence Agency, cia.gov
The World Bank, data.worldbank.org
Frontline, frontlineonnet.com
The Hindu, hindu.com
Historical Iranian Sites and People, historicaliran.blogspot.com
Horizons Unlimited, horizonsunlimited.com
Indian Mountaineering Foundation, indmount.org
International Society for Ecology and Culture, localfutures.org
Shabdkosh: English-Hindi Dictionary, shabdkosh.com
US Department of State, state.gov
Dharmapala Thangka Centre, thangka.de
A View on Buddhism, viewonbuddhism.org
World Health Organisation, who.int
Wikipedia, wikipedia.org

EUROPE

Delgany
Rosslare
Cherbourg
Paris
Stuttgart
Innsbruck
Ljubljana
Zagreb
Belgrade
Sofia
Istanbul
BLACK
Ankara
Göre

ALPS

MEDITERRANEAN SEA